The Princess 1

John Reed Scott

Alpha Editions

This edition published in 2024

ISBN 9789362097347

Design and Setting By

Alpha Editions

www.alphaedis.com

Email - info@alphaedis.com

As per information held with us this book is in Public Domain. This book is a reproduction of an important historical work. Alpha Editions uses the best technology to reproduce historical work in the same manner it was first published to preserve its original nature. Any marks or number seen are left intentionally to preserve.

Contents

I THE RECALL	- 1 -
II TO-MORROW AND THE BOOK	- 15 -
III THE ROYAL COUNCIL	- 29 -
IV THE PRESUMPTION SHIFTS	- 38 -
V THE COMPROMISE	- 46 -
VI THE REWARD OF A MEDDLER	- 55 -
VII THE ARMISTICE OF MOURNING	- 64 -
VIII INFERENCE OR FACT	- 72 -
IX THE RECKLESS GAME	- 79 -
X A QUESTION OF VENEER	- 89 -
XI FIRST BLOOD	- 99 -
XII THE SOLE SURVIVOR	- 109 -
XIII IN THE JAPONICA WALK	- 120 -
XIV AN ENTICING RENDEZVOUS	- 132 -
XV FOUR O'CLOCK AT THE INN	- 140 -
XVI A TOO CONVINCING ARGUMENT	- 155 -
XVII INTO THE TIGER'S CAGE	- 166 -
XVIII ON TO LOTZENIA	- 179 -
XIX LA DUCHESSE	- 188 -
XX THE PRINCESS TURNS STRATEGIST	- 198 -
XXI IN THE DUKE'S LIBRARY	- 208 -
XXII THE BOOK IN THE CLOTH	- 224 -
XXIII THE CANOPY OF SWORDS	- 231 -

I
THE RECALL

For the first time in a generation the Castle of Lotzen was entertaining its lord. He had come suddenly, a month before, and presently there had followed rumors of strange happenings in Dornlitz, in which the Duke had been too intimately concerned to please the King, and as punishment had been banished to his mountain estates. But Lotzenia was far from the Capital and isolated, and the people cared more for their crops and the amount of the tax levy than for the doings of the Court. And so it concerned them very little why the red banner with the golden cross floated from the highest turret of the old pile of stone, on the spur of the mountain overhanging the foaming Dreer. They knew it meant the Duke himself was in presence; but to them there was but one over-lord: the Dalberg, who reigned in Dornlitz; and in him they had all pride—for was not the Dalberg their hereditary chieftain centuries before he was the King!

True, the Duke of Lotzen had long been the Heir Presumptive, and so, in the prospective, entitled to their loyalty, but lately there had come from across the Sea a new Dalberg, of the blood of the great Henry, who, it was said, had displaced him in the line of Succession, and was to marry the Princess Dehra.

And at her name every woman of them curtsied and every man uncovered; blaming High Heaven the while, that she might not reign over them, when Frederick the King were gone; and well prepared to welcome the new heir if she were to be his queen.

At first the Duke had kept to the seclusion of his own domain, wide and wild enough to let him ride all day without crossing its boundary, but after a time he came at intervals, with a companion or two, into the low-lands, choosing the main highways, and dallying occasionally at some cross-road smithy for a word of gossip with those around the forge.

For Lotzen was not alone in his exile; he might be banished from the Capital, but that was no reason for denying himself all its pleasures; and the lights burned late at the Castle, and when the wind was from the North it strewed the valley with whisps of music and strands of laughter. And the country-side shook its head, and marveled at the turning of night into day, and at people who seemed never to sleep except when others worked; and not much even then, if the tales of such of the servants as belonged to the locality were to be believed.

And the revelry waxed louder and wilder as the days passed, and many times toward evening the whole company would come plunging down the mountain, and, with the great dogs baying before them, go racing through the valleys and back again to the Castle, as though some fiend were hot on their trail or they on his.

And ever beside the Duke, on a great, black horse, went the same woman, slender and sinuous, with raven hair and dead-white cheek; a feather touch on rein, a careless grace in saddle. And as they rode the Duke watched her with glowing eyes; and his cold face warmed with his thoughts, and he would speak to her earnestly and persuasively; and she, swaying toward him, would answer softly and with a tantalizing smile.

Then, one day, she had refused to ride.

"I am tired," she said, when at the sounding of the horn he had sought her apartments; "let the others go."

He went over and leaned on the back of her chair.

"Tired—of what?" he asked.

"Of everything—of myself most of all."

"And of everybody?" smiling down at her.

"One usually tires of self last."

"And you want to leave me?" he asked.

She shook her head. "No, not you, Ferdinand—the others."

"Shall I send them away?" he said eagerly.

"And make this lonely place more lonely still!"

"I despise the miserable place," he exclaimed.

"Then why not to Paris to-night?" she asked.

"Why not, indeed?" he answered, gravely, "for the others and—you."

"And you, too?" glancing up at him and touching, for an instant, his hand.

He shrugged his shoulders. "You forget, there is a King in Dornlitz!"

"You would go *incog.* and old Frederick never be the wiser, nor care even if he were."

He laughed shortly. "Think you so, *ma belle*,—well, believe me, I want not to be the one to try him."

The horn rang out again from the court-yard; the Duke crossed to a window.

"Go on," he called, "we will follow presently;" and with a clatter and a shout, they spurred across the bridge and away.

"Who leads?" she asked, going over and drawing herself up on the casement.

He put his arm around her. "What matters," he laughed, "since we are here?" and bent his head to her cheek.

"Let us go to Paris, dear," she whispered, caressingly; "to the boulevards and the music, the life, and the color."

He shook his head. "You don't know what you ask, little one— once I might have dared it, but not now—no, not now."

She drew a bit nearer. "And would the penalty now be so very serious?" she asked.

He looked at her a while uncertainly; and she smiled back persuasively. She knew that he was in disfavor because of his plots against the Archduke Armand's honor and life; and that he had been sent hither in disgrace; but all along what had puzzled her was his calm acquiescence; his remaining in this desolation, with never a word of anger toward the King, nor disposition to slip away surreptitiously to haunts beyond the border. Why should he be so careful not to transgress even the spirit of the royal order?—he who had not hesitated to play a false wife against the Archduke Armand, to try assassination, and to arrange deliberately to kill him in a duel. She remembered well that evening in her reception room, at the Hotel Metzen in Dornlitz, when Lotzen's whole scheme had suddenly collapsed like a house of cards. She recalled the King's very words of sentence when, at last, he had deigned to notice the Duke. "The Court has no present need of plotters and will be the better for your absence," he had said. "It has been over long since you have visited your titular estates and they doubtless require your immediate attention. You are, therefore, permitted to depart to them forthwith—and to remain indefinitely." Surely, it was very general and precluded only a return to Dornlitz.

That the question of the succession was behind it all, she was very well persuaded; the family laws of the Dalbergs were secret, undisclosed to any but the ranking members of the House, but the Crown had always descended by male primogeniture. The advent of Armand, the eldest male descendant of Hugo Dalberg (who had been banished by his father, the Great Henry, when he had gone to America and taken service under Washington) had tangled matters, for Armand was senior in line to Lotzen. It was known that Henry, shortly before his death, had revoked the former decree and restored Hugo and his children to their rank and estates; and Frederick had proclaimed this decree to the Nation and had executed it in favor of Armand, making him an Archduke and Colonel of the Red Huzzars. But what no one knew was whether Lotzen had hereby been displaced as Heir Presumptive. How far did the Great Henry's decree of restoration extend? How far had Frederick made it effective? In short, would the next King be Ferdinand, Duke of Lotzen, or Armand, Archduke of Valeria?

And to Madeline Spencer the answer was of deep concern; and she had been manœuvering to draw it from the Duke ever since she had come to the Castle. But every time she had led up to it, he had led away, and with evident deliberation. Plainly there was something in the Laws that made it well for him to drive the King no further; and what could it be but the power to remove him as Heir Presumptive.

And as Lotzen knew the answer, she would know it, too. If he were not to be king, she had no notion to entangle herself further with him; he was then too small game for her bow; and there would be a very chill welcome for her in Dornlitz from Queen Dehra. But should he get the Crown—well, there are worse positions than a king's favorite—for a few months—the open-handed months.

So she slipped an arm about his shoulders and let a whisp of perfumed hair flirt across his face.

"Tell me, dear," she said, "why won't you go to Paris?"

He laughed and lightly pinched her cheek. "Because I'm surer of you here. Paris breeds too many rivals."

"Yet I left them all to come here," she answered.

"But now you would go back."

She smiled up at him. "Yes, but with you, dear—not alone." Her hand stole into his. "Tell me, sweetheart, why you will not go— might it cause Frederick to deprive you of the succession?"

For a space the Duke made no answer, gazing the while steadily into the distance, with eyebrows slightly drawn. And she, having dared so far, dared further.

"Surely, dear, he would not wrong you by making Armand king!" she exclaimed, as though the thought had but that moment come.

He turned to her with quick sympathy, a look of warm appreciation in his eyes. The answer she had played for trembled on his lips—then died unspoken.

He bent down and kissed her forehead.

"We of the Dalbergs still believe, my dear, that the King can do no wrong," he said, and swung her to the floor. "Come, let us walk on the wall, and forget everything except that we are together, and that I love you."

She closed her eyes to hide the flash of angry disappointment, though her voice was calm and easy.

"Love!" she laughed; "love! what is it? The infatuation of the moment—the pleasure of an hour."

"And hence this eagerness for Paris?"

She gave him a quick glance. "May be, my lord, to prolong our moment; to extend our hour." He paused, his hand upon the door.

"And otherwise are they ended?" he asked quietly.

She let her eyes seek the door. "No—not yet." He slowly closed the door and leaned against it.

"My dear Madeline," he said, "let us deal frankly with each other. I am not so silly as to think you love me, though I'm willing to admit I wish you did. You have fascinated me—ever since that evening in the Hanging Garden when you made the play of being the Archduke Armand's wife. Love may be what you style it: 'the infatuation of the moment; the pleasure of an hour.' If so, for you, my moment and my hour still linger. But with you, I know, there is a different motive; you may like me passing well—I believe you do—yet it was not that which brought you here, away from Paris—'the boulevards and the music.' You came because—well, what matters the because: you came; and for that I am very grateful; they have been pleasant days for me——"

She had been gazing through the window; now she looked him in the eyes.

"And for me as well," she said.

"I am glad," he answered gravely—"and it shall not be I that ends them. You wish to know if I am still the Heir Presumptive. You shall have your answer: I do not know. It rests with the King. He has the power to displace me in favor of Armand."

She smiled comprehendingly. It was as she had feared.

"And the Princess Royal is betrothed to Armand," she commented.

Lotzen shrugged his shoulders. "Just so," he said. "Do you wonder I may not go to Paris?"

She went over to the fireplace, and sitting on the arm of a chair rested her slender feet on the fender, her silk clad ankles glistening in the fire-light.

"I don't quite understand," she said, "why, when the American was restored to Hugo's rank, he did not, by that very fact, become also Heir Presumptive—his line is senior to yours."

There was room on the chair arm for another and he took it.

"You have touched the very point," he said. "Henry the Third himself restored Hugo and his heirs to rank and estate; but it needs Frederick's decree to make him eligible to the Crown."

"And has he made it?"

He shook his head. "I do not know——"

"But, surely, it would be promulgated, if he had."

"Very probably; but not necessarily. All that is required is a line in the big book which for centuries has contained the Laws of the Dalbergs."

She studied the tip of her shoe, tapping it the while on the fender rod.

"When will this marriage be solemnized?" she asked.

He laughed rather curtly. "Never, I hope."

She gave him a quick look. "So—the wound still hurts. I beg your pardon; I did not mean to be unkind. I was only thinking that, if the decree were not yet made, the wedding would be sure to bring it."

He put his arm around her waist and drew her over until the black hair pressed his shoulder.

"Nay, Madeline, you are quite wrong," he said. "The Princess is nothing to me now—nothing but the King's daughter and the American's chief advocate. I meant what you did:—that the marriage will lose me the Crown."

For a moment she suffered his embrace, watching him the while through half closed eyes; then she drew away.

"I suppose there is no way to prevent the marriage," she remarked, her gaze upon the fire.

He arose and, crossing to the table, found a cigarette.

"Can you suggest a way?" he asked, his back toward her, the match aflame, poised before his face.

She had turned and was watching him with sharp interest, but she did not answer, and when he glanced around, in question, she was looking at the fire.

"Want a cigarette?" he said.

She nodded, and he took it to her and held the match for its lighting.

"I asked you if you could suggest a way," he remarked.

She blew a smoke ring toward the ceiling. "Yes, go back to Dornlitz and kill the American."

"Will you go with me?" banteringly.

"Indeed I won't," with a reminiscent smile; "I have quite too vivid a memory of my recent visit there."

"And the killing—shall I do it by proxy or in person?"

"Any way—so it is done—though one's best servant is one's self, you know."

He had thought her jesting, but now he leaned forward to see her face.

"Surely, you do not mean it," he said uncertainly.

"Why not?" she asked. "It's true you have already tried both ways—and failed; but that is no assurance of the future. The second, or some other try may win."

A tolerant smile crossed his lips. "And meanwhile, of course, the American would wait patiently to be killed."

She shrugged her shoulders. "You seem to have forgot that steel vests do not protect the head; and that several swords might penetrate a guard which one could not."

"Surely," he exclaimed, "surely, you must have loved this man!"

She put his words aside with a wave of her hand.

"My advice is quite impersonal," she said—"and it is only trite advice at that, as you know. You have yourself considered it already scores of times, and have been deterred only by the danger to yourself."

He laughed. "I'm glad you cannot go over to my enemies. You read my mind too accurately."

"Nonsense," she retorted; "Armand knows it quite as well as I, though possibly he may not yet have realized how timid you have grown."

"Timid!"

She nodded. "Yes, timid; you had plenty of nerve at first, when the American came; but it seems to have run to water."

"And I shall lose, you think?"

She tossed the cigarette among the red ashes and arose.

"Why should you win, Ferdinand?" she asked—then a sly smile touched her lips—"so far as I have observed, you haven't troubled even so much as to pray for success."

He leaned forward and drew her back to the place beside him.

"Patience, Madeline, patience," said he; "some day I'm going back to Dornlitz."

"To see the Archduke Armand crowned?" she scoffed.

He bent his head close to her ear. "I trust so—with the diadem that never fades."

She laughed. "Trust and hope are the weapons of the apathetic. Why don't you, at least, deal in predictions; sometimes they inspire deeds."

"Very good," he said smilingly. "I predict that there is another little game for you and me to play in Dornlitz, and that we shall be there before many days."

"You are an absent-minded prophet," she said; "I told you I would not go to Dornlitz."

"But if I need you, Madeline?"

She shook her head. "Transfer the game to Paris, or any place outside Valeria, and I will gladly be your partner."

He took her hand. "Will nothing persuade you?"

She faced him instantly. "Nothing, my lord, nothing, so long as Frederick is king."

The Duke lifted her hand and tapped it softly against his cheek.

"*Tres bien ma chère, tres bien*," he said; then frowned, as Mrs. Spencer's maid entered.

"*Pour Monsieur le Duc*," she curtsied.

Lotzen took the card from the salver and turned it over.

"I will see him at once," he said; "have him shown to my private cabinet.... It is Bigler," he explained.

"Why not have him here?"

He hesitated.

"Oh, very well; I thought you trusted me."

He struck the bell. "Show Count Bigler here," he ordered. Then when the maid had gone: "There, Madeline, that should satisfy you, for I have no idea what brings him."

She went quickly to him, and leaning over his shoulder lightly kissed his cheek.

"I knew you trusted me, dear," she said, "but a woman likes to have it demonstrated, now and then."

He turned to catch her; but she sprang away.

"No, Ferdinand, no," as he pursued her; "the Count is coming—go and sit down."—She tried to reach her boudoir, but with a laugh he headed her off, and slowly drove her into a corner.

"Surrender," he said; "I'll be merciful."

For answer there came the swish of high-held skirts, a vision of black silk stockings and white lace, and she was across a huge sofa, and, with flushed face and merry eyes, had turned and faced him.

And as they stood so, Count Bigler was announced.

"Welcome, my dear Bigler, welcome!" the Duke exclaimed, hurrying over to greet him; "you are surely Heaven sent.... Madame Spencer, I think you know the Count."

She saw the look of sharp surprise that Bigler tried to hide by bowing very low, and she laughed gayly.

"Indeed, you do come in good time, my lord," she said; "we were so put to for amusement we were reduced to playing tag around the room—don't be shocked; you will be playing it too, if you are here for long."

"If it carry the usual penalty," he answered, joining in her laugh, "I am very ready to play it now."

"Doubtless," said the Duke dryly, motioning him to a chair. "But first, tell us the gossip of the Capital; we have heard nothing for weeks. What's my dear cousin Armand up to—not dying, I fear?"

"Dying! Not he—not while there are any honors handy, with a doting King to shower them on him, and a Princess waiting for wife."

The Duke's face, cold at best, went yet colder.

"Has the wedding date been announced?" he asked.

"Not formally, but I understand it has been fixed for the twenty-seventh."

Lotzen glanced at a calendar. "Three weeks from to-morrow—well, much may happen in that time. Come," he said good-naturedly, shaking off the irritation, "tell us all you know—everything—from the newest dance at the opera to the tattle of the Clubs. I said you were Heaven sent—now prove it. But first—was it wise for you to come here? What will Frederick say?"

The Count laughed. "Oh, I'm not here; I'm in Paris, on two weeks leave."

"Paris!" the Duke exclaimed. "Surely, this Paris fever is the very devil; are you off to-night or in the morning?"

Bigler shot a quick glance at Mrs. Spencer, and understood.

"I'm not to Paris at all," he said, "unless you send me."

"He won't do that, Monsieur le Comte," the lady laughed; and Lotzen, who had quite missed the hidden meaning in their words, nodded in affirmance.

"Come," he said, "your budget—out with it. I'm athirst for news."

The Count drew out a cigar and, at Mrs. Spencer's smile of permission, he lighted it, and began his tale. And it took time in the telling, for the Duke was constant in his questions, and a month is very long for such as he to be torn from his usual life and haunts.

And, through it all, Mrs. Spencer lay back in sinuous indolence among the cushions on the couch before the fire, one hand behind her shapely head, her eyes, languidly indifferent, upon the two men, her thoughts seemingly far away. And while he talked, Count Bigler watched her curiously, but discreetly. This was the first time he had seen the famous "Woman in Black" so closely, and her striking beauty fairly stunned him. He knew his Paris and Vienna well, but her equal was not there—no, nor elsewhere, he would swear. Truly, he had wasted his sympathy on Lotzen—he needed none of it with such a companion for his exile.

And she, unseeing, yet seeing all, read much of his thoughts; and presently, from behind her heavy lashes, she flashed a smile upon him—half challenge, half rebuke—then turned her face from him, nor shifted it until the fading daylight wrapped her in its shadow.

"There, my tale is told," the Count ended. "I'm empty as a broken bottle—and as dry," and he poured himself a glass of wine from the decanter on a side table.

"You are a rare gossip, truly," said the Duke; "but you have most carefully avoided the one matter that interests me most:—what do they say of me in Dornlitz?"

Bigler shrugged his shoulders. "Why ask?" he said. "You know quite well the Capital does not love you."

"And, therefore, no reason for me to be sensitive. Come, out with it. What do they say?"

"Very well," said Bigler, "if you want it, here it is:—they have the notion that you are no longer the Heir Presumptive, and it seems to give them vast delight."

The Duke nodded. "And on what is the notion based?"

"Originally, on hope, I fancy; but lately it has become accepted that the King not only has the power to displace you, but has actually signed the decree."

"And Frederick—does he encourage the idea?"

The Count shook his head. "No, except by his open fondness for the American."

"I've been urged to go to Dornlitz and kill the American," Lotzen remarked, with a smile and a nod toward Mrs. Spencer.

"If you can kill him," said Bigler instantly, "the advice is excellent."

"Exactly. And if I can't, it's the end of me—and my friends."

"I think your friends would gladly try the hazard," the Count answered. "It is dull prospect and small hope for them, even now. And candidly, my lord, to my mind, it's your only chance, if you wish the Crown; for, believe me, the Archduke Armand is fixed for the succession, and the day he weds the Princess Royal will see him formally proclaimed."

The Duke strode to the far end of the room and back again.

"Is that your honest advice—to go to Dornlitz?" he asked.

The other arose and raised his hand in salute. "It is, sir; and not mine alone, but Gimels' and Rosen's and Whippen's, and all the others'—that is what brought me here."

"And have you any plan arranged?"

The Count nodded ever so slightly, then looked the Duke steadily in the face—and the latter understood.

He turned to Madeline Spencer. "Come nearer, my dear," he said, "we may need your quick wit—there is plotting afoot."

She gave him a smile of appreciation, and came and took the chair he offered, and he motioned for Bigler to proceed.

"But, first, tell me," he interjected, "am I to go to Dornlitz openly or in disguise? I don't fancy the latter."

"Openly," said the Count. "Having been in exile a month, you can venture to return and throw yourself on Frederick's mercy. We think he will receive you and permit you to remain—but, at least, it will give you two days in Dornlitz, and, if our plan does not miscarry, that will be quite ample."

"Very good," the Duke commented; "but my going will depend upon how I like your plot; let us have it—and in it, I trust you have not overlooked my fiasco at the Vierle Masque and so hung it all on my single sword."

"Your sword may be very necessary, but, if so, it won't be alone. We have several plans—the one we hope to——"

A light tap on the door interrupted him, and a servant entered, with the bright pink envelope that, in Valeria, always contained a telegram.

"My recall to Court," laughed the Duke, and drawing out the message glanced at it indifferently.

But it seemed to take him unduly long to read it; and when, at length, he folded it, his face was very grave; and he sat silent, staring at the floor, creasing and recreasing the sheet with nervous fingers, and quite oblivious to the two who were watching him, and the servant standing stiffly at attention at his side.

Suddenly, from without, arose a mad din of horses' hoofs and human voices, as the returning cavalcade dashed into the courtyard, women and men yelling like fiends possessed. And it roused the Duke.

"You may go," to the footman; "there is no answer now." He waited until the door closed; then held up the telegram. "His Majesty died, suddenly, this afternoon," he said.

Count Bigler sprang half out of his chair.

"Frederick dead! the King dead!" he cried—"then, in God's name, who now is king—you or the American?"

The Duke arose. "That is what we are about to find out," he said, very quietly. "Come, we will go to Dornlitz."

II
TO-MORROW AND THE BOOK

Frederick of Valeria had died as every strong man wants to die: suddenly and in the midst of his affairs, with the full vigor of life still upon him and no premonition of the end. It had been a sharp straightening in saddle, a catch of breath, a lift of hand toward heart, and then, with the great band of the Foot Guards thundering before him, and the regiment swinging by in review, he had sunk slowly over and into the arms of the Archduke Armand. And as he held him, there was a quick touch of surgeon's fingers to pulse and breast, a shake of head, a word; and then, sorrowfully and in silence, they bore him away; while the regiment, wheeling sharply into line, spread across the parade and held back the populace. And presently, as the people lingered, wondering and fearful, and the Guards stood stolid in their ranks, the royal standard on the great tower of the Castle dropped slowly to half staff, and the mellow bell of the Cathedral began to toll, to all Valeria, the mournful message that her King was dead.

And far out in the country the Princess Dehra heard it, but faintly; and drawing rein, she listened in growing trepidation for a louder note. Was it the Cathedral bell?—the bell that tolled only when a Dalberg died! For a while she caught no stroke, and the fear was passing, when down the wind it came, clear and strong—and again—and yet again.

And with blanched cheek and fluttering heart she was racing at top speed toward Dornlitz, staying neither for man nor beast, nor hill nor stream, the solemn clang smiting her ever harder and harder in the face. There were but two for whom it could be speaking, her father and her lover—for she gave no thought to Lotzen or his brother, Charles. And now, which?—which?—which? Mile after mile went behind her in dust and flying stones, until six were passed, and then the outer guard post rose in front.

"The bell!" she cried, as the sentry sprang to attention, "the bell, man, the bell?"

The soldier grounded arms.

"For the King," he said.

But as the word was spoken she was gone—joy and sorrow now fighting strangely in her heart—and as she dashed up the wide Avenue, the men uncovered and the women breathed a prayer; but she, herself, saw only the big, gray building with the drooping flag, and toward it she sped, the echo of the now silent bell still ringing in her ears.

The Castle gates were closed, and before them with drawn swords, stern and impassive, sat two huge Cuirassiers of the Guard; they heard the nearing hoof beats, and, over the heads of the crowd that hung about the entrance, they saw and understood.

"Stand back!" they cried; "stand back—the Princess comes!"

And the gates swung open, and the big sorrel horse, reeking with sweat and flecked with foam and dust, flashed by, and on across the courtyard. And Colonel Moore, who was about to ride away, sprang down and swung her out of saddle.

"Take me to him," she said quietly, as he stood aside to let her pass.

She swayed slightly at the first step, and her legs seemed strangely stiff and heavy, but she slipped her hand through his arm and drove herself along. And so he led her, calm and dry-eyed, down the long corridor and through the ante-room to the King's chamber, and all who met them bowed head and drew back. At the threshold she halted.

"Do you please bid all retire," she said. "I would see my father alone."

And when he had done her will, he came and held open the door for her a little way, then stood at attention and raised his hand in salute; and the Princess went in to her dead.

Meanwhile, the Archduke Armand was searching for the Princess. The moment he had seen the King at rest in the Castle, declining all escort, he had galloped away for the Summer Palace, first ordering that no information should be conveyed there by telephone. It was a message for him to deliver in person, though he shrank from it, as only a man can shrink from such a duty. But he knew nothing of the Cathedral bell and its tolling, and when, as he neared the Park, the first note broke upon him, he listened in surprise; then he grasped its meaning, and with an imprecation, spurred the faster, racing now with a brazen clapper as to which should tell the Princess first. And the sentry at the gate stared in wonder; but the officer on duty at the main entrance ran out to meet him, knowing instantly for whom the bell was tolling and for whom the Archduke came.

"Her Highness is not here," he cried. "She rode away alone by the North Avenue a short while ago."

"Make report to the Castle the instant she returns," Armand called, and was gone—to follow her, as he thought, on the old forge road.

"Ye Gods!" the officer exclaimed, "that was the King—the new King!" and mechanically he clicked his heels together and saluted.

Nor did he imagine that all unwittingly he had sent his master far astray; for the Princess had gone but a little way by the North Avenue, and then had circled over to the South gate.

And so Armand searched vainly, until at last, bearing around toward Dornlitz, he struck the main highway and learned that she had passed long since, making for the Capital as fast as horse could run. And he knew that the Bell had been the messenger, and that there was now naught for him to do but to return with all speed and give such comfort as he might. Though what to do or to say he had no idea—for never before had he been called upon to minister to a woman's grief; and he pondered upon it with a misgiving that was at its deepest when, at length, he stood outside her door and heard her bid the servant to admit him.

But if he looked for tears and trembling he was disappointed, for she met him as she had met those in the corridor and the ante-room, dry-eyed and calmly. And in silence he took her in his arms, and held her close, and stroked her shining hair.

And presently she put his arms aside, and stepping back, she curtsied low and very gravely.

"Life to Your Majesty!" she said; "long live the King!" and kissed his hand.

He raised her quickly. "Never bend knee to me, Dehra," he said. "And believe me, I had quite forgot everything except that you had lost your father."

She went back to him. "And so had I, dear, until you came; but now, since he is gone, you are all I have—is it very selfish, then, for me to think of you so soon?"

He drew her to a chair and stood looking down at her.

"If it is," he said, "I am surely not the one to judge you."

She shook her head sadly. "There is no one to judge but—him," she answered; "and he, I know, would give me full approval." She was silent for a while, her thoughts in the darkened room across the court, where the tapers burned dimly, and a Captain of the Guard kept watch. And her heart sobbed afresh, though her lips were mute and her eyes undimmed. At last she spoke.

"Is the Book of Laws at the Summer Palace or here?" she asked.

"I do not know," said Armand, "I have never seen it except the day that the King read old Henry's decree and offered me Hugo's titles and estates."

"Well, at least, he spoke of it to you to-day."

Armand shook his head. "Never a word; neither to-day nor for many days."

A faint frown showed between her eyes. "Didn't he mention to you, this afternoon, the matter of the Succession?"

"No."

She sat up sharply. "It can't be he didn't——"

The Archduke dropped on the floor at her feet and took her hand. "I assure you, Dehra, the King didn't speak a single word to me on such a matter."

"THE KING DIDN'T SPEAK A SINGLE WORD TO ME
ON SUCH A MATTER."

"No, no," she said, "you don't understand. I mean it can not be he didn't make the decree."

"The decree!" Armand exclaimed, though he knew well there was but one she would refer to; and his pulse bounded fiercely and his face grew very hot.

"Yes, dear—the decree—that would have made you Heir Presumptive—and now King."

"And you think it was drawn?"

"I am sure of it."

"The King told you so?"

"Not directly, but by inference. I came upon him late last night in his library, with the Laws open before him and a pen in his hand; and when I ventured to voice my curiosity, he smiled and closed the book, saying, 'You may see it to-morrow, child; after I have told Armand.'"

"Doubtless he intended to tell me after the review."

The Princess leaned over and put her arm around his neck.

"And now you are the King, dear; as he had always intended you should be," she whispered. "Thank God, the decree was made in time."

For a while Armand toyed with her slender fingers, and did not answer. Of course, she was right:—it was the decree they both had been hoping for so earnestly, but which neither had dared mention to the King. And now, when it had come, and in such fashion, was it really worth the while. Worth the turmoil and the trouble, and, may be, the fighting, that was sure to follow his assumption of the royal dignity. Had Frederick lived to proclaim the decree and to school the Nation into accepting him as his successor, the way would have been easy and well assured. But it was vastly different now—with Frederick dead, the decree yet to be announced, and few, doubtless, of those in authority around him, to be depended on to aid him hold the throne. Dalberg though he was, and now, by birth, the Head of the House, yet he was a foreigner, and no people take kindly to a foreign King. Frederick had died too soon—another year——

And Dehra, bending down questioning his abstraction, read his face and understood his thoughts.

"Come, dear," she said, "the crisis is here, and we must face it. Dismiss the idea that you're a foreigner. Only you and Lotzen and I are familiar with our Laws. You forget that the people do not know it required a special decree to make you eligible for the Crown; and to them you have been the next King ever since you were proclaimed as Hugo's heir. And surely they have shown you a rare good will, and an amazing preference over the Duke. He has spent his whole life in cultivating their dislike; do you fancy it won't bring its harvest now?"

He had turned and was watching her with an indulgent smile. It was sweet to hear her argue so; to see her intense devotion to his cause; her passionate desire that he should sit in her father's place and rule the ancient monarchy. And at her first words, and the sight of her loving eyes and flushed cheeks, his doubts had vanished, and his decision had been made. Yet, because he liked to see her so, he led her on.

"But what of the Nobility," he objected; "in Valeria they still lead the people."

"True," she answered instantly, "true; but you forget again that the Nobles are sworn to maintain the Laws of the Dalbergs; and that for centuries none has ever broken faith. No, no, Armand, they will be true to their oaths; they will uphold the decree."

"Don't you think, dear," he smiled, "you are making it rather too assured? If the people are for me (or at least are not for Lotzen) and the Nobles will abide by the Laws, nothing remains but to mount the Throne and seize the sceptre."

"Just about that, I fancy," she replied.

"And, meanwhile, what will Lotzen be doing?"

She frowned. "Whatever the Head of his House orders him to do. As a Dalberg he is bound to obey."

"And you think he will obey?"

"I surely do. I cannot imagine a Dalberg dishonoring the Book of Laws."

"I fear you do not know Ferdinand of Lotzen," said Armand seriously. "He intends to dispute the Succession. I have never told you how, long ago, he warned me what to expect if I undertook to 'filch the Crown,' as he put it. It was the afternoon he insulted me at headquarters—the Vierle Masque was in the evening."

The Princess nodded eagerly. "Yes," said she, "yes—I know—the time he wanted you to toss up a coin for me. What did he say?"

The Archduke reflected a moment. "I can give you his exact words: 'Do you think,' he said, 'that I, who have been the Heir Presumptive since the instant of my birth, almost, will calmly step aside and permit you to take my place? Do you fancy for an instant that the people of Valeria would have a foreigner for King? And even if old Frederick were to become so infatuated with you that he would restore you to Hugo's place in the line of Succession, do you imagine that the House of Nobles would hesitate to annul it the instant he died?'"

When he had finished, Dehra's fingers were beating a tattoo on the chair's arm, and her eyes were snapping—as once or twice he had seen Frederick's snap.

"And I suppose you never told the King?" she exclaimed.

"Naturally not."

"Of course, of course," with a toss of the handsome head. "That's a man's way—his silly, senseless way—never tell tales about a rival. And as a result, see what a mess you have made. Had you informed the King, he instantly would have proclaimed you as his heir, and then disgraced Lotzen publicly and sent him into exile. And you would now be his successor, without a shadow of opposition."

Armand subdued a smile. "You don't understand, Dehra——" he began.

"Quite right," she cut in; "quite right; I don't. Why didn't you tell me? I would have told the King, you may be sure."

"Of course you would, little woman; that's just the reason I didn't tell you."

She shrugged her shoulders, and the tattoo began afresh.

"I've no patience with such nonsense," she declared; "Lotzen deserved no gentlemanly consideration; he would have shown none to you; and besides, it was your duty to your King and your House to uphold the Laws of the Dalbergs and to prevent any attempt to violate them."

"I am very much afraid that lately, between Lotzen and myself, the Laws of the Dalbergs have been sadly slighted."

His bantering jarred upon her. "To me, Armand," she answered gravely, "our Laws are holy. For almost a thousand years they have been our unchallenged rule of governance. I can understand why, to you, they have no sacredness and no sentiment; but Lotzen has been born and bred under them, and should honor them with his life—and more especially as they alone made him the Heir Presumptive. But for the decree of the first Dalberg King, four hundred years ago, I would be the Queen-Regent of Valeria."

"It's a pity, a crying pity!" he exclaimed.

She looked down at him with shining eyes. "No, dear, it isn't; once I thought it was; but now I'm quite content to be Queen-consort."

He took both her hands and held them between his own. "That, dear, is what makes it possible, and worth the struggle; and if Valeria does accept me as its King, it will be solely for love of you, and to get you for its Queen."

A smile of satisfaction crossed her face. "I hope the people do love me," she said. "I would like to feel I may have helped you, even a little."

"A little! but for you, my princess, I'd go back to America and leave the way clear for Lotzen."

She laughed softly. "No, no, Armand, you would do nothing of the sort. A Dalberg never ran from duty—and least of all the Dalberg whom God has made in the image of the greatest of them all."

He glanced in the tall mirror across the room. He was wearing the dress uniform of the Red Huzzars (who had been inspected immediately before the Foot Guards; and he, as titular Colonel, had led them in the march by), and there was no denying he made a handsome figure, in the brilliant tunic and black, fur-bound dohlman, his Orders sparkling, his sword across his knees.

She put her head close beside his and smiled at him in the mirror.

"Henry the Great was not at all bad looking," she said.

He smiled back at her. "But with a beastly bad temper, at times, I'm told."

"I'm not afraid—I mean his wife wasn't afraid; tradition is, she managed him very skilfully."

"Doubtless," he agreed; "any clever woman can manage a man if she take the trouble to try."

"And shall I try, Armand?"

"Try!" he chuckled; "you couldn't help trying; man taming is your natural avocation. By all means, manage me—only, don't let me know it."

"I'll not," she laughed—"the King never——" and she straightened sharply. "I forgot, dear, I forgot!" And she got up suddenly, and went over to the window. Nor did he follow her; but waited silently, knowing well it was no time for him even to intrude.

After a while she came slowly back to him, a wistfully sad look in her eyes. And as he met her she gave him both her hands.

"I shall never be anything but a thoughtless child, Armand," she said, with a wan, little smile. "So be kind to me, dear—and don't forget."

He drew her arms about his neck. "Let us always be children to each other," he answered, "forgetting, when together, everything but the joy of living, the pleasures of to-day, the anticipations of to-morrow."

She shook her head. "A woman is always a child in love," she said; "it's the man who grows into maturity, and sobers with age."

He knew quite well she was right, and for the moment he had no words to answer; and she understood and helped him.

"But this is no time for either of us to be children," she went on; "there is work to do and plans to be arranged." She drew a chair close to the table and, resting both arms upon it, looked up at the Archduke expectantly. "What is first?"

He hesitated.

"Come, dear," she said; "Frederick was my father and my dearest friend, but there remains for him now only the last sad offices the living do the dead; we will do them; but we will also do what he has decreed. We will seat you in his place, and confound Lotzen and his satellites."

He took her hand and gravely raised it to his lips.

"You are a rare woman, Dehra," he said, "a rare woman. No man can reach your level, nor understand the beauty of your faith, the meaning of your love. Yet, at least, will I try to do you honor and to give you truth."

She drew him down and kissed him lightly on the cheek.

"You do not know the Dalberg women, dear," she said—"to them the King is next to God—and the line that separates is very narrow."

"But I'm not yet the King," he protested.

"You've been king, in fact, since the moment—Frederick died. With us, the tenet still obtains in all its ancient strength; the throne is never vacant."

"So it's Lotzen or I, and to-morrow the Book will decide."

"Yes," she agreed; "to-morrow the Book will decide for the Nation; but *we* know it will be you."

"Not exactly," he smiled; "we think we know; we can't be sure until we see the decree."

"I have no doubt," she averred, "my father's words can bear but one construction."

"It would seem so—yet I've long learned that, in this life, it's the certain things that usually are lost."

She sprang up. "Why not settle it at once—let us send for the Book; of course it is at the Palace—it was there last night."

He shook his head decisively. "No, dear, no; believe me it is not wise now for either of us to touch the Book. It were best that it be opened only by the Prime Minister in presence of the Royal Council. We must give Lotzen no reason to cry forgery."

She shrugged her shoulders. "Small good would it do him, as against Frederick's writing and my testimony. However, we can wait—the Council meets in the morning, I assume?"

"Yes; at ten o'clock, at the Palace."

She looked up quickly. "The key?" she asked; "it was always on his watch chain—have you got it?"

"No," said he; "I never thought of it."

She rang the bell and sent for the Chamberlain.

"Bring me King Frederick's watch, and the Orders he was wearing," she said. When they came she handed the Orders to Armand.

"They are yours now, dear," she said. She took the watch and held up the chain, from the end of which hung the small, antique key of the brass bound box, in which the Book of Laws had been kept for centuries that now reached back to tradition. She contemplated, for a moment, the swaying bit of gold and bronze, then loosed it from the ring.

"This also is yours, Sire," she said, and proffered it to him.

But he declined. "To-morrow," he said.

"And in the meantime?"

"If Count Epping is still in the Castle, we will let him hold it."

The Princess nodded in approval. "Doubtless that is wiser," she said, "though quite unprecedented; none but the King ever holds that key, save when he rides to war."

"We are dealing with a situation that has no precedents," he smiled; "we must make some."

As he went toward the bell, a servant entered with a card.

"Admit him," he said.... "It is Epping," he explained.

The Prime Minister of Valeria was one of those extraordinary exceptions that occasionally occur in public officials; he had no purpose in life but to serve his King. Without regard to his own private ends or personal ambition, he had administered his office for a generation, and Frederick trusted him as few monarchs ever trusted a powerful subject. To the Nation, he was honesty and justice incarnate, and only the King and the Princess Royal excelled him in popularity and respect. Seventy years had passed over the tall and slender figure, leaving a crown of silver above the pale, lean face, with its tight-shut mouth, high cheek bones and faded blue eyes; but they had brought no stoop to the shoulders, nor feebleness to the step, nor dullness to the brain.

He saluted Armand with formal dignity; then bent over Dehra's hand, silently and long—and when he rose a tear was trembling on his lashes. He dashed it away impatiently and turned to the Archduke.

"Sire," he said—and Armand, in sheer surprise, made no objection—"I have brought the proclamation announcing His late Majesty's death and your accession. It should be published in the morning. Will it please you to sign it now?"

There are moments in life so sharp with emotion that they cut into one's memory like a sculptor's tool, and, ever after, stand clear-lined and cameoed against the blurred background of commonplace existence. Such was the moment at the Palace when Frederick had handed him the patents of an Archduke, and such now was this. "Sire!" the word was pounding in his brain. "Sire!" he, who, less than a year ago, was but a Major in the American Army; "Sire!" he—he—King of Valeria!

Then, through the mirage, he saw Dehra's smiling face, and he awoke suddenly to consciousness and the need for speech, and for immediate decision. Should he sign the proclamation on the chance that the decree was in his favor, and that he was, in truth, the King? He hesitated just an instant—tempted by his own desires and by the eager eyes of the fair woman before him; then he straightened his shoulders and chose the way of prudence.

He waved the Prime Minister to a chair.

"Your pardon, my lord," he said; "your form of address was so new and unexpected, it for the moment bound my tongue."

The old man bowed. "I think I understand, Sire," he said, with a smile that, for an instant, softened amazingly his stern face. "Yet, believe me, one says it to you very naturally"—and his glance strayed deliberately to the wall opposite, where hung a small copy of the Great Henry's portrait in the uniform of the Red Huzzars. "It is very wonderful," he commented;—"and I fancy it won you instant favor and, even now, may be, makes us willing to accept you as our King. Sometimes, Your Majesty, sentiment dominates even a nation."

"Then I trust sentiment will be content with the physical resemblance and not examine the idol too closely."

The Count smiled again; this time rather coldly.

"The first duty of a king is to look like one," he said; "and sentiment demands nothing else;" and, with placid insistence, he laid the proclamation on the table beside Armand.

The latter picked it up and read it—and put it down.

"My lord," he said, "I prefer not to exercise any prerogative of kingship until the Royal Council has examined the Book of Laws and confirmed my title under the decrees."

The faded blue eyes looked at him contemplatively.

"I assumed there was no question as to the Succession," he remarked.

"Nor did I mean to intimate there was," Armand answered.

"Then, with all respect, Sire, I see no reason why you should not sign the proclamation."

Armand shook his head. "May be I am foolish," he said; "but I will not assume the government until after the Council to-morrow—it will do no harm to delay the proclamation for a few hours. And, in the interim, you will oblige Her Royal Highness and me by keeping this key, which she removed from King Frederick's watch chain, but a moment before you came."

The Count nodded and took the key.

"I recognize it," he replied. "I know the lock it opens."

"Good," said Armand; "the box is at the Palace, and doubtless you also know what it contains. For reasons you may easily appreciate, I desire to avoid any imputation that the Book has been touched since His Majesty's demise. You will produce this key at the meeting to-morrow, explaining how and where you got it; and then, in the presence of the Council, I shall open the box and if, by the Laws of the Dalbergs, I am Head of the House, I will enter into my heritage and try to keep it."

The Prime Minister got up; gladness in his heart, though his face was quite impassive. He had come in doubt and misgiving; he was easy now—here was a man who led, a man to be served; he asked no more—he was content.

"I understand," he said; "the proclamation can wait;" then he drew himself to his full height. "God save Your Majesty!" he ended.

III
THE ROYAL COUNCIL

Count Epping was the last of the five Ministers to arrive at the Council, the following morning. He came in, a few minutes before the hour, acknowledged with grave courtesy, but brief words, the greetings of the others, and when his secretary had put his dispatch box on the table he immediately opened it and busied himself with his papers. It was his way—and none of them had ever seen him otherwise; but now there seemed to be a special significance in his silence and preoccupation.

The failure of the Court Journal to appear that morning had broken a custom that ante-dated the memory of man, and the information which was promptly conveyed to the Ministers that it was delayed until evening, and by the personal order of the Prime Minister, had provoked both amazement and expectancy. It could mean only that the paper was being held for something that must be in that day's issue, and as they had promptly disclaimed to one another all responsibility, the inference was not difficult that it had to do with the new King's first proclamation.

"The Count was at the Castle last evening," Duval, the War Minister, had remarked, "and I assumed it was to submit the proclamation and have it signed."

Baron Retz, the Minister of Justice, shrugged his shoulders.

"May be you assumed correctly," he remarked.

The others looked at him with quick interest, but got only a smile and another shrug.

"Then why didn't he sign it?" Duval demanded.

The Baron leaned back in his chair and studied the ceiling. "When you say 'he,' you mean——?"

"The King, of course," the other snapped. "Who the devil else would I mean?"

"And by 'the King,'" drawled Retz, "you mean——?"

There was a sudden silence—then General Duval brought his fist down on the table with a bang.

"Monsieur le Baron," he exclaimed, "you understand perfectly whom *I* meant by the King—the Archduke Armand. If he is not the King, and you know it, it is your duty as a member of the Council to disclose the fact to us forthwith; this is no time nor place to indulge in innuendoes."

The Baron's small grey eyes turned slowly and, for a brief instant, lingered, with a dull glitter, on the War Minister's face.

"My dear General," he laughed, "you are so precipitate. If you ever lead an army you will deal only in frontal attacks—and defeats. I assure you I *know* nothing; but to restate your own question: if the Archduke Armand be the King, why didn't he sign the proclamation?"

Steuben, the grey-bearded Minister of the Interior, cut in with a growl.

"What is the profit of all these wonderful theories?" he demanded, eyeing Retz. "The ordinary and reasonable explanation is that the proclamation is to be submitted to us this morning."

"In which event," said the Baron, "we shall have the explanation in a very few minutes," and resumed his study of the ceiling.

"And in the meantime," remarked Admiral Marquand, "I am moved to inquire, where is the Duke of Lotzen?"

Steuben gave a gruff laugh. "Doubtless the Department of Justice can also offer a violent presumption on that subject."

"On the contrary, my friend," said Retz, "it will offer the very natural presumption that the Duke of Lotzen is hastening to Dornlitz; to the funeral—and the coronation."

"Whose coronation?" Duval asked quickly.

"My dear General," said the Baron, "there can't be two Kings of Valeria, and it would seem that the Army has spoken for the Archduke Armand."

"And the Department of Justice for whom?" the General exclaimed.

A faint sneer played over Retz's lips. "Monsieur le General forgets that when the Army speaks, Justice is bound and gagged."

It was at that moment that Count Epping had entered.

When the clock on the mantel chimed the hour the Count sat down and motioned the others to attend.

"Will not the King be present?" Retz asked casually, as he took his place.

The Prime Minister looked at him in studious comprehension.

"Patience, monsieur, patience," he said softly, "His Majesty will doubtless join us in proper time. Have you any business that requires his personal attention?"

The Baron shook his head. "No—nothing. I was only curious as to what uniform he would wear."

A faint smile touched the Count's thin lips.

"But more particularly curious as to *who* would wear it," he remarked dryly.

Retz swung around and faced him.

"My lord," he said, "I would ask you, who is King in Valeria: the Archduke Armand or Ferdinand of Lotzen?"

The old Minister's smile chilled to a sneer.

"That is a most astonishing question from the chief law officer of the kingdom," he said.

"But not so astonishing as that he should be compelled to ask it," was the quick answer.

"Is there, then, monsieur, any doubt in your mind as to the eldest male of the House of Dalberg?"

"None whatever; but can you assure us that he is king?"

"What has my assurance to do with the matter?" the Count asked. "By the laws of the Dalbergs the Crown has always passed to the eldest male."

The Baron laughed quietly. "At last we near the point—the Laws. There is no doubt that, by birth, the Archduke Armand is the eldest male; yet what of the decree of the Great Henry as to Hugo? As I remember, Frederick explained enough of it to the Council to cover Armand's assumption of his ancestor's rank and estates, but said no word as to the Crown." He leaned forward and looked the old Count in the eyes. "And I ask you now, my lord, if, under the decree, Armand became the Heir Presumptive, why was it that, at all our sessions, the Duke of Lotzen, until his banishment, retained his place on the King's right, and Armand sat on the left? Is it not a fair inference, from the actions of the three men who know the exact words of the decree, that, though it restored Hugo's heir to archducal rank, it specifically barred him from the Crown?"

The Prime Minister had listened with an impassive face and now he nodded curtly.

"There might be some weight to your argument, Monsieur le Baron," he said, "if you displayed a more judicial spirit in its presentation—and if you did not know otherwise."

"I shall not permit even you——" Retz broke in.

The Count silenced him with a wave of his hand. "You have sat at this board with us, and since the Duke of Lotzen's absence, at least, you have seen our dead master treat the Archduke Armand, in every way, as his successor; and on one occasion, in your hearing and to your knowledge—for I saw you slyly note the exact words, on your cuff—he referred to him as the one who would 'come after.' Hence, I say, you are not honest with the Council."

"I felicitate your lordship on your powers of observation and recollection," said Retz suavely; "they are vastly more effective and timely than mine, which, I confess, hesitate at miracles. But with due modesty, I submit there is a very simple way to settle this question quickly and finally. Let us have the exact words of Henry's decree. I am well aware it is unprecedented for any but a Dalberg to see the Dalberg Laws; but we are facing an unprecedented condition. Never before has a Dalberg king failed to have a son to follow him. Now, we hearken back for generations, with a mysterious juggle intervening; and it is for him who claims the Throne to prove his title. Before the coming of the American there was no question that Lotzen was the Heir Presumptive. Did he lose the place when Armand became an Archduke? The decree alone can determine; let it be submitted to the Royal Council for inspection."

"The Minister of Justice is overdoing his part," said the old Count, addressing the other Ministers. "It is not for him nor his Department to dictate the method by which the Dalbergs shall decide their kingship, nor does it lie in the mouth of any of us to demand an inspection of the Book of Laws. So much for principle and ancient custom. It may be the pleasure of the Archduke to confirm his right by exhibiting to us the Laws; or the Duke of Lotzen may challenge his title, and so force their submission to us or to the House of Nobles for decision. But, as the matter stands now, the Council has no discretion. We must accept the eldest male Dalberg as King of Valeria; and, as you very well know" (looking directly at Retz) "none but a Dalberg may dispute his claim—do you, Monsieur le Baron, wish to be understood as speaking for the Duke of Lotzen?"

Retz leaned back in his chair and laughed.

"No, no, my lord, no, no!" he said. "I speak no more for Lotzen than you do for Armand."

"So it would seem—though not with the same motives," the Count sneered—then arose hastily. "The King, my lords, the King!" he exclaimed, as the door in the far corner opened and Armand entered, unattended, and behind him came a manservant bearing a brass-bound, black-oak box, inlaid with silver.

Never had any of the Council seen it, yet instantly all surmised what it contained; and, courtiers though they were, they (save the old Count) stared at it so curiously that the Archduke, with an amused glance at the latter, turned and motioned the servant to precede him.

"Place it before His Excellency, the Prime Minister," he said; and now the stares shifted, in unfeigned astonishment to Armand—while the Count's thin lips twitched ever so slightly, and, for an instant, his faded blue eyes actually sparkled, as they lingered in calm derision on the Baron's face.

And Retz, turning suddenly, caught the look and straightway realized he had been outplayed. He understood, now, that the Count had been aware, all along, of the Archduke's purpose to produce the Laws to the Council, this morning, and that he, by his very persistence, had given the grim old diplomat an opportunity to demonstrate, in the most effective fashion, the unprecedented honor Armand was now doing them. It was irritating enough to be out-manœuvered, but to have his own ammunition seized and used to enhance another's triumph was searing to his pride; and, in truth, this was not the first time that the Prime Minister had left his scar and a score to settle between them.

"Be seated, my lords," said Armand, "and accept my apologies for my tardiness," and he took the chair at the head of the table.

Count Epping drew his sword and raised it high.

"Valeria hails the Head of the House of Dalberg as the King!" he cried.

And back from the others, as their blades rang together above the table, came the echo:

"We hail the Dalberg King!"

It was the ancient formula, which had always been used to welcome the new ruler upon his first entrance to the Royal Council.

And it had come as yet another scar to Retz, for it put him to the choice—whether to play the fool now, or the dastard later—and that with every eye upon him, even the Archduke's, whose glance had instinctively followed the others'. Yet he had made it instantly, smiling mockingly at the Count; and his voice rang loud and his sword was the last to fall.

But Armand knew nothing of this old ceremony, and the surprise of it brought him sharply to his feet, with his hand at the salute, while his face and brow went ruddy and his fingers chill. It was for him to speak, he knew, yet speak he could not. But when led by Count Epping, they crowded close about him and bent knee and would have kissed his hand, he drew back and waved them up.

"I thank you, my lords, I thank you from my heart," he said gravely, "though not yet will I assume to accept either the homage or the greeting. They belong to him who is King of Valeria, and whether I be he I do not know. As the eldest male, the presumption is with me; yet as the monarch has full power to choose his successor from any of the Dalbergs, it may have been his pleasure, under the peculiar conditions now existing, to name another as his heir. Hence it is my purpose to submit to you the Book of Laws, that you may inspect the decrees and ascertain to whom the Crown descends. I am informed this is a proceeding utterly unknown; that the Dalberg Laws are seen only by Dalberg eyes. Yet, as I apprehend there will be another claimant, who will have a hearty following, and as, in the end, it is the Laws that will decide between us, it is best they should decide now. If, by them, I am King of Valeria I will assume the Crown and its prerogatives; and if I am not King, then I will do homage to him who is, and join with you in his service."

He paused, and instantly General Duval flashed up his sword.

"God save Your Royal Highness!" he cried. "God grant that you be King."

And as the others gave it back for answer, their blades locked above the Archduke's head, the corridor door behind them swung open, and Ferdinand of Lotzen entered and, unnoticed, came slowly down the room.

All night, with a clear track and a special train, he had been speeding to the Capital, anxious and fearful, for in an interregnum hours count as days against the absent claimant to a throne. But when, at the station, he learned from Baron Rosen that the Proclamation had not yet been issued and the Council had been called for ten o'clock, the prospect brightened, and he hurried to the Palace.

Yet there was small encouragement in the scene before him, though the words of the acclaim and the black box on the table puzzled him. Why, with the Laws at their disposal, should there be any doubt as to who was King! So he leaned upon a chair and waited, a contemptuous smile on his lips, a storm of hate and anger in his heart. Those shouts, those swords, those ardent faces should all have been his; would all have been his, but for this foreigner, this American, this usurper, this thief. And his fingers closed about his sword's hilt and, for the shadow of an instant, he was tempted to spring in and drive the blade through his rival's throat. But instead he laughed—and when at the sound they whirled around, he laughed again, searching the while every face with his crafty eyes, and, save in Retz's, finding no trace of confusion nor regret.

"A pretty picture, messieurs," he jeered, "truly, a pretty picture—pray don't let me disturb it; though I might inquire, since when has the Royal Council of Valeria gone in for private theatricals!"

And Armand promptly gave him back his laugh.

"Our cousin of Lotzen appears in good time," he said very softly. "Will he not come into the picture?"

Ferdinand shook his head. "In pictures of that sort, there can be but one central figure," he answered.

The Archduke swung his hand toward the Ministers.

"True, quite true," said he; "but there is ample space for Your Royal Highness in the background."

Lotzen's face went white, and he measured Armand with the steady stare of implacable hate, though on his lips the sneering smile still lingered.

And presently he answered: "I trust, monsieur, you will not mistake my meaning, when I assure you that there isn't space enough in such a picture to contain us both."

"It is a positive pleasure, Monsieur le Duc," returned Armand quickly, "to find, at last, one matter in which our minds can meet."

And so, for a time, they stood at gaze, while the others watched them, wondering and in silence. Then the Archduke spoke again:

"And now, my dear cousin, since we understand each other, I suggest we permit the Royal Council to continue its session. Be seated, messieurs;" and with a nod to the Ministers, he resumed his place at the head of the table.

Instantly Lotzen stepped forward.

"My lords," he cried, "as Heir Presumptive I claim the Throne of Valeria. I call upon you, in the name of the House of Dalberg, to acknowledge me and to proclaim my accession."

"Upon what does Your Royal Highness rest your claim?" Count Epping asked formally.

The Duke pointed to the box; he saw now it was shut tight and the key not in the lock—and this, with what had occurred as he entered, undoubtedly indicated either that the Book had not yet been examined or that it contained no decree fixing the Succession. In either event, he stood a chance to win; and, at least, he had need for time.

"Upon the Laws of the Dalbergs," he replied, raising his hand in salute; "and under which, as you all well know, I have been the Heir Presumptive since my father's death."

"And you will accept them as final arbiter between us?" asked Armand quickly.

Ferdinand turned and looked at him fixedly.

"For the Crown, yes," he said very softly; and not a man but understood the limitation and the challenge.

And the Archduke smiled, and answered in a voice even softer and more suave.

"So be it—I will chance the rest." Then he addressed the Council. "His Excellency, the Prime Minister, has the key to the box; with your permission I will ask him to explain when and under what circumstances he got it."

And the Count took care that Armand should lose nothing in the telling, and when he had finished, he drew out the queer little key, and holding it so all could see looked at the two Dalbergs inquiringly.

"Shall I unlock the box?" he asked; and both nodded.

But the key would enter only a little way; and while the Count worked with it, Armand remembered suddenly the unusual motion Frederick had used the day he showed him the Laws.

"Turn the bit sidewise and push down and in," he said. And at once the key slipped into place and the lock snapped open.

At the sound, the Ministers eagerly craned forward; but the Count did not offer to lift the lid until he received the Archduke's nod; then he slowly laid it back, and leaning over peered inside. And he peered so long, that Lotzen grew impatient.

"The Laws, Epping, the Laws," he said sharply; "let us have them, man."

The Count looked at him and then at Armand.

"The box is empty," he said.

IV
THE PRESUMPTION SHIFTS

Into the silence of amazement that ensued, came the Duke's sneering laugh.

"Surely, surely, you didn't think to find it otherwise!" he said.

His insinuation was so apparent that the Archduke turned upon him instantly.

"Don't be a coward, Ferdinand of Lotzen," he said. "Speak plainly; do you mean to charge me with having removed the Book from the box?"

The Duke bowed. "Just that, Your Royal Highness," he said; "just that, since you must have it—you Americans are so blunt of speech."

Armand leaned forward. "The only way to deal with a liar," he answered, "is to put him where he can't lie out."

Ferdinand shrugged his shoulders deprecatingly. "You play it very cleverly, cousin mine, but the logic of elimination is against you. I assume you will not accuse our dear dead master of having hid the Laws; and since his decease, the key, you admit, has been with only you and His Excellency, the Prime Minister. I assume also you will acquit Count Epping—I am quite sure I will—and so we come back to—you."

The Archduke had long ago learned that in an encounter with Lotzen it was the smiling face that served him best; so he controlled his anger and turned to the Ministers.

"His Highness overlooks the logic of opportunity," he said. "I was not in the Summer Palace, since the King's death, until this morning."

Ferdinand laughed again. "Naturally not; you're not such a bungler."

Baron Steuben, who had been pulling thoughtfully at his beard, eyeing first one and then another, here broke in, addressing Armand.

"Would Your Highness care to tell us when you last saw the Book of Laws?" he inquired.

"I shall gladly answer any question the Council may ask. The only time I ever saw either Book or box was the day the King offered me my inheritance as the heir of Hugo."

And once again came Lotzen's sneering interruption.

"And yet you could instruct Count Epping just how to manipulate the key:—'turn the bit sidewise and push down and in.'"

Retz half closed his eyes and smiled; Epping's lips grew tighter; Duval and Marquand frowned; Steuben, with a last fierce tug at his beard, relapsed into silence.

But Armand met the issue squarely.

"It is my word against your inference," he said. "I am quite content to let the Council choose. They, too, have seen that key used but once, and yet I venture that a year hence they also will remember the peculiar motion it requires."

"They are much more likely to remember your ready wit and clever tongue," Lotzen retorted.

The Archduke turned from him to the Council.

"My lords," he said, "there is small profit to you in these personal recriminations. The question is, who is King of Valeria, Ferdinand of Lotzen or myself—and as only the Book of Laws can answer, I ask that you, yourselves, search King Frederick's apartments and interrogate his particular attendants."

Count Epping arose. "Will the Minister of Justice aid in the search," he said—"and also Your Royal Highness?" addressing Lotzen.

The latter smiled. "No; I thank you—what is the good in searching for something that isn't there!"—then he turned upon Armand. "I assume you brought the box here," pointing to the table, "and that you found it in the vault, where it is always kept—may I inquire how you got into the vault?"

"Through the door," said the Archduke dryly.

"Then you know the combination—something the King never told even me. Observe, my lords, the logic of opportunity!"

But Armand shook his head. "No," said he, "I do not know the combination."

And Lotzen, seeing suddenly the pit that yawned for him if he pursued farther, simply smiled incredulously and turned away.

The old Count, however, saw it too, and had no mind to let the opportunity slip.

"Who opened the door?" he asked bluntly.

"Her Royal Highness the Princess," said the Archduke.

And Epping nodded in undisguised satisfaction; while Ferdinand of Lotzen, sauntering nonchalantly over to the nearest window, cursed him under his breath for a meddler and a fool.

As the Duke had predicted, the search of the King's apartments and the vault proved barren; and then, his particular servants and such attendants as were in the Palace were summoned and examined, and also without result; indeed none of them remembered having seen either box or Book—save one: Adolph, Frederick's valet. He said that, recently, his master had spent many hours in the evenings studying the Laws, going through them with great care, making notations and marking certain pages with slips of paper; that no one else was ever present at such times, and once, when he had unthinkingly approached the desk, the King had angrily bade him leave the room. Asked when he had last seen the Book, he answered the fourth day before His Majesty's demise; which, he added, he felt sure was also the last time it had been used; but admitting, frankly, when pressed by the Archduke, that his only reason for so thinking was that he had not seen it in that interval.

"Oh, as to that, my dear cousin," said Lotzen from the window, the instant the valet had gone, "I am altogether willing to admit, and for the Council to assume, that the Book was safely in the box and the box safely in the vault when Frederick died. Don't try to obscure the point at issue—what we want to know is what you have—I beg your pardon—what has happened to it since that time."

Armand waited with polite condescension until the Duke had finished, then he ignored him and addressed the Council.

"My lords," he said, "you are confronted by a most unpleasant duty: Valeria must have a King, and you must choose him, either Ferdinand of Lotzen or myself. We cannot wait until the Laws are found. I claim the throne by presumptive right; he, by a right admitted to be subordinate to mine. In the absence of the decrees my title is paramount, and the royal dignity falls on me. If the Laws be recovered, and under them I am not King, I will abdicate, instantly."

Lotzen had come back to the table and resumed his favorite attitude of leaning over the back of a chair.

"Charming, indeed, charming!" he chuckled. "Make me King, and if the Laws unmake me I will abdicate when they are recovered—when—they—are—recovered! Do you fancy, messieurs, they would ever be recovered?"

Count Epping saved the Archduke the necessity of answer.

"Your Highness' argument," he observed, "is predicated on the hypothesis that the Archduke Armand has possession of the Book of Laws and is concealing it because it would, if exhibited, prove him ineligible to the Throne."

"Admirably stated!" said Lotzen.

"But," Epping went on, "you cannot expect the Council to accept any such hypothesis"—and all the Ministers nodded—"we must assume that neither you nor the Archduke knows aught of the Book, and whatever action we do take must be, upon the distinct condition, agreed to, here and now, by you both, that when the Laws are found—as found they surely will be—the Succession shall be determined instantly by them. Are you willing,"—addressing Lotzen—"that the Council, of which you are one, shall settle it, pending the recovery of the Laws?"

"No, I am not," said the Duke abruptly; "but pending election by the House of Nobles, I am content."

The Prime Minister watched the Duke meditatively for a moment, then turned to the Archduke inquiringly.

"I am content, even as His Highness of Lotzen," said Armand; he saw where the play was leading, and the other's next move, and he was not minded to balk him; there was likely to be a surprise at the end.

The Count faced the Council.

"The matter is before you," he said. "Having in view the Laws and circumstances, as we know them, to whom shall we confide the government?" and with a bland smile, he looked at the

Minister of Justice—who, as the junior member, would have to vote first.

Retz stirred uneasily and glanced furtively at Lotzen. He was not inclined to go so rapidly, or, at least, so openly. Had he apprehended any such proceeding he would have remained at home, ill, and let his dear colleagues bear the unpleasant burdens. It was an appalling dilemma. He wanted to vote for Lotzen—yet he was sure that Armand would be chosen. If he voted for Armand, he would bear the Duke's everlasting enmity, and, in the end, the Laws or the Nobles might give him the Crown. If he voted for Lotzen, and Armand were chosen, he lifted himself out of the Council, and ended his career if eventually the American won. He ran his eye around the table and caught the smile on every face, and mentally he consigned them all to death and perdition. Then he heard Epping's voice again:

"We are waiting, Monsieur le Baron."

But Lotzen came to his relief—quite unintentionally; he alone had not noted Retz's embarrassment, having been reading a paper he had taken from his pocket-book.

"One moment, if you please," he said. "I take it, that what may give the Archduke Armand preference over me in his claim for the Crown, is the presumptive right of the eldest male. If, however, by the Laws, he is specifically deprived of that right and made ineligible to the Crown, save under two conditions, I assume the presumption would be reversed, and he would be disqualified for the Succession until he had proved, by the Laws themselves, his rehabilitation?"

The words were addressed to Epping, and the answer was prompt and to the point:

"Your proposition begs the situation," he said; "it needs the Laws to prove it."

The Duke laughed. "No, it doesn't. I will prove it out of the mouth of the Archduke Armand himself." He held up the paper. "Here is a copy of the Great Henry's decree reinstating Hugo. I made it months ago, being, it would seem, wiser than I knew. With the first portion the Council is already familiar, Frederick having quoted it to you the day the Archduke Armand was presented; but of the last sentence, unfortunately, he made no mention; and it is that which governs now. His Royal Highness is fully acquainted with the original, and if my copy is not accurate he can make denial—nay, further, if he deny, I will accept whatever correction he may offer.... Surely, cousin, that is fair and honest—shall I read it—or will you?"

Armand smiled indifferently. "You can do it with much better effect," he answered.

"Will you have all of it or only the last sentence?"

"All of it."

Lotzen smiled maliciously. "The sweet as well as the bitter, cousin mine, with the bitter at the end." Then he tossed the paper across to Epping. "Will Your Excellency read it?" he said.

With a glance at the Archduke for permission, the Count complied:

> "'Section one hundred twenty-fifth—Whereas, we have learned that our second son, Hugo, hath served with much honour in the American Army under General Washington, and hath, since the termination of hostilities, married into a good family in one of the said American States, called Maryland, and hath assumed residence therein; and whereas he hath never sought aid from us nor sued for pardon; Now, therefore, in recognition of his valour and self reliance and true Dalberg independence, it is decreed, that Section one hundred twenty-one, supra, be annulled; and Hugo's name is hereby reinstated on the Family Roll in its proper place, the same as though never stricken therefrom. And it is further decreed that the marriage of Hugo and the marriage of his descendants shall be deemed lawful, the same as though their respective consorts were of the Blood Royal. The titles conferred upon Hugo shall, however, remain in abeyance until claimed anew by him or by his right heir male——'"

"And now, my lords, attend," Lotzen cut in. "Your pardon, Monsieur le Comte, pray proceed."

The old man paused a moment in rebuke, then resumed:

> "'Nor shall the latter be eligible to the Crown unless hereinafter specifically decreed so to be—or in event of a vacancy in the royal dignity without such decree

having been so made, then, by special Act of the House of Nobles.

"'Henry III., Rex. "'Ye 17th of September, A.D. 1785.'"

The Prime Minister slowly put down the paper, and every one looked at the Archduke—what would be his answer? There was no doubt that Lotzen had scored heavily, so heavily, indeed, that Retz made no effort to restrain his smile.

"Does His Royal Highness deny the correctness of the copy and that the decree is as read?" the Duke asked.

"I have never seen the decree," said Armand, "and my—pray have the courtesy, sir," (as Lotzen laughed and shrugged his shoulders) "to wait until I've finished—and my only knowledge of it is from hearing it read by the King, the day he offered me my inheritance; but if my recollection be accurate, the decree is as you have it."

In a flash the situation had become reversed, and it was now Armand against whom the presumption ran; and it was he, and not Ferdinand, who required the Laws to prove his claim.

A heavy silence followed. Then into the stillness cut the Duke's taunting laugh.

"Exit the American," he sneered. "Vale the foreign pretender."

It was, he knew, into Armand's most vulnerable spot and, like the *coup de grâce*, he had saved it until last; yet, to his astonishment, it brought only a contemptuous smile and an ignoring stare.

"His Grace of Lotzen seems to have discovered a mare's nest," said Armand. "The decree that is required to make me eligible to the Crown and to restore me to my proper place in the Line of Succession was executed by Frederick the Fourth the night before he died."

And once again came Lotzen's taunting laugh.

"The night *after* he died, you mean, cousin," he exclaimed.

The Prime Minister turned upon him with a frown.

"Your Royal Highness will permit me to suggest," said he, "the propriety, under the circumstances, of neither you nor the Archduke addressing each other."

And Lotzen, discerning that the Council was of the same mind, nodded easily.

"I cry pardon," he replied. "Your Excellency is quite right—but you will understand, I deny the existence of this suspiciously timely decree. As to it, at least, there is no presumption of execution—the Laws alone can prove it."

The Count turned to the Archduke. "Your Highness has seen the decree?" he asked.

"I have not."

"Did the King tell you it was executed?"

"He did not—but he told another."

"And that other——?"

"Is the Princess Royal," said the Archduke.

The Count paused a moment to give the situation emphasis—and Lotzen, chagrin and anger consuming him, yet smiling and unabashed, drew out a cigarette and carefully lit it.

"Do you think Her Highness would honor the Council with the facts?" Epping asked.

"I will acquaint her with your desires," said Armand.

V
THE COMPROMISE

The Princess' suite was across the corridor from the King's, and in a moment the Archduke was with her.

"Your Majesty!" she cried, and curtsied.

He raised her quickly. "Not yet, sweetheart," he said, "not yet—and, may be, never."

She stepped back and regarded him in puzzled surprise.

"You are jesting, dear," she said; "surely, you are jesting!"

He shook his head and went toward her.

"But the decree—the decree!" she exclaimed, again stepping back.

"The Laws have disappeared," he said, "the box is empty and the Book cannot be found."

In bewildered amazement she let him lead her to a chair, and listened, frowning and impatient, to his story. Only once did she interrupt—when he mentioned the Duke's unexpected entrance—then she struck her hand sharply on the table at her side. "Lotzen! Oh, Lotzen!" she cried, and with such threatening vehemence that Armand looked at her in sudden wonder.

At the end, she sprang up.

"Come!" she commanded. "Come; take me to the Council—I can at least assure they won't make Lotzen king," and seizing his hand she made for the door.

He slipped his arm around her waist and detained her.

"Are you sure, Dehra, you ought to mix in this unfortunate squabble?" he asked. "Is it——"

She turned upon him sharply. "Squabble! Do you call a contest for Valeria's Throne a squabble?"—then suddenly she smiled—that sweet, adorable smile she ever had for him. "Be very careful, sir, or I shall tumble both you and Lotzen aside, and take the Throne myself.... Now, will you escort me!"

He looked at her thoughtfully, then smiled and patted her cheek.

"Come, Your Majesty," he said; "come, and claim your Crown; it's yours by right, and I shall be the first to swear allegiance."

"And the first to rebel, dear," she laughed.

They entered the council chamber through the King's cabinet, and as the Princess halted a moment in the doorway the Ministers sprang to their feet and stood waiting, while Ferdinand of Lotzen advanced and bowed low; not offering, however, to take her hand, fearing it would not be given, and having no notion to risk a snub in such company.

To his astonishment, Dehra extended her hand and let him kiss it.

"You come on a sad errand, cousin," she said.... "I would you were still in Lotzenia." The words were so innocently fitting, yet the double meaning was so deliberate.

The Duke slowly straightened, discomfiture and amusement struggling for control, while Armand smiled openly and the Ministers looked away.

Meanwhile, the Princess passed on serenely to the table and took the chair at its head. Then, led by Count Epping, the Council came forward and made obeisance. She received them with just that touch of dignified sadness which the circumstances demanded, and which, with men, a woman must measure with the exactness of fine gold. And with it there was the low, sweet voice, the winning graciousness, and the dazzling smile—now softened just a trifle—that never yet had failed to conquer, and that had made her the toast of the Army and the pride of the Nation. And Armand had watched her, with glistening eyes, as one after another she sent the Ministers back to their places, bound to her chariot wheels; captive and content.

And Ferdinand of Lotzen, seeing, understood; and for the first time he realized fully what her aid meant to his rival, and how little chance he had to win, save with the Laws. And straightway the last faint scruple perished, and he set his cold heart against her, as well. Henceforth, for him, there was but one object in life—the Crown of his ancestors, and for all who interfered there would be neither consideration nor mercy.

And the Princess' eye, resting for an instant on his face, read something of his mind, and with a lift of the chin and a careless smile she turned to the Council.

"My lords," she said, "His Royal Highness has acquainted me with your desires, and I am glad indeed if I can serve you. His Majesty, the night before he died, executed the decree necessary to make the Archduke Armand his successor."

"You saw the decree?" Count Epping asked.

"No, I did not, but what I know is this. Late that night I went into the King's library; he was sitting at his desk, with the Book of Laws open before him and a pen in his hand. He was blotting a page as I entered. 'You have made Armand's decree?' I cried, and went to his side to read it; but he laughed and closed the Book, saying: 'You may see it to-morrow, child, after I have told Armand.'"

"And he did not tell you the words of the decree," the Count asked, after a pause, "neither then nor the following day?"

The Princess closed her eyes and lowered her head. "No," she said; "no—I never saw my father again—alive."

There was a distressing silence—then Armand spoke:

"The Council will understand that His Majesty had no opportunity to tell me of the decree. I was with him yesterday only at the review; naturally he would not speak of it then."

"And that was, I suppose, the last time you saw the Book of Laws?" Epping asked, addressing the Princess, who had recovered her composure.

"Yes—it was lying on the table when I left."

"May I ask Your Highness," said Steuben, "why, when you saw that His Majesty had been writing in the Book of Laws, you assumed, instantly, that it was 'Armand's decree,' as you put it?"

"You must know, my lords," she responded, "that it is rare, indeed, that a new law is made for the Dalbergs, there have been but five in the last hundred years, and the making is ever due to some extraordinary circumstance, which is known, of course, to all the family. We had been anticipating the decree, restoring Armand to his rightful place in the Line of Succession as Hugo's heir, and hence it was very natural to assume it was that which His Majesty had written." She paused, and, for an instant, her glance strayed to the Duke of Lotzen. "But it was particularly natural," she went on, "inasmuch as the King had mentioned the matter to me twice within the week, the last time that very morning, and referring to it as 'Armand's decree.'"

Steuben nodded. "I am satisfied," he said—and Duval and Marquand nodded.

The Prime Minister turned to Ferdinand.

"We would be glad to hear Your Royal Highness," he said.

The Duke laughed softly in sneering amusement. He was still standing behind his chair, and now he tilted it forward and leaned across it, his arms folded on the rail.

"Small chance have I against such a Portia," he answered. "Yet I would remind the Council that, where kingdoms are concerned, a pretty woman is a dangerous advocate to follow—and thrice dangerous when against her is the written Law and with her only—conjecture."

"Our cousin of Lotzen does not mean to question my veracity?" the Princess asked quickly.

"Your veracity?—never, I assure you—only your inferences."

"And yet, sir, what other inferences can be drawn?"

He shrugged his shoulders and turned to the Prime Minister.

"I reiterate my claim to the Crown," he said; "and the only Law of the Dalbergs that is before you confirms it. I cannot conceive that the Royal Council of Valeria will arrogate to itself the right to annul a decree of Henry the Third."

"His Highness of Lotzen misses the point," said Armand. "I do not ask the Council to annul that decree, but only to assume from Her Royal Highness' story that it was duly and legally annulled by Frederick the Fourth."

"Exactly, my lords, exactly," the Duke retorted; "inference against fact—guesses against an admitted Law."

Then Armand made the play he had had in mind since it was certain that the Book of Laws was lost. He was standing behind the Princess' chair—now he stepped forward and addressed the Duke.

"Cousin," he said, "we are putting a grievous burden on the Ministers in obliging them to choose between us, with the proofs seemingly so strong on either side. It is not fair to them to drive them to the embarrassment nor to the misfortune that would attend a mistake. There ought to be no doubt in the mind of the Nation as to the title of the king; he who occupies the Throne should have his tenure unquestioned; and such cannot be if the one of us who is to-day made king is liable to be displaced to-morrow by the other. Besides, as I understand Henry the Third's decree, the Council has no jurisdiction except by our agreement. You assert the decree of eligibility was not made by Frederick. If that be true, then, there being 'a vacancy in the royal dignity without such decree being made,' it is for the House of Nobles to enact my eligibility and so give me the Crown, or to refuse and so give it to you. Therefore, I propose that for the space of a year, or pending the recovery meanwhile of the Book of Laws, we let the question of succession remain in abeyance. If, at the end of the year, the Book has not been found, then the House of Nobles shall choose between us. And as in the interval there must be some one in supreme authority, let Her Royal Highness be proclaimed Regent of Valeria."

Never before had there been such instant, open and cordial unanimity among the Ministers of the Royal Council. Here was a complete solution of the vexing problem, and one, moreover, that would relieve them of a most undesirable duty. Baron Retz's smile was positively gleeful, and the others nodded enthusiastically and turned to the Duke expectantly.

And Lotzen saw that he was losing—and with rage and hatred in his heart, but with calm face and voice softer even than usual, he made his last play, knowing well that though it might not win, it would at least work a sweet revenge upon his rival.

"An admirable compromise for you, cousin mine," he laughed; "and clever, very clever—you and Dehra are to be married on the twenty-seventh. What difference, think you, will there be between you as King and you as Consort of the Princess Regent?" Then he faced the Council and flung his last card: "Otherwise, my lords," he said with suave frankness, "I would willingly accept His Highness' proposition—or I will accept it, if it is engaged that the wedding shall abide the termination of the Regency ... how say you, cousin?"

Once again had the Duke turned the situation by his devilish cleverness, and Armand's fingers itched to take him by the throat and choke the life out of him; and Lotzen, reading something of this in his eyes, grinned malevolently.

"How say you, cousin?" he repeated, "how say you?"

The Archduke deliberately gave him his back. "My lords," he said, "it seems the Duke of Lotzen would force you to the choice."

But the old Count did not intend to forego the compromise. He wanted Armand for king because Armand was, *de facto*, the Head of the House, because he was convinced the decree had been executed, because it would make Dehra the Queen, and because he despised Lotzen. With the Princess as Regent, there would be ample means to swing the Nobles to the Archduke, and to prepare the public for his accession. Of course, it would also give Lotzen time to campaign, yet he who fights the government has a rough road to travel, and usually falls by the way. Leastwise, the Count was very ready to adventure it. But he needed aid now; and aid that could come from but one quarter and which he could seek only by indirection—Dehra alone controlled the situation.

"The compromise suggested is admirable," he said, "and though there is force in the objection made to it, yet, my lord," (addressing Lotzen) "you cannot expect the Archduke to accept your amendment. It is not for the man to change the wedding day——"

The Princess sat up sharply. When Armand had suggested her as Regent she had leaned forward to decline, but catching Epping's eye she had read an almost imperious order to wait; and having full faith in him, she had obeyed. Now she saw what he wanted; and though it was against her heart's desire and a cheerless business, yet her own judgment told her he was right.

"It is not for the man," the Count repeated, looking at her hard, "to change the wedding day, and least of all——"

"Wait, monsieur," she broke in. "It seems that unwittingly I have been drawn into the situation, and put in a position where I am obliged to speak. Does the Royal Council approve this compromise, and desire me to become Regent of Valeria?"

The Count smiled in supreme satisfaction.

"I can assure Your Highness we are of one mind that, in this exigency, it is your duty to assume the office."

The Princess arose. "Then, my lords," she said gravely, "I accept, hereby engaging that my wedding shall abide the termination of the Regency."

The Archduke made a gesture of protest, but Dehra flashed him her subduing smile and shook her head, and there was naught for him to do but to smile back—and add one more to the score that, some day, Ferdinand of Lotzen would have to settle.

The Prime Minister looked at the Duke with a bland smile of triumph, and then at Armand.

"Is it your joint wish," he asked, "that we ratify the stipulation and proclaim the Regency?"

"It is," said the Archduke; but Lotzen only bowed.

Count Epping drew his sword.

"Valeria hails the Princess Dehra as Regent," he cried. It was the ancient formula changed to fit the occasion.

And this time Armand's blade rang with the others across the table, and his voice joined exultantly in the answer that echoed through the room.

"We hail the Princess Regent!"

As the sound died Ferdinand of Lotzen stepped forward and bent knee.

"God save Your Royal Highness!" he said, and again Dehra gave him her hand.

"And grant me strength," she answered.

"Amen," said the Count gravely. "Amen."

It was Lotzen who broke the stillness.

"With Your Highness' permission I will withdraw," he said; "there are pressing personal affairs which demand my presence elsewhere." He turned to go.

"One moment, cousin," said she—then to the Prime Minister: "Will the Council need His Highness?"

There was the same gracious manner, the same soft voice, and yet, in those few words, she warned them all that there was now a Regent in Valeria—and a Dalberg regent, too.

"There is nothing now but to draw the Proclamation for your signature," said the Count—"the other matters can abide for the time."

And Lotzen, at the Princess' nod of permission, went slowly from the room, his surprise still stronger than his anger; though, in the end, it was the latter that lingered and left its mark in his unforgiving soul.

While the Count was drafting the Proclamation made necessary by the changed conditions, the Princess sat in silence, gazing in abstracted contemplation through the window. Regent of Valeria! the second the kingdom had known; the first had been a woman, too—Eleanor, mother of the infant, Henry the Third of glorious memory—yet, was it wise—was it in fact her duty—her duty to her House; to her beloved? Surely it was not to her pleasure—she who had been happy in her nearing wedding day—her lover placed next the Throne—his bright future and her joy for it. And now—the wait—the struggle—the obligation of right, of justice; the putting off the woman, the putting on the ruler where the woman interfered. Her father! she turned that thought aside sharply—she had turned it aside many times since yesterday, as he had bade her to do:—"When I go, child, do not grieve." Yet, when two have been comrades for years it is not easy.

The Count ceased his writing and, laying aside the pen, looked up.

"Will it please Your Highness to sign?" he said quickly—he had little liking at any time for a woman's reverie, and none at all when it was of the sort he knew this reverie to be—and the woman had work to do.

And Dehra, preoccupied though she was, had missed nothing that was doing at the table, and she let him know she understood him, by a smile and a shake of her handsome head. It was not exactly a reproof, and yet neither was it an encouragement to do the like again.

"Please read it," she said.

It was very brief—reciting the death of Frederick the Fourth, the disappearance of the Book of Laws, the stipulation of the Archduke and the Duke relative to the Succession remaining in abeyance, the creation of a Regency during the inter-regnum and the Princess' acceptance of the office.

When he had done, she asked if there were any suggestions, and none being offered, she signed it and returned it to the Count. Immediately the Council arose and she and Armand retired, by the same way they had entered.

As they passed through the library, Dehra went over to the desk.

"Here is where the King sat that last night," she said, "and here the Book of Laws lay, and here was the box. I can't imagine what he did with the Book—nor why he removed it from the box—and the box was in its usual place in the vault when I gave it to you to take to the Council——"

A door latch clicked, and Adolph, the valet, came in hurriedly.

"Well?" said the Archduke, seeing he wished to speak.

"The box, my lord," he answered; "you left it in the council-chamber—is it to remain there?"

"No," said the Princess—"bring it here at once." She went to the vault and opened it.... "Put it on the shelf in the rear," she ordered, when Adolph returned. He obeyed and gave her the key.

"There was no need to lock it," she remarked.

"It has a spring lock, mademoiselle," said the man. "It snapped when I closed the lid."

Dehra nodded indifferently. "So it has.... Shut the vault door." Then motioned to him in dismissal.

"It's of small consequence," she remarked to Armand, as she gave the combination a twirl, "the box is of little use without the Book."

As she turned away, her glance fell on the big portrait of her father that hung high on the opposite wall—and of a sudden the reaction came, and the tears started, and her lips twitched. She reached out her hand appealingly to Armand. In silence, he put his arm around her and led her quickly from the room.

VI
THE REWARD OF A MEDDLER

When Ferdinand of Lotzen left the Council, he passed leisurely down the corridor toward one of the private exits. The pressing business that was demanding his immediate attention seemed to bother him no longer, and he even took the trouble to acknowledge the salute of the guard who paced before the main stairway; whereat the man stared after him in unfeigned surprise, until the Duke, suddenly looking back, caught him in the act—and with a frown sent him to the about-face and the far end of his beat.

So no one saw His Highness step quickly over and try the door of the King's library, and, when it opened to him—as he had anticipated it would, the Princess having come that way to the Council—go in and close it softly behind him. Dropping the lock, he went to the door of the private cabinet (which was between the library and the room used for the Council meetings) and listened. Hearing nothing, he opened it very cautiously and peered inside; no one was there and he fixed the door a bit ajar, so as to be warned if anyone entered from the Council.

The library was a large room, paneled ceiling and sides in wood painted an ivory white; the great, wide windows were half hidden by the Gobelin blue tapestries that hung in folds to the floor; heavy bookcases of carved mahogany lined the walls; the furniture was of the massive Empire style, but the desk was a big, oblong, flat-topped affair that had been made over Frederick's own design—and which more than compensated in utility for what it lacked in artistry. It pleased its owner and so fulfilled its mission. It stood a little way back from the center of the room, the great crystal chandelier above its outer edge, and all the doors directly in focus of the revolving chair behind it.

It was to this chair that the Duke went and began hurriedly to go through the papers on the desk, yet taking the utmost care not to disturb their arrangement, and replacing them exactly as he found them. Evidently whatever he was seeking was of the sort that needed no examination to prove it, for he passed over letters and written documents without a glance at their contents. It was not on the desk and he began on the drawers, none of which was locked. One after another was searched without success, and the Duke's brow went blacker and blacker, until, as the last proved barren, he flung himself into the chair, and again ran over the documents on top—and again without finding what he sought.

"It was only a chance," he muttered, sending his glance around the room, "only a feeble chance;... 'He was blotting a page as I entered,' was what she said ... and if it were a fresh blotter it might tell the story." He went over to the vault, the front of which was painted white and paneled to correspond to the walls, and tried the door.... "Locked, of course——"

Suddenly he turned toward the King's cabinet, listening; then sprang quickly behind one of the window curtains; and its swaying had not ceased when the Princess and Armand entered, on their return from the Council.

Unseen, he was also unseeing; yet hearing, he had little need for eyes—it was easy to picture all that occurred:—Dehra's pointing out the positions of the King, the Laws and the box; the entry of Adolph; the opening of the vault; the valet's return with the box; his dismissal; the locking again of the vault. But what then happened always puzzled the Duke—that it was something unexpected was proved by the sudden silence, and pause, before either of them moved, followed at once by the closing of the corridor door.

He waited a moment, until he was sure they had gone, then went to the desk. What had disturbed the American and the Princess—why had their talk ceased so abruptly—why did they wait, unmoving, and then go out together and still unspeaking?... Had they seen him?... Impossible; even the window did not show through the tapestry; and he had been against the wall.... His gloves—had he let them lie somewhere?... no, they were drawn through his sword belt.... He studied the desk top—the floor—the chairs.... They told him nothing;... and, yet, it was very queer.... Had any part of him been exposed beyond the curtain? He went back and got behind it ... it completely covered him—and as he stood there the cabinet door opened and Adolph came in softly.

He glanced around quickly, then went straight to the vault and began to turn the knob, while the Duke, one eye just beyond the curtain's edge, watched him curiously. Could it be that this servant was familiar with the combination of the lock, that only the King and Dehra were supposed to know! If so ... the bolts shot back, the door opened, and the valet disappeared in the vault. In a moment he came out with the box; but Lotzen did not see him, having drawn behind the curtain; nor did he venture again to look out except when assured that Adolph's back was toward him.

Placing the box on the desk, the valet laid back the lid and with another furtive look around, went swiftly across to the wall, where hung the big, life-sized portrait of the King, the escutcheon, on the top of the heavy gold frame, almost against the ceiling. Under it was a tall, straight-backed chair, with high arms; and, mounting on them, Adolph reached behind the picture and, from the space between it and the wall, drew out an ancient book, leather-bound and metal-hinged:—the Laws of the Dalbergs.

With a faint chuckle, he sprang down and started toward the box; then stopped—the Book slipped from his fingers—he gasped—his eyes widened in terrified amazement—his face took on the gray pallor of awful fear; for the Duke of Lotzen had emerged from behind the window curtain and was coming slowly toward him.

"You seem startled, Adolph," said the Duke, with an amused smile, "doubtless you thought you were alone." He sat down in the revolving chair. "May I trouble you to give me the Book—the floor is hardly the place for the Laws of the Dalbergs."

The valet's composure had returned, in a measure, at the tone of the other's voice, but his hand still trembled as he picked up the Book and carried it to the desk.

"Thank you, Adolph," said Lotzen, "thank you ... you seem a trifle shaky, sit down and rest" (indicating a chair near by). "I shall need you presently."

He watched the man until he had obeyed, then opened the Laws and turned quickly to the last decree.

Across the page lay a fresh, white blotter, used but twice, he noticed, as he turned it over. He had come for this very bit of paper, that Dehra had casually mentioned in her story to the Council—hoping vaguely that the King had let it lie, and that it had not been destroyed by the servants who cared for the desk. He would have been amply satisfied with the faint chance it might give him of guessing the decree from the few words the mirror would disclose. But, now, he had no need for guesses nor mirrors; and with a light laugh he laid the blotter aside. Surely, the Goddess of Fortune was with him! And to Ferdinand of Lotzen this meant much; for to him there was only one other Divinity, and that other was a female, too.

Thrice he read Frederick's decree; first rapidly, then slowly, then word by word, as it were.

And all the while Adolph watched him covertly, a sly smile in his small, black eyes. He had quite recovered from his fright—though he might be led to pretend otherwise—indeed, now that he had time to think, he could find no reason why the Duke should punish him; rather did he deserve an ample reward for having kept the Laws from the Council. In fact, why should he not demand a reward, if it were not offered?—demand it discreetly, to be sure, but none the less demand it. And, as the Duke read, and re-read, the reward piled higher, and visions of Paris (it is strange how, under certain conditions, the thoughts of a certain sort of people turn to Paris as instinctively as the needle to the Pole) danced before his eyes.... And presently he forgot the Duke, and the Laws, and Dornlitz—he was sitting at a little table along the Boulevard des Italiens, an absinthe at his hand, a merry girl, with sparkling eyes and perfumed hair, at his elbow, a sensuous waltz song in his ears, and light, and life, and love, and lingerie in every breath of air....

"Dreaming, Adolph," said Lotzen, "dreaming?... of what, pray?"

"Of Paris, my lord," he answered unthinkingly.

The Duke regarded him in frowning surprise.

"Paris!" he muttered, "Paris! has everyone gone Paris mad?"

"It was of the Boulevards, my lord—the music and the lights and the———"

"Shut up!" exclaimed Lotzen; "to the devil with your Paris and its Boulevards!... How did this Book get behind that picture?"

"I put it there, monsieur."—The reward was not piled quite as high as he had fancied.

"Why?"

"To hide it, monsieur—until I could replace it in the box."—The reward was dwindling marvellously fast.

"Then you stole the Laws of the Dalbergs?"

Adolph did not answer.... It was queer how chilly the room had got. It had seemed warm enough, a moment ago.

The Duke regarded him meditatively.

"Come," he said presently; "tell me how you managed it. My time is short—speak up."

The valet slunk a furtive look at his face; it was expressionlessly pitiless.—The reward had disappeared.

"Your Highness will believe me?" he asked.

"Believe you, Adolph! surely—a valet never lies! Go on."

The man gulped—ran his tongue over his lips—gulped again—then began, his voice husky, full of quavers and sudden stops; while the Duke, with steady gaze and searching eye, drove him on as with a lash.

"Your Highness heard my story to the Council," said Adolph; "all of it was true except as to the last time I saw the Book of Laws.... I happened to witness the scene between Her Royal Highness and the King. It was just as she related it, monsieur. When she had gone, His Majesty sat, doing nothing—and presently he dropped asleep.... I came to the room a number of times, and always that Book stared at me, and my curiosity as to the decree grew hotter every minute. After a while, the King awoke and told me to put the Book in the box and return it to its place in the vault—then he went over to the sideboard and poured out a drink.... Here, monsieur, was my opportunity—I laid the Book in the box and lowered the lid, but slipped in an envelope to prevent it locking, then put it in the vault—which the King himself closed. After he had retired, I opened the vault and got out the Book——"

"How did you know the combination?" the Duke asked.

"By—by—watching the King, monsieur ... I had picked up the numbers one by one ... long ago."

Lotzen tossed him a bit of paper and a pencil.

"Write out the combination," he ordered—and smiled at the servant's trembling hand and labored motions.... "Thank you;"—glancing at the paper and dropping it carelessly in his pocket—"proceed—you had just got the Book out of the vault."

"While I was examining it, monsieur," Adolph resumed, "I thought I heard the King moving about in his room. I sprang inside the vault, drew the door shut, but not quite tight, and tried to put the Book in the box. But I must have been nervous, monsieur, for, in some way, I struck the lid and knocked it down; and it locked, leaving the book in my hand. I could not open the box—the only key was under the King's pillow, on his watch chain. What was to be done? I dared not try for it that night; the King was too light a sleeper;—nor did I dare leave the Book in the vault, there was no place to conceal it, and he was sure to go in there in the morning. What was to do, monsieur? I listened—everything seemed quiet; I opened the door very slowly—no one was in the room—I stepped out, and the King's portrait confronted me—I stared at it a moment, frightened as though it were my master—then, of a sudden, I knew I had found the hiding place, and I sprang up and put the Book behind the picture.... And in the morning, monsieur, I forgot the Book—forgot it until His Majesty had gone to the city.—Then, in desperation, I tried every key I could find—tried to pick the lock—in vain.... I knew the Archduke Armand was to dine here that evening, and from what the King had said to the Princess I knew, also, the Book would have to be in the box before then. I felt, however, that I would have a good chance at the key when my master dressed for dinner. Then, my lord, came the awful news of his death, and once again I forgot the Book—nor ever thought of it, until I saw the Council gather—and then——" he threw up his hand, expressively.

"And, now, what were you about to do?" asked Lotzen.

"Put the Book in the box, monsieur, and return it to its place in the vault."

The Duke looked at him in surprise.

"Clever, clever, indeed," he muttered.... "I thought you gave the key to Her Highness."

Adolph smiled—his spirit was never long in travail. "I did, monsieur—I didn't need it;—and it was a good play to give it up at once. Never having had the key to the box, it could not be I who replaced the Book."

Lotzen studied the little valet a bit.

"Clever," he repeated, "clever ... quite too clever, I fear." He leaned across and tried the closed lid of the box; it lifted to his hand—and out on the desk dropped the little square of folded paper that had held the lock just out of catch.

"Altogether, too clever," he concluded, picking it up and looking at it.

"I fixed that in the Council chamber," Adolph explained; then he stared knowingly at the Duke—"monsieur was behind the curtain when I brought back the box."

Decidedly, this fellow was not to Lotzen's liking. He made no reply beyond a quick, sidelong glance, drumming with his finger tips softly on his knee. Then he turned to the desk and tapped the Book of Laws.

"You read this, I suppose, Adolph?" he remarked indifferently.

"King Frederick's, you mean?—yes, my lord, I did; but that is all—I had no time to read more."

The Duke nodded, his eyes on the Book.

The valet was becoming uneasy; he fidgeted in his chair, locked and unlocked his hands, listened toward all the doors.

"My lord," he said, at length, "we may be found here!"

Lotzen closed the Book. "True, Adolph, true," he answered, getting up and stepping back. "Put the Laws in the box—don't let it lock."

The valet sprang to obey; and as he leaned across the desk—his back to the Duke—and dropped the Book into the box, Ferdinand of Lotzen whipped out his sword, and, with the sure hand of the skilled fencer, drove the rapier-like blade through the man's heart.

Without cry or struggle, Adolph sank forward; and the box locked, as the lid fell under him.

For a moment, the Duke held the body with his sword; then he slowly drew out the blade and wiped it on his handkerchief; while the dead man slipped from the desk and crumpled on the floor.

Lotzen looked down at him and shrugged his shoulders.

"You poor fool," he muttered—"why did you read what didn't concern you!"... He stooped and turned the body on its face. "No blood!—a neat thrust, truly."

THE DEAD MAN SLIPPED FROM THE DESK.

He knew the room overlooked the King's private gardens, and, going to a window, he cautiously raised the sash. It was as he had thought:—below was a thick hedge of box-wood, that grew to within a foot of the palace wall, which at that point was blank. Fortune was still his friend, it seemed; and, with a smile, he carried the valet's body to the window and—after a quick survey of the garden to assure that no one was in sight—balanced it an instant on the casement, then dropped it behind the hedge.

Drawing down the window he rearranged the curtains and returned to the desk.

"Damnation!" he exclaimed, as his eyes fell upon the box—"Locked!—the fool must have fallen on it."

He stood looking at it, frowning in indecision. He had intended to take the Book with him, trusting to conceal it under his short cavalry cape—but the box was impossible; not only was it considerably larger than the Laws, but its weight was amazing for its size.... Then he saw the open vault, and what to do was plain—he would follow the valet's plan. None now would look in the box, and, for a time, the Book would be safer there than with him; later, he could arrange to get it—he knew the combination.... He laughed cynically—it was a pretty game, and the pleasanter because it would be played directly under the American's eye.

He carried the box into the vault, closed and locked the door, and, returning to the desk, put in place the papers disarranged by the valet's fall. Among them lay the blotter that had been in the Book of Laws. He studied it a moment ... made as though to tear it ... then folded it and put it in the inside pocket of his jacket. A last glance around the room assured him that everything was as he had found it. With a satisfied smile, he turned toward the corridor door, and his eyes rested on the portrait of His late Majesty. He stopped, and the smile changed to a sneer, and doffing his cap he bowed mockingly.

"My thanks, Sire, for dying so opportunely," he said; "may the devil keep you."

VII
THE ARMISTICE OF MOURNING

And so Frederick the Fourth of Valeria slept with his fathers, and Dehra, his daughter, ruled, as Regent, in his stead.

In the great crypt of the Cathedral, among the other Dalbergs, they had laid him away, with all the pomp and circumstance that befit a king—within, the gorgeous uniforms and vestments, the chanting priests, the floating incense; without, the boom of cannon, the toll of bells, the solemn music of the bands, the click of hoofs, the rumble of the caissons, the tramp of many feet.

When it was all done, the visiting Princes hurried away, the governmental machinery sped on, the Capital took up its usual routine, and all that remained externally to remind the people of a ruler just and righteous, were the draped buildings and the crape upon the troops. And, at the dead's own express behest, even these had vanished on the fifteenth day after his demise. "Let the period of mourning be limited strictly to a fortnight, both for the Nation and my House," he had written, in his own hand, as a codicil to his Testament; and the Regent, with no shade of hesitation, had ordered it as he wished. She knew it was Frederick's last kindness to his subjects. A Court in sackcloth buries the Capital in ashes, drives the tradesmen into insolvency, and bores the Nobility well nigh into insanity or revolt.

And as she ordered, so she did—though sadly and regretfully—and, with a blessing upon her, the Court resumed its accustomed life and garb, and Dornlitz its gayety and pleasures. Yet Valeria was sorry enough at Frederick's demise—sorrier far than he would have believed it could be. At the best, a King is of use, these days, only as a head for the Government—and when the new head is capable and popular, the old one is not missed for long.

As it was, the people had scarcely realized that Frederick was dead when they were met with the amazing Proclamation of Dehra's Regency; with the result that usually follows when sorrow and joy mingle, with joy mingling last.

In the interval, there had been no developments as to the Book of Laws. The Duke of Lotzen had observed the very strictest of mourning; not transgressing, in the slightest particular, the most trivial canon of propriety. He had remained practically secluded in his big residence on the Alta Avenue, appearing in public only at intervals. He had paid his brief visit of condolence to the Princess and had been greeted by her with calm and formal dignity. He had made his call of ceremony upon the Governor of Dornlitz—the Archduke Armand—and had been received by him in the presence of half his Staff. Then, after the funeral of the dead King, he had settled down to wait the termination of the two weeks of enforced inactivity. He could well afford, for that long, to dally with the future. So he subdued his natural indisposition to quiet and orderly living, and sternly bade Bigler and the others do likewise, telling them that the search for the Laws and the removal of the American could abide for the time.

But never a word did he speak to them of having seen the Book and what Frederick had written the night before he died.

Sometime before midnight, of the day that Adolph, the valet, had been killed, the sergeant of the guard, in making his rounds, saw a man skulking in the private garden. At the order to stand, the fellow had dashed away, and, seemingly unharmed by the shot sent after him, he leaped the low wall into the park, where among the trees and bushes, he had little difficulty in escaping. The matter was duly reported to the officer of the day and an entry made of it, but as such occurrences were rather frequent in the park, due sometimes to petty pilferers from the town, and sometimes to soldiers out without pass, it received no special attention, beyond a cursory inspection of the locality the following morning.

Two days later, Adolph's body was discovered by a gardener who was clipping the hedge; and then it was remembered that the valet had not been seen since the morning after Frederick's death. No one had given him a thought—in truth, no one cared anything about him. Like most of his class under such circumstances, he had won the cordial hatred of every one about the Court—a spoiled, impudent and lying knave. Busy with the royal funeral, and the great crowds it brought to the Capital, the police gave the matter scant regard—the fellow was known to them as a night prowler and a frequenter of questionable resorts, and to have had numerous escapades with married women; and the autopsy indicating he had been dead at least thirty-six hours, they had promptly ascribed the death to the skulker shot at by the sergeant. There was no other clue to work on, so, after a perfunctory search, they shrugged it over among the other unsolved. What was the use of bothering about a valet, any way! Besides, it was a case to let alone, unless special orders came from higher powers.

So they saw to it that the affair was entirely suppressed—such happenings around royal palaces are not for the public—and the information was casually given out that the King's valet was so distressed, by his royal master's death, he found it quite impossible to remain in Dornlitz, and had returned to France.

Once again, had the fickle Goddess smiled upon the Duke of Lotzen, still captivated, doubtless, by the very debonairness of his villainy and his steady gambler's nerve.

And all unwittingly the Archduke Armand had played directly into Lotzen's hands. Out of consideration for the Princess, he had insisted that they forget the Book of Laws until the period of mourning were passed, and Dehra, against her better judgment, had consented, though only upon condition that they two should first make a thorough search of her father's apartments, which they did the following morning; she even climbing up and looking behind the large pictures—much to Armand's amusement; he asking what would be the King's object in concealing the Book in such a place; and she retorting that, as there was no reason at all for concealing it, the unreasonable place was the most likely.

And in that she was very right; for the box itself was now the most unreasonable place, yet even her woman's fancy stopped short of it.

The period of official mourning expired on the twentieth, and on the twenty-first, the Princess telephoned to the Archduke to ride out to the Palace for luncheon that day, and to bring the American Ambassador with him—unless Mr. Courtney would object to being with Helen Radnor—and that the day being very warm they would be served under the trees near the sun dial, below the marble terrace—and that he and Courtney should join them there—and that Helen was with her now. And Armand had laughed and readily promised for them both.

As he hung up the receiver, Colonel Bernheim stood in the doorway, and he nodded for him to come in.

Bernheim saluted and crossing to the desk put down a small package, about as large as one's fist.

"My lord," he said, "here is the steel vest."

The Archduke leaned back and laughed.

"You say that as naturally as though it were my cap or gloves," he commented.

"And why not, sir—Ferdinand of Lotzen is in Dornlitz, and the truce is ended."

"The truce?"

"The truce of mourning—you were quite safe so long as it lasted; Moore and I made sure of that."

"Really, Colonel, you surprise me," said Armand. "How did you make sure?"

"By having some one buy Bigler plenty of wine, at the Club—and then putting together stray words he let slip."

The Archduke shook his head in mock reproof.

"You and Moore are a wonderful pair," he said. "You think for me more than I think for myself."

A smile touched Bernheim's stern mouth and impassive face.

"We need to, Your Highness," he answered. "You don't think at all; you leave it to Lotzen." He pushed the package a little nearer—"You will wear it, my lord?"

Armand took it, and, cutting the wrapper, shook out the wonderful steel vest, that had saved his life at the Vierle Masque when, from across the hedge, the assassin's dagger had sought his heart. It was, truly, a marvellous bit of craftsmanship; pliable as silk and scarcely more bulky, the tiny steel links so cunningly joined they had the appearance of dark gray cloth. He bent and twisted it in admiring contemplation. Verily, those armorers of old Milan understood their art—never could modern hand have forged and knit so perfect a garment. He found the mark on the back, where the bravo's weapon struck—only a scratch, so faint it was almost indistinguishable, yet the blow had sent him plunging on his face.

"It served you well that night," said Bernheim.

The Archduke smiled. "And as its owner always does;" he smiled—and the old Aide bowed—"but there is no Masque to-night."

"Every night, now, is a Masque for Lotzen—and every day, too."

"Heaven, man! you wouldn't have me wear this constantly?"

"No—not in bed;" then seriously—"but at all other times, sir."

Armand pushed the vest back on the desk and frowned.

"Has it come to this, then—that my life isn't safe here—nor in my house, nor on the street! Is this civilization or savagery?"

Bernheim shrugged his shoulders.

"Neither," he said, "neither—it's Hell. It's always Hell where Lotzen plays. Surely, sir, you have not forgot the past."

"No—no—but that was a Masque, and assassination went with the costumes and the atmosphere; yet now, in Dornlitz of the twentieth century—I can't bring myself to believe ... why don't you threaten me with poison or a bomb?"

"Poison is possible, but not a bomb—it is not neat enough for Lotzen."

Armand looked at him in puzzled amusement.

"I see," he said, "I see—he murders artistically—he doesn't like a mess."

"Just so, sir; and the most artistic and least messy is a neat hole through the heart.... You will wear the vest, my lord?"

The Archduke's glance wandered to the window—electric cars were speeding down the avenue—an automobile whizzed by—and another—and another.

"Look," said he, "look! isn't it absurd to talk of steel vests!"

Bernheim shook his head. "Lotzen does not belong yonder—he is a remnant of the Middle Ages."

"Well, I'm not; so no armor for me, my dear Bernheim—I'll keep my eyes open and take my chances. I don't believe the crown of Valeria will be the reward of an assassin."

Disappointment shone in the Aide's eyes.

"I'm something of a Fatalist, myself, sir," he said, "but I wouldn't play with a tiger after I had goaded him to fury."

Armand smiled. "The case isn't exactly parallel."

"No—not exactly:—the tiger *might* not kill me."

The Archduke picked up the letter knife and slowly cut lines on the blotter.

"You need not go into the tiger's cage," he remarked.

"There isn't any cage—the beast is at large."

"Nonsense, Colonel; this fellow Lotzen has got on your nerves. I thought you hadn't any."

"The pity of it is, sir, that he hasn't got on yours."

"And when he does," said Armand kindly, "will be time enough for the chain-mail."

Bernheim took the vest and deliberately laid it on the blotter.

"For the sake of those who love you, my lord," he said—"and"—turning to a picture of the Princess, which hung on the opposite wall, and saluting—"for her whom we all serve."

The Archduke looked at the picture in silence for a moment.

"Send the vest to the Epsau," he said; "I will wear it—sometimes."

And Bernheim knew he had to be satisfied with the sometimes—though as even that was more than he had dared to hope for, he was well content.

The Archduke and the American Ambassador met by appointment at the outer gate of the City, and as the former had been delayed, they rode at speed to the Summer Palace. It was the first time they had been together, informally, since the King's death, but beyond the usual friendly greeting and an occasional word en route there was no conversation. There was much that Armand wished to discuss with his friend, but this was not the place for it—it needed a quiet room and the other aids to serious consultation.

"I want a word with you, Dick, before you go back to town," he remarked, as they dismounted.

And Courtney nodded comprehendingly.

"As many as you wish, my boy," he said.

But the Princess also wanted a word with Courtney; she knew his keen insight into motives and men; his calm judicialness of judgment; his critical analysis of facts, and, most important of all, his influence with Armand, and she desired his counsel and his aid. She had not forgot the part he had played in the recent past; that but for him there would be no Archduke Armand; that, indeed, it was this quiet diplomat whom she had to thank for the happiest days of her life, and the happy prospect for the days to come; and, but for whom, there would be to her only the memory of that ride in the forest with the American Captain Smith; and Ferdinand of Lotzen would be King; and she—she might even be his Queen—and have yet to learn his vileness and his villainy.

All this she knew, and her heart warmed to Courtney as now it warmed to none other save Armand himself. And that very morning, as the two men crossed the terrace and came toward them, she had told Lady Helen Radnor, with the smiling frankness of a comrade, that if she sent this man away, no act in all her life would equal it in folly; then without waiting for an answer she had gone to greet her guests.

Now, when the luncheon was ended, she dismissed the servants and turned to Courtney.

"Will you do something for Armand?" she asked.

"Don't you think I have already done him service enough?" he said, looking at her with a significant smile—"more than he deserves or can ever appreciate."

"Well, may be you have," she smiled, catching his humor, "so do this for me—help me to make him King."

"What can I do?" he asked.

She leaned a bit nearer. "Keep him firm for his birthright; don't let him fling it aside in disgust, if the struggle drags out, for long."

Courtney nodded. "I understand," he said; "but you need have no concern; you yourself will keep him firm—it's the only way he can make you Queen." He paused and tapped his cigarette meditatively against his glass. "You think there isn't any doubt as to the decree in his favor?" he asked.

"None—absolutely none."

"Then all you have to do is to find the Book—that shouldn't be so very difficult."

"True enough; it shouldn't—but it will be."

"You seem very positive," he said.

"A woman's intuition."

Courtney smiled. "Which isn't infallible."

"Will you try to prove that?" she asked. "Will you help us find the Book?" And without waiting for his answer she turned to the Archduke. "Armand," she said, "tell Mr. Courtney what we know as to the Laws; I want his advice."

Armand laughed. "I fancy he already knows it, my dear—it's his business to know things."

"And it's also particularly his business," she retorted, "never to betray that he knows—therefore, we must tell him."

"Bear with him, Your Highness," said Courtney—"I assure you he will learn in time.... Meanwhile, Monsieur le Prince, I'm all attention."

Armand leaned over to Lady Helen. "His manners are rather crass," he remarked, in a confidential whisper, "but he really means well." Then he pushed the cigarettes across to Courtney.

"Take a fresh one, old chap; the story may be a bit long."

VIII
INFERENCE OR FACT

Through the story Courtney sat with half closed eyes, pulling at his gray imperial, the unlighted cigarette between his lips. With the main facts he was already familiar, as was every Embassy in Dornlitz, but much of the small details were new to him; and at the end, for a while, he was silent, fitting the incidents together in his mind.

"Do you care to tell me what the police make of it?" he asked.

"Nothing, as usual," Armand answered. "Their intelligence doesn't run beyond a hidden panel, and sounding every wall and floor in the Palace; they scorn any theory but that His Majesty concealed the Book."

"Which is perfectly absurd," Dehra added; "why should he conceal it, with the box and the vault at hand?"

"Why don't you make them take another lead?" Lady Helen asked.

"Because I'm sick of them and their ways.—I've sent them away—and away they stay; in another day there wouldn't have been a wall in the Palace."

"She told the officer in charge the only way he could ever find the Book was not to search for it," Armand laughed. "And then gave him a grade in rank to salve the words."

"Don't interrupt, sir!" the Princess exclaimed. "And remember I can't give *you* a grade."

"Was any one with the King after you left him that night?" Courtney asked.

"Only Adolph, the valet," Dehra replied. "I'm quite sure he would receive no one at that hour."

"And what did Adolph say as to the Book?"

"That he hadn't seen it for four days prior to Frederick's death," said Armand.

"Who told you that?" the Princess asked quickly.

"He told the Council."

"Then he deliberately deceived you; he saw it the night I did—the last night;—he came to the door just after the King spoke of Armand's decree."

Courtney struck a match and carefully lit the cigarette.

"Where is Adolph?" he asked.

"He has gone back to France, I think."

Courtney sent a quick, inquiring look at Armand, which the latter missed, having turned toward Lady Helen.

"Oh, I remember," he replied; "there was a stray line about him in the paper—grief and so forth. At the time, I inferred he had been banished by the police, for some reason."

"We can have him back," she interjected.

The Archduke looked around. "Adolph is dead," he said. "His body was found behind the hedge under the King's library windows three days after Frederick's demise."

"But his return to France?" Dehra exclaimed.

"A fiction of your police, doubtless," said Courtney dryly; "they are very clever.... He was—killed, of course?"

"In the Park, the night the King died; a dagger wound in the heart," the Archduke explained.

"Do you know that to be the fact; or is it the police theory?"

"*I* don't know anything—indeed, it was only yesterday I learned of it and sent for the papers in the case."

"And the—killer, I assume, has not been apprehended."

"Naturally not," said Armand; and proceeded to explain the matter as the police viewed it.

"What do you think, now?" Dehra demanded, at the end.

A bit of a smile crept into Courtney's face.

"I think," he said, "that the only circumstance which relieves the police from utter imbecility is their not knowing that the valet had lied to the Royal Council as to the Book."

The Princess' finger tips began to tap the table, and the little wrinkle showed between her eyes.

"Don't, my dear, don't," laughed Armand; "you can't give the entire Bureau a grade in rank—and besides, they are not to blame. I called the Chief down hard yesterday, only to have him tell me it was the ancient and rigid custom never, except by special order, to investigate a crime that touched the royal household, nor to follow any clue which led inside the Palace. And I apologized—and instantly abolished the custom."

"They were specially ordered to search for the Book of Laws," the Princess insisted; "wouldn't that lead them to Adolph?"

"Under their theory Adolph had nothing to do with the Book," said Courtney.

"Just so," the Archduke remarked; "and between their rotten theories and customs the business has been sadly bungled."

"Their fatal fallacy," said Courtney, "was, it seems to me, in assuming that no one but His Majesty and Her Highness could open the vault.—I have no doubt the valet had discovered the combination."

"But the box," Dehra objected; "it was locked when I got it, and Adolph could not have had the key."

"He might have had a duplicate."

"I think not," said Armand; "it is a trick lock with a most complicated arrangement, and to make a duplicate would have required the original key."

"Well, however that may be is not essential," said Courtney; "the fact remains that, between eleven o'clock of one night and ten o'clock of the second day thereafter, the Book disappeared; and the last time it was seen, to our knowledge, it was lying under the King's own hand, on the table in his library, with the open box beside it; and that the latter was found, closed and locked and empty, in its place in the vault, while the most thorough search for the Book has been ineffectual except, it seems, to prove that it is not in the Palace. We can safely assume that His Majesty did not hide it; hence he returned it to its place; and whoever took it, got it out of a locked box in a locked vault. For this, Adolph had the best opportunity."

"But what possible motive?" the Princess exclaimed.

Courtney smiled. "If I could tell you that, we would be far toward finding the Book; yet he had a motive—his lie to the Council proves it."

"You think he stole the Laws?" she asked.

Courtney sent a smoke cloud shooting upward and watched it fade.

"I think," said he, "that if Adolph didn't steal them, he knows who did; his lie can bear no other construction."

"And his death?" the Archduke asked.

Courtney watched another smoke ring and made no reply.

"Come," insisted Armand; "answer."

The other shook his head.

"I stop with the lie," he said. "Indeed, I can't get beyond it. The valet would have but one reason for stealing the Book—to sell it to—Some-one, who would have every reason to conceal or even to destroy it. Every logical inference points to this Some-one; and yet, for once, logic seems to be at fault."

"You mean the Duke of Lotzen?" said the Princess.

Courtney smiled, but made no answer.

"Your pardon," she said, "but at least you can tell us why the logic is at fault."

"Because," said he, "the actual facts are otherwise. As Armand knows, I like to play with mystery, and when I may help a friend I like it all the more. The logical solution of the matter, in view of the decree, is a knowing valet, and a ready buyer; yet the latter was not in Dornlitz, when the Book was stolen, nor has my most careful investigation disclosed any communication, by Adolph, with him or his friends. On the contrary, the evidence is absolutely conclusive against it; and hence acquits the Some-one of having had any hand in the theft."

"You knew, then, of Adolph's death?" Armand asked.

"Yes—though not all the details as you related them."

The Archduke smiled; there were very few details missed when Courtney started an investigation.

"Your argument, Richard," he said, "is based upon the hypothesis that Adolph is the thief, which appears most probable; yet did your examination suggest no other solution?"

"Absolutely none—and, more peculiar still, I was unable to find the slightest trace of the valet outside the Palace, between the time he left the Council and the discovery of his dead body behind the hedge—though you and Her Highness saw him in the library after the Council adjourned."

"And that is the last time I ever saw him," said Dehra.

"And more than that," Armand added, "it's the last time any one saw him in the Palace; I had that matter looked into yesterday. The Council rose about noon and afterward not a servant nor soldier so much as laid eyes on him."

"Isn't there something particularly significant in the place where Adolph was found?" the Princess asked. "Mightn't he have been killed in the library and then, from the window, the body dropped behind the hedge?"

Courtney's hand went to his imperial reflectively.

"A very reasonable and a very likely explanation," he said; "and the nature of the wound supports it; it was a noiseless assassination;—but, again, that eliminates the Some-one."

"Very true," said the Archduke; "he left the Council before it adjourned, to return at once to town."

"But *did* he return at once?" Dehra persisted. "Mightn't he have remained and killed Adolph—some how, some way—I don't know, but mightn't he?"

Armand shook his head. "I think not," he said. "I looked into that too, and there seems to be no doubt Lotzen was in Dornlitz before one o'clock; and every moment of his time, until Adolph was found, has been accounted for; so, even assuming he didn't leave the Palace immediately, he would have had to kill the valet within half an hour after we saw him in the library; and that, under all the conditions, is utterly incredible."

"Nothing's incredible where Lotzen is concerned," she answered. "So let us assume he did kill Adolph, in the King's library, during that very half hour between noon and twelve-thirty, and answer me this: *Why* did he kill him?"

"Either to get the Book of Laws or because Adolph knew too much concerning it," said Armand, smiling at her earnestness.

"Exactly; and, therefore, Lotzen either has the Book or he knows where it is.... Am I not right?" she demanded, turning to Courtney.

"Undoubtedly, Your Highness—according to your premises."

"You don't admit the premises?"

"I can't—they are too improbable—and the facts are against them."

"Oh, facts!" she exclaimed, "facts! I don't care a rap for facts. Lotzen killed Adolph and Lotzen has the Book."

Courtney looked at her curiously—the idea was preposterous, naturally, but the very arbitrariness of her conclusions was softened by her earnestness and evident faith in their truth. It was, of course, just another case of woman's intuition, that begged every question and tore logic into tatters; yet, sometimes, he had known it to guess truly, despite the most adverse facts— might it be that here was just another such guess?

The table stood back a little way among the trees, and was hidden from the Palace by the hedge of rhododendron, that flanked the roadway where it swept around the great marble pergola; and so they did not see the man in undress cavalry uniform, who came slowly along the terrace, and, descending the steps, took the path leading to the sun-dial. At it he paused, with desultory interest seemingly, to read the shadow; bending over, the while, to blow away the dust.

As he did so, the Princess saw him, through a rift in the hedge. First she frowned, then a quizzical smile settled on her lips, and she glanced again at Courtney.

"Do you still doubt?" she asked.

Courtney, preoccupied, looked at her a moment without replying.

"Yes," he said; "being a man and intuitionless, I still must doubt."

At that moment, the officer passed the hedge and they all saw him.

"Cousin!" the Princess called,—"cousin!"

The Duke of Lotzen faced about sharply, then doffed cap and approached.

"Your Highness spoke?" he said, bowing.

Dehra leaned on the table, her chin in her hand, and studied him a bit, while the others wondered, and Armand's anger rose.

"Cousin," she said, "I have just asserted that you killed Adolph and have the Book of Laws—is it not the truth?"

Lady Helen gasped; Armand half rose from his chair; even Courtney's studied immobility of countenance was not impervious to his surprise.

The Duke alone met the situation with perfect imperturbability. He neither started, frowned, nor changed expression in the slightest; the pleasant smile, that was on his lips, lingered unabated, while the hand that rested on his sword hilt was as steady as the cold, blue eyes which gave back the Princess' gaze. Then, gradually, the smile broadened, creeping slowly upward, until it touched the cold blue eyes, though warming them not a whit; presently, he laughed, gently, and with just a trace of jeer.

"It is not for a subject to contradict the Regent of Valeria," he said—and with a bow and a salute he turned languidly away.

And the Princess did not stop him, but in silence, chin still on hand, she watched him out of sight.

IX
THE RECKLESS GAME

The Princess was the first to speak. "Tell me, Your Excellency," she said, "do you admit my premises, now?"

"Are you, yourself, quite as sure of them, as you were?" he asked.

"Sure!—sure! I'm absolutely sure—I saw the truth in his eyes—didn't you, Armand?"

"No," said the latter, "I didn't—I never saw truth anywhere in Lotzen."

"If he were innocent, why should he plead guilty?" she demanded.

"And if guilty, why should he admit it?" the Archduke asked.

"Because in this case the truth is more misleading than a lie—he had no notion we would believe him."

"He is a very extraordinary man," observed Courtney; "his mental processes are beyond belief. Your question was the most amazing I ever heard, and should have been instantly decisive of his guilt or innocence; instead, it has only clouded the matter deeper for you and cleared it completely for him. Your cards are exposed—his are still stacked."

"They are not stacked to me," said Dehra; "he is guilty."

"Then, in that aspect, he has deliberately asked you what you're going to do about it."

"I'm going to get the Book—for Adolph I don't care—I'm glad he killed the little beast."

"And how," said Armand, "are we to get the Book? No ordinary means will suffice. Imprisonment would only make a martyr of him and strengthen him enormously with the Nobles and the people; and banishment is absurd; he may be the King."

"If he has the Book, he would welcome banishment," said Courtney; "it would relieve him of your espionage. But, Your Highness, let me ask, why should he have it now? Armand admitted to the Council he is ineligible without King Frederick's decree, so why would Lotzen preserve that decree? The Book is not essential to *his* title."

The Princess shook her head incredulously. "Ferdinand of Lotzen is a knave but I won't believe that of him.... A Dalberg destroy the Dalberg Laws! Inconceivable!—oh, inconceivable!"

"So, between the Crown of Valeria and the Book of Laws, you think he would chose the latter; and hand the Crown to Armand?"

"He would conceal the Laws—he wouldn't destroy them," she insisted.

The Archduke reached over and took her hand.

"Little woman," he said, "your mistake is in rating Lotzen a Dalberg—he isn't; he's a vicious mongrel; if he had the Book, you can rest assured he destroyed it."

But she shook her head.

"Your facts proved him innocent;" she smiled, "and so they don't appeal to me to-day. I'm as sure he won't destroy the Laws as I am that he killed Adolph; what troubles me is how to recover them."

"We have a year——"

"I don't intend to wait a year for your crowning, Sire," she broke in. "Nor half a year, either."

He smiled indulgently, and pressing lightly the small fingers that still lay in his.

"The little Kingmaker," he laughed.

"No, no!" she said, "not I; Mr. Courtney is your Warwick and Valeria's benefactor—he saved us from Lotzen."

"Then, your work is not finished, old man," the Archduke remarked; "there's a lot of saving to be done, I fear."

Courtney nodded rather gravely; he was quite of the same mind.

"Warwick will hold to the work," he answered, "and aid you all he may; but, for the immediate present, I would advise that we sit tight and give the enemy a chance to blunder. And in the meantime, Armand, I suggest you change the combinations on all the vaults here, and at the Castle."

"It was done ten days ago."

"The Book isn't in any vault," the Princess remarked; "they all have been thoroughly searched."

"But something else may be in them, which will be needed—one can never know," the Ambassador answered. "Leastwise, it won't hamper us, and may hamper Lotzen—or some one."

"It's only a wise precaution," the Archduke added—"the vault in the King's library, both here and at the Castle, is filled with records and other valuables, and upon both I changed the combinations myself—I didn't trust it to a workman, who could be found and bribed."

And it was this change of combination that the Duke of Lotzen had discovered that afternoon.

At the Archduke's firm insistence, Colonel Moore, his junior Aide, had been detached from his staff and assigned as Adjutant to the Regent; and a portion of the King's suite, including his library, allotted to him for quarters. This, also, was at the Archduke's personal order—he, himself, might not be there always to guard Dehra, so he gave her the gallant Irishman, with the best sword in the Kingdom and a heart as true as his sword. Lotzen's bravos and his blandishment would be alike powerless against him.

And the Duke, when he saw the order, smiled in quiet satisfaction; and Bigler chuckled and read it to Rosen at the Club—"Thank Heaven we shan't have the other damned foreigner to contend with when we go after the American," he had said.

But when the Duke learned who occupied the library, he cursed Moore and the luck that had put him there—with the Book in the vault, and to be got, and none but him to get it. For no one, not even his closest associates, might know he had found it—he could not trust even their loyalty against the fetish of the Laws. So it was for him alone to obtain it; and now the task—delicate enough at best—had become almost impossible for one man. Under every precedent, the King's suite should have remained unoccupied, awaiting his successor; but, instead, this Irishman; this fellow with the quickest sword and surest eye in the Army; this devoted follower of the American, and, after him, the one man in Valeria whom he hated the fiercest and feared even more; he was—though thank God he did not know it!—guarding the Book for his master.

It was, in truth, the first faint frown of his Goddess, but Lotzen was too good a gambler to flout her at the loss of a single turn. It meant either a little more careful play or a little more recklessness. And, on the whole, the recklessness was rather more appealing than the care. If he could not easily recover the Book, he could, at least, adventure leaving it where it was—and let the Regent's Adjutant guard it for him, too. And he smiled his cold smile—and longed to make a second Adolph of the Irishman, knowing well that he, skillful fencer though he was, could never reach Moore's heart save from the rear.

And that day, he had thought to take a reconnoissance, and he had come to the Summer Palace, trusting for an opportunity to gain admission to the library, to open the vault. There was a possibility that the King's effects had been removed from it, and the box might also have been taken; and, if so, it might be lying in some room, quite unguarded. Yet he deluded himself little on that score; the chance was too slight even to consider seriously; there was really no occasion for emptying the vault; on the contrary, Moore's presence was the very best reason for leaving it untouched. Nevertheless, it was well enough to make sure.

And here again luck bent to him. As he turned the corner of the corridor at the end farthest from the King's suite, Colonel Moore came out and hurried down the stairway opposite, without a glance aside.

Lotzen smiled, and went on to the library door—and smiled still more broadly when he saw it was open wide. Really, the thing was getting too easy! He stopped and tapped lightly on the jamb with his sword hilt—then stepped in and glanced quickly around. The shades were half drawn, but there was enough light for him to see that the room was empty. Going swiftly to the vault, he whirled the knob through the combination that Adolph had given him, dropped it at the final number and seized the handle.... The bolts refused to move. With a frown, he spun the knob again; and again they stood firm. A third time he tried, carefully and slowly, not overrunning the marks by the shade of a hair—and still the bolts stayed fixed.

With a muttered curse he stepped back, and from the paper in his pocket verified the formula he had used—though he knew he had made no mistake.... Could the valet have lied—have given him a wrong combination—have actually played him for a fool to his very face!... Impossible—quite impossible—he could recognize fear when he saw it; and no servant ever lied adroitly under such terror as had gripped Adolph at that moment. He stared at the vault and at the paper ... and, then, of a sudden, he understood—the combination had been changed.... Why—by whom, did not matter now. Enough, that behind that iron door the Book was surely lying, and he powerless to obtain it.... Well, so be it—he must chance the risk; the reckless game had been forced upon him by his enemies, and he would play it out. They did not imagine the Book was in the box—they would seek it elsewhere—and the American would lead in the seeking—on—on—on to Lotzenia, and the castle on the mountain, high above the foaming Dreer—and then!... A fell smile crossed his face, and his eyes narrowed malevolently—there would be no need for the Book, when they came back to Dornlitz.

As he stepped into the corridor, the door opposite, in the Princess' suite, opened and Mademoiselle d'Essoldé came out.

"Your Highness!" she said, dropping him a bit of a curtsy.

"My lady!" he answered, bowing over her hand; then motioned behind him. "Who occupies his Majesty's apartments?" he asked.

"The Adjutant to Her Royal Highness," she answered, knowing well he knew.

"True," said he; "I quite forgot. Colonel Moore has pleasant quarters," and he smiled.

His inference was too evident to miss. She was of the Regent's Household and Moore was her most persistent suitor. She made no pretense to conceal her displeasure, though she echoed his laugh.

"Yes, very pleasant," she answered, "yet they won't be his for long—he but holds them for another."

"And the other?" maliciously driving her to the choice between the Archduke and himself.

She raised her eyebrows.

"There could be but one, my lord," she answered, looking at him with calm directness.

He laughed. "May be we do not guess alike; and I fear me, when *my* other comes, the dashing Colonel will have to make a far move—beyond the border."

The blue eyes snapped. "I can well believe Your Highness," she retorted. "When you move in, Colonel Moore would scorn to stay this side the border."

Elise d'Essoldé never forgot the look that came in Lotzen's eyes. It was, she said afterwards to the Regent, as though he had actually struck her in the face. And, for a little while, he did not speak. Then as she drew back into the room, he bowed, his hand upon his heart.

"My thanks, my lady, my thanks for your candor," his voice soft and very kind—"I shall see to it that your Colonel does not go alone."

"Small danger," she replied, as she slowly closed the door, "Your Highness has been seeing to that with fine success, these many years—*au revoir, mon Prince*," and the latch clicked between them.

With a shrug, the Duke turned away. What a vixen she was!—and how very sure Dehra must be of the American's succession, when one of her Household would venture to flout Ferdinand of Lotzen to his face. His mouth hardened. Damn the woman who played with statecraft—who meddled with the things she knew nothing of—who would impose a foreigner upon an ancient Kingdom, just because he was her lover. Damn the whole tribe—they were fit only to play with clothes, and to serve man's idle moment....

The rattle of a sword and click of spurs sounded on the stairway, and the Regent's Adjutant turned the corner.

"Ah, Colonel, well met!" said Lotzen briskly, as Moore came to attention and salute; "I took the liberty, as I passed your quarters, of looking at His late Majesty's portrait; I wish to have a copy made—the door was open, so I assumed I might go in," and with a pleasant smile and nod he passed on—then stopped. "My congratulations on your promotion—though as the smartest soldier in the army it belonged to you."

Moore looked after him thoughtfully.

"What particularly fine bit of deviltry are you up to now," he muttered; "and what were you really doing in the library?"

Half way down the corridor Moore met Elise d'Essoldé.

"Whither away, my lady, whither away?" he asked, sweeping the floor with his cap.

"I'm not your lady," she answered, making to pass by, but smiling sidelong at him.

"Egad, I wish you wouldn't tell me that so often—have some regard for my poor heart."

She tossed her head. "Your heart, indeed! which heart? An Irishman has a hundred and a different girl for every one."

"This Irishman has a million hearts—and the same girl for them all."

She put the tip of her parasol to the wall, and leaned lightly against it.

"And how many hearts has she?" she asked.

He shook his head sadly. "None—none—not the faintest trace of one."

She bent further over, and tightened the bow of blue ribbon on the staff.

"May be you're not the one to find it," she smiled—"another man——" and the merry eyes glinted gaily through the long lashes.

"Oh, I'm the man—and she knows it."

A little laugh rippled forth—"And does she know, also, your stupendous self sufficiency?"

"Yes, she knows that, too—and likes me just the same."

"Which would seem to be very little—as it should be.... My parasol if you please, I'm going."

He kept his hold.

"You little witch," he said; "I don't know why I let you walk upon me so."

The saucy mouth drooped at the corners. "Nor I why I walk—the way is surely very stony.... My parasol, I said."

He glanced up and down the corridor.

"Do you know," he said seriously, "I believe that hat is so big I could kiss you, and no one see us."

She dropped the sun-shade and sprang back.

"Yes, I believe you could—and I believe you actually would—but you shan't."

He opened the parasol, and drew the circle close behind his head.

"It's not quite so large as your hat," he went on, "but I think, if you don't struggle too much, I can manage to hold it properly."

He went slowly toward her—she retreated.

"Come," she commanded;... "cease this foolishness ... my parasol;... I'm going...."

He did not answer.

"Ralph," she exclaimed, "are you crazy!"

He shook his head and came on.

She was on the stairway now—a glance:—no one was below her. She lifted her skirts with both hands, and backed down the steps, smiling up at him the while, tantalizingly.

"Come on," she said, as he halted at the top; "I need the parasol; come on."

"You little devil," he laughed; "You'll tempt me once too often.... Here, take your sun-shade—I may have need of it another time."

"*Merci*—*amant, merci*," she inflected softly, then flung him a kiss from her finger tips—"and you take that—I won't need it another time—and, if I do, I've others."

"Many others?" he asked.

She faced about, and raising the parasol swung it between them.

"A million—for your hearts," she answered, and ran quickly down the steps.

Meanwhile the Duke of Lotzen, passing along the lower corridor, had caught, in a mirror, the reflection of the scene on the stairs, and had paused to watch it.

"A pretty picture, Mademoiselle; truly, a pretty picture," he said, as they met; "and most charming from the rear—and below—oh! most charming."

Her cheeks and brow went red as flame, as she caught his meaning.

"You vile peeper," she exclaimed; "doubtless, you're an experienced judge," and dropping the parasol in his face, nor caring that the silk struck him, she hurried by.

The Duke looked after her contemplatively. Really, this girl was worth while—he must take a hand in the Irishman's game—that hair, those eyes, that walk, that figure—oh, decidedly, she was quite worth while.

With an evil little laugh, he put her out of his mind, for the moment, and turned toward the terrace and to business. He had learned of the alfresco luncheon near the pergola, and he appreciated that there was the place to make the first move in his new plot.

Yet when, from the sun-dial, as he feigned to study it, he saw the Princess, through the rhododendrons—with the American across the table from her, where he himself ought to have been; and watched her lavish upon Armand the adorable smile that should have been his; and knew, afresh, that, come what may, the glorious woman yonder was lost to him forever—his anger welled so high he dared not risk a meeting, lest in his rage he wreck his cause completely. So he braced his shoulders against the fierce desire that tugged him toward them, and went on, giving no glance aside.

Then the Princess called him; and when the only voice able, hitherto, to touch a soft chord in his heart, struck now a jarring dissonance, the fury passed; and again he was the man of cold, calm hate and ruthless purpose. So he turned aside, and to his enemies—her and the foreigner—deliberating how to make his play quickly, yet naturally and with seeming inadvertence. The faintest blunder would be fatal with Courtney watching; Armand he despised.

And at Dehra's sudden question, he had almost laughed aloud—was it always to be so easy! But he bound his face to his part, and made his answer, and went his way; whistling softly, and all unknowingly, a little song, that a slender, sinuous woman, with raven hair and dead-white cheek, had sung to him in the North.

And when, presently, it came to him whose the song was, and where he had heard it, he laughed gaily.

"An omen!" he said aloud, "an omen! On to Lotzenia—and a dead Archduke."

X
A QUESTION OF VENEER

The Archduke Armand tossed the end of his fourth cigar into the grate and looked at the big clock in the corner. It was only a bit after eleven, and that was, he knew by experience, the blush of the evening at the American Embassy, where there were no women-folk to repress the youngsters nor to necessitate the closing of the house at conventional hours. Courtney had only bachelors in his official family; and he housed them all with him in the big residence on Alta Avenue, and gave them free rein to a merry life, fully assured they would not abuse the liberty; he had known every one of them as boys, and their fathers before them.

The Archduke reached over and pressed a button.

"Bring me a cap and a light cape," he said to the servant;—"and a stick."

The man went out, and Armand crossed to a window and drew aside the curtain.

"Put them on a chair," he said without looking around, as the door opened again. "You may go."

The door closed. For a little while he watched the gay street, stretching southward for half a mile to the center of the city, where the lights blazed variegatedly and brightest. The theatres had tossed out their crowds, and below him the van of the carriage column was hurrying homeward, to the fashionable district out the Avenue, or to the Hanging Garden above the Lake. Occasionally a face, usually a woman's, would lean close to the door and look at the Epsau curiously—it housed the man who was likely to be King. And the man smiled with half bitter cynicism, and wondered what words followed the look, and who spoke them, and to whom. Once, he recognized Count Epping's lean visage, and in that carriage, at least, he felt that the words were friendly; a moment later, the snake eyes of Baron Retz went glittering by—but never a glance did he turn aside.

"You little reptile," the Archduke muttered aloud, "you ought to crawl, not ride."

He dropped the curtain and turned away—then stopped, and his lips softened; and presently he laughed. Just inside the door, and standing stiffly at attention, was Colonel Bernheim, holding the cape and cap and stick the servant had been sent for.

"Now what's the trouble?" Armand demanded.

"Your Highness desired these?" said Bernheim.

"Yes—but I didn't send for you." The tone was very kindly.

"But you are going out, sir?"

"Yes."

"And I'm on duty to-night."

"You're excused—go to bed."

The old soldier shook his head. "I'm going with you."

"Nonsense," said Armand, "nonsense! I'm for only a short walk up the Avenue."

"I must go with you, sir," the Aide insisted.

The Archduke looked at him in some surprise.

"Positively, Bernheim," he said, "if you keep this up you will have nervous prostration. Quit it, man, quit it." He flung on the cape, and taking cap and cane went toward the door. "Good night."

The Colonel stood aside, hand at the salute. "Your pardon, sir—but I must go with you—it is the Regent's personal order."

"What!"

"She telephoned me this evening always to see that you had an escort, after dark."

The Archduke sat on the end of the writing-table and laughed until the tears came—and even old Bernheim condescended to emit, at intervals, a grim sort of chuckle.

"What hour are you to put me to bed, nurse?" Armand asked.

"The orders did not run to that point, sir,"—with a louder chuckle—"but I should say not later than midnight."

"Then I've a few minutes' grace, and I'll spend them playing on the sidewalk, while you warm the sheets and get the milk," and with another laugh he went out. "Don't forget the milk," he added over his shoulder.

Bernheim held open the door.

"I'll not, sir," he said, and followed him.

At the street, Armand stopped.

"Where are you going, Colonel?" he asked.

The heels clicked together and the hand went up.

"For the milk, sir."

He recognized the futility of further opposition; with the Regent's command to sustain him, Bernheim would not be denied.

"Come, along, then," he ordered—"and if they have a cow at the American Embassy I'll set you to milking it, or I'm a sailor."

The old fellow answered with the faintest suggestion of a grin.

All Dornlitz was familiar with the features of the Great Henry, and so it was quite impossible for the Archduke Armand to escape recognition—and to-night, as he and Bernheim went out the Avenue, the people made way for him with a respect and deference that even he could not but feel was honest and sincere, and of the quietly enthusiastic sort that is most dependable.

"Does it look as though I had need for an escort?" he asked.

"Not at this moment," the Aide agreed.

"Nor at any moment on Alta Avenue;" he put his hand on the other's arm—"you know, Bernheim, it's not you I object to, it's the idea. I always like you with me."

The Colonel's face flushed, and for an instant he did not reply; when he did, his voice was low and faintly husky.

"Sire!" he said, "Sire!"

The Archduke glanced at him in quick surprise, and understood; sometimes Bernheim's intense devotion overflowed.

"Brace up, Colonel," he exclaimed, with sudden gayety, "brace up! you won't have to milk that cow."

Then both men laughed, and the normal situation was resumed.

The bells began to chime midnight, as they reached the Embassy.

"Don't wait for me," Armand said; "I may be late. Go back and send an orderly."

The other smiled. "I'll wait, myself, sir, if you will permit; they have a game here I rather like."

"Take care, Colonel; those boys will skin you out of your very uniform—better look on."

"I do, sir, when I've a poor draw;" he answered seriously, and wondered at the Archduke's chuckling laugh.

Courtney greeted his friend with a nod and a wave of his hand.

"I'm glad you came in," he said. "I've been thinking about you—sit down.... Scotch?"

"No, rye—and seltzer, please." He took the chair across the desk from Courtney and waited until the man had placed the decanters and glasses and retired. "And I've been thinking about you, too," he said. "You got me into this infernal mess, and now it's up to you to help me out."

Courtney slowly lit a cigarette and scrutinized the coal, critically.

"I see," he remarked, "that you have already developed the ungratefulness of kings—I have high hopes for your reign ... if you live to reign."

The Archduke put down his glass and regarded him in exasperated surprise.

"Damn it, man, you too?" he exclaimed. "If I were given to nerves I would be seeing daggers and bullets all around me—Bernheim croaks death; and so does Moore; and now you join the chorus—pretty soon the boys will be whistling it on the Avenue."

Courtney picked up an Embassy official envelope that lay before him, and tossed it across to the Archduke.

"I've done a little work on my own account, lately," he said, "and here is what I got this evening. I have always found this—agent, reliable."

It was only a few words, scratched hastily in pencil on a sheet torn from a small note-book:—

> "Danger very imminent—under no circumstance go out at night without an escort."

"Nice sort of country this, you brought me to," said Armand.

"It's not the country, my dear boy," Courtney observed; "it is beyond reproach. The trouble is that one of your own family still is a barbarian; and you insist upon treating him as though he were civilized. For my part, I have no patience with your altruism; you've had quite sufficient warning—he tried twice to kill you at the Vierle Masque; and he has told you to your face that you would never be king. Yet you persist in regarding him as fighting square and in the open. Bernheim and Moore are wise—they know your dear cousin—and you,—well, you're a fool if you don't know him, too."

It was a very long speech for Courtney, and Armand had listened in surprise—it was most unusual for his imperturbable friend to grow emphatic, either in voice or gesture, and it impressed him as Bernheim and Moore never had. In truth, he had no particular scruples against meeting Lotzen in the good, old-fashioned, cloak-and-dagger way; but what irked him was the necessity of being always on the *qui vive* to resist assault or to avoid a trap; and the seeming absurdity of it in Dornlitz of the twentieth century. It made him feel such a simpleton, to be looking for bravos in dark alleys, or to wear steel vests, or to be eternally watchful and suspicious of every one and everything.

"What do you want me to do," he asked; "go down to Lotzen's palace and stick my sword through him?"

"It's a pity you may not—it's what he would do to you, if he could—but that's not our way; we're civilized ... to a certain point. But what you may do is to take every precaution against him; and then, if you get the chance in fair justification, kill him as unconcernedly as he would kill you."

The Archduke sat silent, his cigar between his teeth, the smoke floating in a thin strand across his face, his eyes upon the desk before him.

"Of course, my boy," Courtney went on, after a pause, "I assume you are in the game to the end, and in to win. If you're not, the whole matter is easy of adjustment—renounce the

Crown and marry the Princess ... and live somewhere beyond the borders of Valeria—come back to America, indeed; I'll see that you have again your commission in the Engineer's——"

Armand's lips closed a bit tighter on his cigar, his fingers began to play upon the chair-arm, and his glance shifted for an instant to the other's face, then back to the desk. And Courtney read his mind and pressed on to clinch the purpose.

"But if you're in to win—and it's your duty to your friends to win; it's your duty to your friends to win, I repeat—your first obligation is to keep alive; a dead archduke is of no earthly use in the king business we have in hand. You may go straight to Glory, but that won't help out the poor devils you leave here in Lotzen's clutches, and who have been true to you, never doubting that you would be true to them. Your life belongs to them, now; and you have no right to fritter it away in silly, stubborn recklessness.... There, I've spoken my mind, and quite too frankly, may be; but I'll promise never to bother you again. After all, it's for you to decide—not for a meddling friend."

The Archduke smiled. "And just to prove that the friend isn't meddling, I shall accept his advice—bearing in mind, however, that this is particularly an exigency where prudence must be subordinate to daring. Prudence is all very well in the abstract, but it is more dangerous to our success than recklessness. I'm playing for a Crown and a Nation's favor—let my personal courage be questioned for an instant, and the game is lost as surely as though I were dead. As for my dear cousin of Lotzen, I assure you I've not the least scruple about killing him, under proper opportunity. In fact, I'm inclined to think I should rather enjoy it. I admit now that there have been times when I regret I didn't run him through at the Vierle Masque."

Courtney nodded. "It would have saved you all this trouble—I wanted to call to you to make an end of him."

"I can't do murder; I had disarmed him. Next time, I'll make a different play."

"There won't be a next time, if the Duke has the choosing. He isn't the sort to seek death, and he knows you are his master. You'll have to kill him in a melée, or manœuvre him into a position where he has no option but to fight."

"He is manœuvring himself into a position where he will have to contend with a far more formidable blade than mine."

Courtney's eye-brows lifted expressively. Than the Archduke himself there was but one better swordsman in the kingdom.

"What has Lotzen been doing to Moore?" he asked.

"Insulting Elise d'Essoldé."

"By making advances?"

Armand nodded. "And in a particularly nasty way."

"He isn't bothered about Moore," said Courtney. "He thinks he is safe from any one that isn't of his station."

"He doesn't know the Irishman—Moore would kill him without a thought."

"I'm not so sure," said Courtney. "Moore is bred to respect for royalty; he would hesitate to use sword against one of the Blood except in defense."

"Lotzen would best not bank much on that for immunity if he pursue d'Essoldé."

"Well, so much the better; between you, the trick should be turned; though, as a matter of abstract justice, it's your particular work."

"And I shan't shirk it," said Armand—then he laughed—"on the whole, I'm something of a savage myself; Lotzen hasn't got all of it for the family, it would seem."

Courtney shrugged his shoulders. "We all are savages at the core—it's only a question of the veneer's thickness."

"Of its thinness, I should say. However, now that you have saved my precious life, and dedicated me to care and prudence and to killing my enemies, we can get down to business. You had something to tell me."

"I have told you," said Courtney. "I wanted to show you that note and save your precious life."

The Archduke picked up the paper, and read it again.

"May be the party who wrote this," he said, "can help you answer the question I came to ask: what brought Lotzen to the Summer Palace, this afternoon; and, in particular, why did he go into the King's library?"

Courtney lit a fresh cigarette and watched the match burn to a cinder.

"Isn't your second question the answer to the first?" he asked.

"Doubtless; but what's the answer to the second?"

Courtney shook his head. "I pass—unless you can give me some details."

"Here's everything I know," said Armand. "Moore, as Adjutant to the Regent, occupies part of the King's suite as his quarters. This afternoon, he went out, leaving open the corridor door of the library. A little later Mademoiselle d'Essoldé saw Lotzen come from the library—subsequently he met Moore and casually remarked to him that, as he passed his quarters, the door being open, he had taken the liberty of looking at His late Majesty's portrait, which he wished to have copied."

Courtney considered a bit.

"It's really most interesting to study your cousin's methods," he said presently. "He seems to take particular pleasure in telling one what he knows will not be believed. It was quite absurd to offer such a fool explanation, if he really wished to explain—and none knows it better than Lotzen. It was just as though he had said to Moore: 'Tell the Archduke Armand, I've been in the library, I've accomplished what I went for, and he may go to the devil, with my compliments.'"

"That's very well, as an exposition of Lotzen's methods," said Armand; "but what concerns me is his motive; what was it he went for?"

"The Book of Laws, possibly," Courtney replied.

"Nonsense—he knows it's not in the library—if it were, I would have had it days ago."

"And how does he know you haven't got it?"

"How! Because I'd have produced it to prove my title."

Courtney smiled. "Certainly you would—if it proved your title; but if it didn't?"

"You overlook Frederick's decree."

"No, I don't—you overlook the fact that no one has ever seen that decree, and that Lotzen is entitled to assume it was not executed—that the whole story is fabricated, and that you have made away with the Book in order to throw the election into the House of Nobles; and so to have a chance for the Crown, when, in reality, you are entitled to none."

"Lotzen understands perfectly that Dehra told the truth," said Armand; "and that I've not got the Book—for my part, I'm almost ready to accept her notion that he has it."

Courtney leaned back in his chair, and studied the smoke rings he sent whirling upwards.

"I can't agree with you," he said; "indeed, since his visit to the library, I'm more convinced than ever that he hasn't the Book. He pretends to have it, so as to mislead you in your search."

"More likely, in your view of him," said Armand, "it is to decoy me into a trap where he can make an end of me."

"I believe you've guessed it," said Courtney, after a moment's thought; "and what is more, it's the key to Lotzen's plan of campaign, and it proves conclusively his murderous purpose. I'd be very shy of information that points Book-ward, unless you know the informant; above everything, don't be fooled by the device of a rendezvous, or a tattling servant."

"True enough; and yet I must not let slip any chance that might lead to the recovery of the Book; my equivocal position demands that it be found, both to vindicate Dehra's story and to justify my own claim to the Succession. Indeed, to my mind, I have no chance whatever unless Frederick's decree is produced. However, Lotzen won't use such hoary artifices; he will have some simple little plot that will enmesh me by its very innocence. As a schemer against him I'm not even an 'also ran.'"

"And, therefore, my dear Armand," said Courtney quickly, "you must be prepared to cut the meshes when they close; an escort—a sword—a pistol—a steel vest—there's where you get your chance at him. Between the schemer and the ready fighter, I'll gamble on the fighter every time.... It's a pity you've lost Moore—you and he would make a famous pair. Bernheim is a good sort, but Moore is worth twenty of him in this business."

The Archduke's eyes brightened—the Irishman and he together could make a merry fight—an altogether worth-while sort of fight—a fight that the Great Henry himself, in his younger days, would have sought with eager blade and joyful heart—a quick, sharp fight that gave the enemy no rest nor quarter—a thrust—a fall—a careless laugh—a dripping point wiped on a handkerchief. He saw it all, and his fingers tingled and his eyes went brighter still.

And across the table Courtney blew ring upon ring of smoke, and watched him curiously, until the intent look waned and passed.

"Well," he said, "did you kill him?"

"Yes, I killed him ... and even wiped my sword—much ground have I to cast reproach at Lotzen." He got up. "I'm going; if I sit under your tutelage any longer, I'll be jabbling holes in the good citizens I meet on the Avenue."

"With that stick?" Courtney asked.

"I forgot—the good citizen is safe to-night."

"But you're not. Let me give you a sword or a revolver." And when both were declined, he held up the paper: "Danger imminent," he warned.

"Bernheim will take care of me," said Armand; "and a light stick isn't a bad sort of rapier, if it is handled properly. I'm glad for this talk, and to have learned how very thin my veneer is.—I'm going back to the Epsau now, and teach Bernheim the scalp dance. Good night."

"And trade him to the Regent for Moore, the first thing in the morning," Courtney urged.

The Archduke paused at the threshold:

"Well, may be I shall," he said; "I believe he is a bit more the savage." He faced about. "As for you, my dear Dick, you're cut out for a typical missionary—you would have the natives killing one another within an hour after you landed."

"Danger imminent!" called Courtney, and the door swung shut.

XI
FIRST BLOOD

The Archduke knew where to find his Aide, so he waved aside the servant and went on to the billiard room.

"Don't mind me, boys," he said, as they sprang up; "go on with the deal—unless," motioning toward Bernheim's big pile of chips, "you want to be relieved of the beginner."

"Your Highness is ready to go?" Bernheim asked.

Armand nodded. "But that mustn't take you away; luck's with you, it's a crime to desert her—I know the way home."

The Colonel pushed his winnings into the centre of the table.

"I have to thank you for a delightful evening, messieurs," he said, with his stiff, military bow; "and since I must leave before the end of the game, I make a John-pot of these for you."

The Archduke took him by the arm.

"You may not do that, Colonel," he laughed; "they cannot let you. You must cash in, and give them a chance some other time."

"But it is my pleasure, sir, for them to have back what I won."

"And it will be their pleasure to take it back," said Armand kindly, "but not in that way—they must win it back from *you*."

Bernheim drew himself up. "I understand, sir," he said.—"Messieurs, I salute you."

When they came out on the Avenue, a fine rain was blowing in clouds, but the Archduke declined the servant's offer to ring the stables for a carriage. The street was deserted; not a pedestrian, nor even a cab, was in sight, either way. Both men wrapped their capes around them, and strode off toward the Epsau.

"A dirty night, sir," the Colonel observed—"it might have been well to take the carriage."

"I like it," said Armand; "to walk in the rain or to ride in the snow."

"The snow, yes—but we don't have much of it in Dornlitz—one must go to the mountains in the North—to Lotzenia—for it."

"My dear cousin's country!"

"His titular estates—but not his country," said Bernheim. "He has the old castle on the Dreer and a huge domain—that King Frederick's father gave to Lotzen's father in a foolish moment of generosity—but he hasn't the heart of a single inhabitant; indeed, until his banishment there, I think he had never even seen the place. But with the old castle of Dalberg, across the valley—the cradle of your race, sir—it's very different. Who rules there is the idol of the Lotzenians; he is their hereditary lord; and they can never forget that he belonged to them before he took the Crown, and that they helped him in the taking."

"And now that there is no king, whom will they serve until the new lord comes?"

Bernheim raised his cap.

"Her Royal Highness the Regent—until they serve you."

No man could be quite insensible to all that this implied of kingly power, and the traditional homage of inherited devotion, the hot love for him who was born their chief—given them of God, and their own before all others. The Archduke's fingers closed a bit tighter on his stick, his blood pulsed faster, and the stubborn spirit of old Hugo awoke to new life; and in that moment, in the dead of night, with the rain whipping around them, as it wrapped the city in a cloud of glowing mist, he turned his face forever from his old life, its memories and methods, and passed finally into the New, its high destiny, its privileges, its responsibilities, its dangers and its cares. He would make this fight in the Duke's own fashion, and end it in the Duke's own way; if he fell in the ending, he would see to it that the Duke fell first; not that he cared for his company in the outgoing—though, doubtless, it would matter little then—but because it were not well to leave him behind to plague the kingdom with his viciousness.

They now had left the more modern portion of the Avenue and were in the older section, where the houses were smaller and stood only a little way from the sidewalk; though occasionally a more pretentious one was set far back, with trees and shrubbery around it, and a wall before, hiding it almost entirely from the street.

In front of one of these residences, the Archduke suddenly stopped and caught Bernheim's arm.

"Listen!" he said, "I heard a cry."

Bernheim, too, had heard it, but he was not minded to let his master know.

"It was the wind, doubtless, sir," he said.

"No, it wasn't the wind—it was a voice, and a woman's voice, I thought."

A blast of rain and mist swept by them and through the trees, stirring the leaves into a rustling as of the sighs of disembodied spirits, while the swaying street lights flung the shadows hither and thither like pursuing cerecloths struggling to re-shroud them in their forsaken garb.

Bernheim looked around to fix the location.

"It's the De Saure house," he said, "and has been unoccupied for months—Your Highness must have been mistaken."

The Archduke moved on. "Doubtless, the wind plays queer tricks with sound on such a night; yet my ears rarely deceive me."

They were passing the wide entrance gates, and he went nearer and peered within—and as though in answer, from out the darkness came the shriek of one in awful terror.

"Don't strike me again! For God's sake don't strike me!"

The Archduke seized the gate.

"Come on, Bernheim," he exclaimed; "it *is* a woman."

The Aide caught his arm.

"Don't, sir," he said; "don't—it is nothing for you to mix in—it is for the police."

Armand made no answer; he was trying to find the latch.

"I pray Your Highness to refrain," Bernheim begged; "an Archduke—"

"Help! For God's sake help!" came the cry.

The latch yielded, and Armand flung back the gate.

"Come on," he ordered, "I'm a man, and yonder a woman calls."

He sprang down the path toward the house, which he could see now in black forbiddingness among the trees far back from the street.

Again Bernheim ventured to protest.

"It may be Lotzen's trap, sir," he warned.

For the shadow of an instant the Archduke hesitated; and at that moment the voice rang out again.

"*Don't strike me! Don't str—*" and a gurgling choke ended it.

"To the devil with Lotzen!" he exclaimed, and dashed on.

And Bernheim, with a silent curse, went beside him, loosening his sword as he ran, and feeling for the small revolver he had slipped inside his tunic, before they left the Epsau. To him, now, everything of mystery or danger spelled Lotzen—but even if it were not he, there was trouble enough ahead, and scandal enough, too, likely; scandal in which the Governor of Dornlitz, an Archduke, may be the King, had no place, and which could serve only to injure him before the people and in the esteem of the Nobles. Better that half the women in Dornlitz should be beaten and choked than that his master should be smirched by the tongue of calumny. He had no patience with this Quixotism that succored foolish females at foolish hours, in a place where neither the female nor they had any right to enter—and where, for her, at least, to enter was a crime. If he were able, he would have picked the Archduke up bodily, and borne him back to the palace, and have left the infernal woman to shift for herself, and to save herself or not, as her luck might rule.

Then they brought up suddenly in front of the house; and as they paused to find the steps, a light flashed, for an instant, from the upper windows, and disappeared—as if an electric switch had been turned on, and off again. But its life had been long enough to show the broad entrance porch, and the big doors beyond it—and that they were open wide.

At the sight, Bernheim swore a good round oath and seized the Archduke's arm.

"It's a trap, my lord, it's a trap!" he exclaimed.

And again Armand hesitated; and again the cry came, though muffled now and indistinct.

"We will have to chance it," he said, "I can't desert a woman who calls for help."

"Very well, sir," said Bernheim, knowing that further opposition was useless, "but if it is a trap, she'll be the first I kill."

They went softly up the steps and into the vestibule; not a sound came from within.

"Are you familiar with this house?" the Archduke whispered.

"Very, sir; I've been in it scores of times—salon on right, dining room and library opposite."

"And the stairs?"

"In the rear, on the left."

"Can you find the electric switch?"

The Colonel drew his revolver and stepped quickly inside; he knew there was a row of buttons near the library door, and he found them readily. With a single motion he pushed them in, and every chandelier and side-light in the entire lower floor sprang to life—illuminating rooms, solitary and undisturbed.

Over the mantel in the library hung a pair of beautiful old duelling rapiers, and the Archduke snatched one down and tried its balance; then took the other and handed it to Bernheim.

"Take it, man," he said, as the Colonel touched his own sword; "take it, it's worth an armory of those; its reach alone may save your life, if we are crowded." He made a pass in the air and laughed—it was sweet any time to feel the hilt of such a weapon, but now it was doubly sweet, with danger ahead and the odds he knew not what. He pointed upward.

"Come along," he said—"now for the next floor and the clash of steel."

But Bernheim shook his head.

"I pray you, my lord, be prudent," he urged—"remember, to us you are the King."

Faintly, from somewhere above, the cry came—weak and suppressed, but audible.

"Help! oh help!"

"Damn the woman!" Bernheim exclaimed, dashing forward to go first; and failing, by four steps.

The upper hall was dark, save for the reflection from below, but Armand caught the sheen of a switch plate and pressed the key. Five closed doors confronted him—without hesitation he chose the rear one on the right, and sprang toward it.

As he did so, the lights on the first floor went out, the front doors closed with a bang, and a key turned in the lock and was withdrawn. Instinctively he stopped and drew back; at the same moment, Bernheim reached over and turned off their lights also, leaving the house in impenetrable darkness.

The Archduke stepped quickly across toward Bernheim, and bumped into him mid-way.

"It's a trap," he whispered; "the locking of the door proves it—these rooms are empty, but we'll have a look and not be caught between two fires."

"Damn the woman!" said Bernheim.

Armand laughed softly. "Never mind her, we have other work on hand now. You keep the stairway; put your sword into any one who tries to come up; I'll go through the rooms," and he was gone before the Colonel could protest.

Bernheim tip-toed over to the head of the stairs and, leaning on the rail, listened. He could detect no sound in the hall below; the silence was as utter as the blackness. He stooped and felt the carpet on the stairs; it was soft and very thick, the sort that deadens noise. Behind him, a door closed softly, and he saw the gleam of a faint light along a sill, and, in a moment, along another further toward the front. Evidently, the Archduke had met no misadventure yet. And so he stood there, tense and expectant, while the darkness pressed hard upon his eyes, and set them burning with the strain of striving to pierce through.

Presently he felt that some one was coming toward him, and then the faintest whisper spoke his name. He reached out, and his fingers touched the Archduke's shoulder.

Armand put his mouth close to his Aide's ear.

"Rooms deserted," he whispered—"what's on the third floor?"

"It's a mere garret; the servants quarters are in a detached building in the rear."

"We'll chance the garret—I laid a chair across the foot of those stairs—and also at the head of the back stairs—anything doing below?"

"Quiet as the grave, sir."

"An apt simile, Bernheim," said the Archduke; "there is going to be a death or two down there to-night, if we can manage it—just as a gentle notice to our cousin of what he may expect."

The old soldier's hand sought impulsively his master's.

"You mean it, my lord?" he asked eagerly.

"I do; I'm——" a stair creaked very faintly—"they're coming," he ended.

Both men bent forward listening ... the seconds passed ... no sound came to them. Then Bernheim bethought himself of the rail, and laid his ear upon it. Instantly he was up.

"They are coming," he whispered, "I could hear them distinctly."

"Good," said Armand. "We will give them the steel as soon as they're within reach—be ready—I'll take the right."

The stairway was of more than medium width, and straight-away almost to the lower floor, the turn being at the bottom. While the lights were on, Bernheim had noticed a heavy oak chest against the wall near where they were standing. Now it suddenly occurred to him how it could be used. Asking the Archduke to bear aside a moment, he seized it in his powerful arms, and carrying it to the head of the stairs hurled it, with all his strength, down into the darkness.

There was a heavy thud as of human bodies struck, wild shrieks of pain and terror, and then a deafening crash, as the chest broke asunder against the wall below, followed directly by moans, and curses, and struggles to get free.

Although Armand had not seen what his Aide had done, he could picture it all now, and he laughed aloud.

"Clear away the débris, gentlemen!" he called. "On to the charge! Don't be a lot of quitters; we've plenty of ammunition left; *en avant!*"

But only the moans answered him. He drew Bernheim closer.

"What do you suggest," he asked; "shall we go down?"—And the upsetting of the chair at the rear stairs answered him.

"Turn on the lights when I whistle," he ordered, and stole swiftly to the rear of the hall.

Doubtless the purpose had been to attack them simultaneously in front and rear, and here was the chance to give this detachment, also, a surprise. He heard the chair being set carefully aside, followed by foot-falls such as are made only by shoeless feet. The darkness was impenetrable, but he knew they paused at the door, and then came slowly forward, passing him so closely he could have touched them with his hand. The next instant he gave the signal.

As the lights blazed out, disclosing three masked men with drawn swords, the Archduke leaped forward and, with the hilt of his rapier, struck the one nearest him behind the ear. The rogue dropped in his tracks. At the same moment, Bernheim's pistol cracked, and another went down, shot through the head. The third stood irresolute; and him the Archduke addressed.

"It's the pistol, yonder, or the sword, here," he said; "which will you choose?"

The fellow chanced to be almost in line with the front stairs, and for answer he sprang across the hall and dashed down them. Bernheim's gun spoke thrice: the first bullet struck the wall; the second, the newel post; the third, fired into the semi-obscurity below, and as the knave's head was almost on a line with the floor, brought an answering cry; but it did not disable him; they heard him stumble over the broken chest, then the key was thrust into the lock, the front door was flung back, and he crossed the porch at a run.

"He's the last of them, I fancy," said Armand.

Bernheim looked at the pistol in disgust.

"I never did have any patience with these toys," he growled; "three shots across a blanket, and only a touch!"

The Archduke pointed to the dead body.

"You did pretty well there," he said.

"Luck, pure luck." He went over to the stairs. "I don't hear anything," he said; "the chest seems to be very quiet—what about the lights; shall I turn them off?"

"First take a look at these gentlemen," said Armand; "do you know them?"

The Aide stooped over the one he had killed and jerked off the mask that covered his upper face—then did the same with the other, and shook his head.

"I never saw either of them," he said; "but they look the part—you hit this one exactly on the spot; he is paralyzed or dead."

"We will leave him to find out for himself which it is," the Archduke answered—"unless, Colonel, you wish to search further for the lady—as I remember, you promised her the first killing."

Bernheim laughed.

"I rather imagine your lady is a man—I think we shall find her at the foot of the stairs."

He ran quickly down, vaulted over the débris with the aid of the rail, and turned on the light.

The Archduke had followed him as far as the turn.

"It looks as though you got her, Colonel," he remarked, pointing with his rapier to two men who lay among the fragments of the chest. One was dead—face and head mashed flat, the crimson splotch on the white wall marking where the heavy missile had crushed them. The other, both legs broken at the ankles, and half his ribs driven in, was pinned in the corner, unconscious—a singularly repulsive creature, with huge, protruding teeth, pimply face, an enormous red nose, and a mouth like a fish's.

Bernheim looked him over.

"Positively, I'd be ashamed to employ such carrion," he remarked. "I don't understand Lotzen; he is an aesthete, even in his crimes."

The Archduke stepped carefully into the hall, and laid his rapier on the table.

"Let us be off," he said; "there is nothing more to do." He turned toward the door—then stopped and reached for the sword.

"Others are coming," he said;—"we'll fight it out right here."

There was the quick tramp of feet on the porch, and a sergeant and two police entered. Their looks of bewildered surprise, as they recognized the Archduke and his Aide, were so comical that even Bernheim smiled, though his words were curt enough.

"Salute, men!" he said, "don't you know His Royal Highness?"

The sergeant's hand went up.

"Your pardon, sir," he stammered, "but we heard shots—and this house is supposed to be unoccupied. I am sorry——"

Armand motioned him to silence.

"There is nothing to pardon, sergeant," he said; "you are doing your duty very properly, and you come in good time. You will search this place thoroughly, including the grounds; remove the dead and wounded immediately; see that all knowledge of the affair is suppressed, and report to me at noon to-morrow."

The officer saluted again. "Yes, Your Highness."

"Where are our capes, Colonel?"

"In the library—I'll get them."... He dropped the Archduke's about his shoulders, and the sergeant did the same for him.

As they gained the Avenue, the cathedral bell struck three.

"A nice hour for an old man like you, Bernheim, to be going home," said the Archduke.

A quizzical smile came into the Aide's stern face.

"A lady called me," he replied.

XII
THE SOLE SURVIVOR

Ferida Palace, the residence of His Royal Highness the Duke of Lotzen, on the Alta Avenue half a mile or so beyond the Epsau, is a great, rambling pile of gray stone, of varying height and diverse architecture, set in the midst of grounds that occupy two entire squares, and are surrounded by a high, embattled wall, pierced with four wide entrances, whose bronze gates are famous in their craftsmanship.

Here the Duke lived in a splendor and munificence almost rivaling the King himself, and with a callous indifference to certain laws of society, that would have scandalized the Capital had it become public knowledge. But in his household, the servant who babbled, never babbled twice; he left Dornlitz quite too suddenly; and those who were wise learned quickly that they lost nothing in wage nor perquisite by being blind and dumb. For Lotzen did not skimp his steward—all he required was skillful service, and that what occurred within the Palace must not go beyond the walls. Nevertheless, in conduct, he was not the habitual libertine and roué,—the contrary was, in truth, the fact—but he proposed to have the opportunity to do as he liked when the fancy moved him—and to have no carping moralist praying over him and then retailing his misdeeds with unctuous smirks of pious horror. Not that he cared a centime for their horrors or their prayers, but because it were not well to irritate unduly the King, by doings which he might not countenance, if brought formally to his attention—though the Duke was well aware that Frederick troubled himself not at all how he went to the devil, nor when, save that the quicker he went the better.

And so it was, that he had not hesitated to bring with him the woman of raven hair and dead-white cheek, and to install her in the gorgeous suite in the west wing of the Ferida, where others, as frail but far less fair, had been before her—and the world never the wiser—just as now it was not the wiser as to Madeline Spencer's presence. The time was not yet for her to show herself, and in the meantime she had remained secluded; she was too well known in Dornlitz to escape recognition; and even Lotzen dared not, at this exigency, so spurn public sentiment as to sponsor the adventuress whom he had procured to pose as wife to the Archduke Armand.

She had come with him to the Capital with deep misgiving, and only after much urging and jeweled caresses; though not the least of the inducements was the hope of annoying the Princess Dehra—for whom she had conceived the most violent hate. By herself it would, of course, have been a fatuously foolish hate, but with Lotzen, and under the peculiar situation existing at Court, there was a chance—and it was this chance she meant to play for and to seize. And besides, it promised the excitement and ample financial returns that were the mainsprings of her existence.

And though it fretted her beyond measure to dawdle in idleness and tiresome inanition, even in the luxury of the Ferida, yet she endured it with amazing equanimity; and amused herself, the while, by flirting with the Duke's friends, when the Duke was not in presence—and sometimes when he was. And then, when he sulked or stormed, a soft arm would slip around his neck, and a pair of red lips smile close to his face; and, presently, he was caressing the one, and pleading for the others—and there was peace, and on her terms. The marvel of it all, was how she held him—as no woman had ever held him hitherto; she made no pretense of love, nor tried for it from him—a pleasant camaraderie was all she gave, and all she asked for; favor-free to-day, favor-cold to-morrow; elusive as a moon-beam; fickle as the wind; tempting and alluring as a vestal; false and faithless as the Daughter of the Foam.

And though Lotzen knew it—and knew it well—for she had told him frankly what she was and what she lived for, yet her fascinations negatived her words; while her indifference as to whether she stayed or went—and which he was thoroughly aware was not assumed—only captivated him the more, who had been used to easy conquest and clinging hearts.

He had explained fully to her the complication produced by the disappearance of the Laws, recounting in detail the scene at the Royal Council, when the compromise was forced; but as to Adolph and the incidents of the King's library he said never a word. To her prompt query, as to how he accounted for the Book's disappearance, he answered that the American, knowing it contained no decree in his favor, had stolen and, doubtless, destroyed it—and that the Princess Royal's story was a clever lie—"just such a lie as you, yourself, would have told for me, in a similar exigency," he had added; and she had smiled an acquiescence—thinking, the while, that for the American she would have done much more than lie, and gladly, if he would but let her.

Since the day when, as Colonel Spencer's bride, she had come to the old fort on the Missouri, and had first set eyes on Captain Armand Dalberg, there was but one man who might have stirred her cold heart to an honest beat; and though he had ignored her overtures, and finally had scorned them with scarring words, yet it had not entirely killed the old desire; and even now, after all that she had done against him, and was ready yet to do, a single word from him would have brought her to his side. Yet, because she knew that word would never come, and that another woman claimed him honestly and without fear, she would go on with her part; and all the more willingly that it enabled her to strike through him the woman who had won him.

And now, after the two weeks quiescence, the restless fever was upon her, and the Duke had caught the signs; next would come the call to Paris; and he knew the second call would win. If he were to hold her, it was time to start the campaign she had come to assist—and that very day was his visit to the Summer Palace, and the sudden determination of his plan. But when, in the evening, he had gone to her apartments to tell her of it, and to discuss the opening moves, she had sent him the message that she was indisposed and had retired, and that he should breakfast with her the next day.

And in the morning he had found her in her boudoir, in the most enticing of soft blue gowns, and no touch of dishabille nor carelessness in all her attire, from the arrangement of the raven hair to the shoeing of the slender feet. Madeline Spencer was much too clever to let a man see her in negligée when, to him, the hour for negligée was passed.

She met him with a smile, and let him kiss her cheek.

"I am sorry about last night, dear," she said, "but I was quite too wretched to see even you—and I wanted to see you."

He sat on the arm of the chair, playing softly with her hair.

"I wish I could believe that it was just I you wanted," he said.

She shot him an upward glance of her siren eyes.

"I have been thinking about this business that we have on hand," she continued; "and, Ferdinand, if you wish my aid, you must get busy—I can't endure this stagnation longer. I'm a wild beast that would die in confinement; I need the jungle and the air and sky."

He laughed, and pinched her ear.

"Your jungle, little one, is the Champs Élysées and *cher Maxim's*; *la chaleur communicative du banquet*,—your air and sky, the adulation of the masculine and the stare of admiring eyes."

"Yes, it is; and I've been away a long, long time; yet I want to stay with you until this work is ended—because" (taking his hand and smiling up at him) "you have been good to me, and because it promises excitement of a novel sort—only, dear, do let us be at it."

A door swung back. "Madam is served!" came the monotone.

As they went in, the Duke slipped his arm around her slender waist.

"We're going to be at it," he said; "send the servants away and I'll tell you my plan; it was for that I came last evening."

"Now, tell me!" she exclaimed, as the door closed behind the footman.

"We are going back to Lotzenia," he said.

She paused, and the black eye-brows went up.

"We?" she inflected.

He nodded. "That is where the game will be played out."

"And why not here, in Dornlitz?"

"Because it's easier there—and surer."

She made to shiver. "So, for me, it's only out of a charming mausoleum into a common grave."

He laughed. "It will be a rarely lively grave, my dear Madeline, and, I promise you, exciting enough for even your starved nerves."

"When do we start?"

"Soon, I trust—there is work to be done here first."

"And I may help?"

"Yes, you may help—the plan needs you."

"And the plan?" she asked eagerly.

"The very simplest I could devise," said he; "to lure the American to Lotzenia and——"

She smiled comprehendingly. "Why take all that trouble—why not kill him in Dornlitz?"

He flung up a cautioning hand. "Softly, my dear, softly—and not so blunt in the words—and as I said, it's easier there and surer."

"But it would be so much prettier to play the game out here," she half objected; "and more accordant with your taste, I fancy."

"Very true," said he. "It's always more artistic to run a man through with a rapier than to kill him with a club; but in this business it's the end alone that concerns me. Yet the primary essential, in either method, is opportunity and freedom of movement; neither is here; both will be plentiful in the North."

"And, of course, at your friendly invitation, the American will gladly accompany you to Lotzenia and permit himself to be— offered up."

"Practically that."

An impatient smile shone in her eyes.

"I do not understand, Ferdinand, why you persist in underrating your enemy; it's the climax of bad generalship. The American may be reckless and a bit headstrong, but assuredly he is not a fool."

The Duke shrugged his shoulders. "He can fight, I grant you— but he can't scheme nor plot—nor detect one, though it's as evident as the sun."

"And yet—" she waved her hand toward the Epsau—"it is he you're fighting for the Crown."

"Luck!" he scoffed—"a dotard King, a damn Huzzar uniform, and a silly girl."

"Is his luck any the less now, with the girl Regent of Valeria?" she asked.

"Possibly not," he said; "and hence another reason for the mountains—she won't be with him there."

She gave it up—she had tried repeatedly, but it was impossible, it seemed, to arouse him to Armand's real ability—when hate rides judgment, reason lies bound and gagged.

"Why should the Governor of Dornlitz go to far off Lotzenia?" she asked.

He glanced around the room suspiciously; then scribbled a line in pencil on his cuff and held it over to her.

She read it, and looked at him in puzzled interrogation.

"I don't understand," she said; "you told me that he——"

He had anticipated her question.

"So I did," he interrupted quickly, "but I have no proof; and lately I have come to doubt it. At any rate, this will disclose the truth. If my scheme works, he will follow into Hell itself."

"A strikingly appropriate name for your Castle, dear," she laughed.

He nodded and smiled.

"And what if the scheme doesn't work?" she asked.

"In that event, the laugh is on me, and we must devise another means to draw him there."

"Which will be quite fruitless, I can assure you."

"Then we will fight it out here," he said, "and I shall doubly need you."

"And you'll get me, doubly welcome."... She lit a cigarette and passed it to him; and lit another for herself. "Now, how are we to contrive to set the trap?"

A footman entered and handed the Duke a visiting card, with something penciled on it....

"It's Bigler," he said, "and he asks to be admitted immediately—he's always in a rush. Tell Count Bigler I'll see him presently."

She stayed the servant with a motion; she did not intend to lose Lotzen until he had told her the whole plot.

"Why not have him here?" she asked; "and then let him go."

"By all means, if you will permit," and he nodded to the footman.

Most women would have called Count Bigler handsome; and not a few men, as well. He was red-headed and ruddy, with clean-cut features, square chin, and a laughing mouth, that contrary to Valerian fashion was not topped by a moustache. Since boyhood, he had been Lotzen's particular companion and intimate; and, as is usual in such instances, he was almost his antipode in temperament and manner.

He saluted the Duke with easy off-handedness, and bent with deferential courtesy over Mrs. Spencer's hand; but pressing it altogether more tightly than the attitude justified.

She answered with the faintest finger tap and a quick smile, and waved him to a chair.

"If I'm *de trop*," she said, "I'll vacate."

"Madame is never *de trop*, to me," he answered, taking the cigarette she offered and smiling down at her, through the smoke, as he lit it.

When he turned to sit down, the left side of his face was, for the first time, toward the Duke, showing the ear bound with strips of surgeon's plaster.

"In the name of Heaven, man," said he, "what have you been doing with yourself?"

The Count laughed. "Trading the top of my ear for a day or two more of life."

"Duel?" Lotzen asked.

"Yes, after a fashion, but not exactly under the code."

The primeval woman stirred in Mrs. Spencer.

"The story, Count, the story!" she demanded, coiling her lithe arms behind her head, and leaning far back in languorous gracefulness.

"It's the story that brings me here so early," he replied.

The Duke was frowning. Duelling was a serious crime in Valeria, even in the Army, and it was a particularly unfortunate moment for Bigler to offend; and especially as only the Governor of Dornlitz or the Regent could save him from punishment.

"How did you manage to get into such a mess just at this time?" he asked sharply. "Was any one killed?"

The Count nodded. "Four, I think; I didn't stay to examine them."

"Four! four! God, man, was it a massacre?"

"Almost—I'm the sole survivor on your side."

Lotzen's frown grew.

"On *my* side!" he echoed.

"I was assuming to act for you," Bigler explained.

"For me!—who was on the other side?"

"The American—the American and Bernheim."

For a space the Duke smoked in silence; then he gave a faint chuckle.

"They came rather close to making it five, didn't they?" He touched his ear—"Bernheim, I suppose?... Of course, the American would have made it five. What a fool you are, Bigler, to go into such a thing without telling me."

"I'm telling you now," the Count grinned.

"And I'm exceedingly grateful to my dear cousin for leaving you to tell it. It's the only service he has ever done me. I assume it isn't necessary to ask if you got him—or even wounded him?"

"Quite unnecessary."

Madeline Spencer had been chafing at the delay; now she arose, and, going over to a divan, sank sinuously among the pillows, one trim, blue silk ankle shimmering far below her skirts.

"If you were as slow in the fight, Count, as you are in getting at the story," she remarked, "it's a wonder to me how Bernheim missed you."

Both men laughed, and Bigler's glance lingered a moment in open admiration.

The Duke swung his hand toward her.

"Madame grows impatient," he said. "Proceed, Monsieur Edmund."

The Count took a fresh cigarette.

"It was this way," he began, pivoting his chair around on one back leg, so that he would have both his auditors within his direct vision. "The two weeks we were bound to idleness mourning for old Frederick, I spent in watching the American. I soon discovered that it was his custom, every few days, to visit, very late at night, his friend, the American Ambassador, and that he invariably not only walked the entire distance from the Epsau and back, but also went unattended. It seemed to me very simple to waylay him, some night on his return; the streets were usually deserted then, and he should be an easy victim, if set upon by enough men to assure success. And I had about arranged the matter, when I chanced to remember that the De Saures were still in the country and their house closed. It stands far back from the Avenue, you know, and a safer and surer plan occurred to me:—I would lure him into this house, and leave him there for burial. In the dark, my four rogues could put enough steel through him, from behind, to insure his quick demise. I proposed to take no chances with such a swordsman by giving him a light; and besides, it was just as well that the men should not know their victim. Nor did they ever see me unmasked. For decoy, one of the rogues procured a woman——"

"What!" exclaimed the Duke,—"one of their women!"

"It was voice, not beauty, I wanted—the cry of a female for help."

Lotzen nodded and smiled. "Rather clever."

"For a week we met at the house at eleven o'clock every night, but the American didn't go to the Embassy. Then, last night, at twelve, he went, and old Bernheim with him. That didn't bother me much, however, and we waited for their return. They came about two, through driving rain and wind; and the woman played her part perfectly. Such piteous cries I never heard. 'Don't strike me again—don't strike me again—help—help;' reiterated in tones that would have moved even your heart, my dear Duke. I was concealed near the gate and they moved me— and they caught the American instantly, though Bernheim scented danger and protested vigorously. 'It may be a trap of Lotzen's,' he warned. 'Damn Lotzen!' was the prompt answer, as the girl wailed again—I tell you she was an artist at it; she, herself, must be used to beatings. They ran up the path to the house, I following; and here the whole scheme was almost upset by some fool having left the front door open. Bernheim protested that it proved the trap; and even the American was hesitating, when again the woman wailed. That settled it; and I dashed around the house to the rear entrance.

"My purpose was to draw them upstairs and finish the job there. They searched the first floor—we were on the second—then, leaving all the electric lights burning, they ascended—and we went down the back way, turned off the lights and closed and locked the doors. They promptly extinguished the lights they had set going above, and the house was in the densest darkness I have ever known. We could hear them whispering in the upper hall; and I sent two of my rogues up the front stairs and led the others up the rear, intending to snap an electric torch for the instant it would require to do our work; and which seemed all the easier because I had observed, at the gate, that the American was without his sword. When we were half way up, I heard a crash from the front, followed by the American's laugh. I paused an instant, then hurried on, and fell over a chair that had been placed at the head of the stairs. Everything remained quiet, however, and we went forward into the hall. My finger was on the key of the torch when there came a shrill whistle, and the lights went on. I saw Bernheim in front of us, pistol in hand; it flashed, and the man on my left went down. At the same moment, the American sprang at us from behind and felled the other fellow with the hilt of a sword—where he got it the devil only knows. As for me, I admit I was dazed with surprise; I heard the American offer me the choice: pistol or sword—I took the pistol. I had retained enough sense to know I hadn't the faintest chance with him. The front steps were near; I made the leap of my life, and plunged down them. Bernheim fired three times—this (indicating his ear) was the last; the first two missed."

"What had become of your other pair of rogues?" the Duke asked.

"Dead. I fell over them at the foot of the stairs, buried under a huge chest."

"Flung upon them, doubtless, as they were ascending," said Lotzen.

Bigler nodded. "That was the crash I heard." He took another cigarette, and lighted it carefully. "And that, madame, is the story," he ended, looking at Mrs. Spencer.

She flashed him a bright smile.

"The nicest thing about it, my dear Count," she said, "is that you are here to tell it."

"Even if he doesn't in the least deserve to be here," the Duke interjected. "Such a—my dear Edmund, don't do it again. You're too young and innocent to die. Leave the strategy to me—and my lady, yonder; we will give you enough of fighting in due time—and soon."

The Count laughed in good natured imperturbability.

"I'm done," he said frankly. "I'm ready to take orders from you or my lady—particularly from my lady."

The Duke gave him a quick, sharp glance.

"The orders will come through me," he said, rather curtly.

Madeline Spencer held out her hand to the Count.

"When His Highness grows jealous," she said, languidly arising and shaking down her skirts, "it's time, you know, for you to go—come back when he is not here;" and with a provoking smile at the Duke, she flung the Count a kiss—"for your wounded ear, my lord."

XIII
IN THE JAPONICA WALK

The Regent signed the last document, and, pushing it across the table, laid aside the pen.

"How much better it would be if that were 'Armand, Rex,'" she said.

The Prime Minister was putting up his papers.

"And better, still, if it were 'Dehra, Regina,'" he returned, closing the portfolio and locking it.

She made a gesture of dissent.

"There would be no need for the Book, then," he continued; "and no danger of Lotzen becoming king. It is God's blessing on Valeria that you were you, and could assume the government—otherwise, we would have had civil war. Your Highness has no conception of the sentiment in the Army; it is two to one for the Archduke; but Lotzen's third is unduly powerful because of a coterie of high officers, who are jealous of the 'American,' as he is styled, and their readiness to precipitate a contest; and Armand's contingent is unduly weak, because they do not feel assured that he would countenance war. In a word, the rogues and rascals are for Lotzen—they recognize a kindred leader and the opportunity for high reward. But they would accept you for Queen with enthusiasm—even rogues and rascals love a pretty woman who can rule them with a heavy hand."

Dehra looked at her hand, slender, soft, small, and smiled.

Count Epping nodded. "Very pretty," he said, "very pretty, but it's a Dalberg hand, you know—and they know, too."

"And as they shall experience," she remarked, eyelids narrowed just a trifle, "if they show a disposition to forget it.... And in the experience they may learn that the Governor of Dornlitz also has a Dalberg hand."

"There will be no civil war now," said the Count; "your regency has quite obviated any such catastrophe; and if the Book be found, its decision will be accepted without protest by the Army, as well as by the people at large. What I fear is the contest in the House of Nobles—the margin there will be very narrow, I apprehend; and that involves high feeling and fierce antagonism and smoldering family hate fanned into fire; and then, if Lotzen lose, the new king may have a chance to show his hand."

"Armand the First will show it, never fear," she said, with the pride a woman always has for him she loves.

"I have no fear," he said; "if I had, I would not help to make him king—yet, if I may be permitted, Henry the Fifth would be a title far more pleasing to the nation than Armand the First. He bears the Great Henry's features, let him bear his name, as well."

She sprang up.

"He shall, he shall!" she exclaimed; "he will do it for me, I know."

The old Count's face softened in one of its rare smiles.

"He would be a poor sort of man, indeed, my lady, who would deny anything to you," he said, and in his stately, old-fashioned way he bent and kissed her hand.

As he arose, the Princess suddenly slipped an arm around his neck, and for the briefest moment her soft lips rested on his forehead.

The Prime Minister kept his face lowered; when he raised it, the tears still trembled in his eyes.

"Don't tell the Archduke," she laughed gayly, seeing how he was moved.

"No," said he, laughing with her now, "I'll not tell him—and lose all chance for another."

"I'll give you another now," she cried, and, springing on the chair beside him, she kissed him on the cheek. "Now go— you've had more than your share—but you shall have a third the day Armand is king."

He took her hand, and gallantly helped her down.

"You give me another object in life," he said.—"I shall claim it if the King permit."

"You may claim it, before him and all the Court," she answered.

After Count Epping had gone, the Princess turned to the table, and sitting on the corner, one foot on a chair, the other dangling, took up some papers he had left with her for examination. In the midst of it the Duke of Lotzen was announced.

"I am engaged," she said curtly; "I cannot see him ... or stay, admit him."

After her question and his answer in the garden near the sundial, two days before, she had decided she would receive him only upon occasions of ceremony, when, to exclude him, would have required a special order; but this unexpected and, for him, amazingly early visit, piqued her curiosity too sharply to resist.

But there was no cordiality in her look nor attitude, as he bowed before her in the intensely respectful manner he could assume so well. She made no change in her position, nor offered him her hand, nor smiled; her eyes showed only polite indifference as, for a space, she let him wait for leave to speak. When she gave it, her voice was as indifferent as her eyes.

"Well, Your Royal Highness," she said, "how can we serve you?"

Not a shade of her bearing had missed the Duke, and though his anger rose, yet his face bore only a placid smile of amused unconcern.

"I desire the Regent's permission," he said, "to absent myself from the country for an indefinite period."

"It is granted—a year, if you wish."

The Duke laughed softly, almost mockingly, indeed.

"I fear I may not stay quite so long," he answered, "much as it would please me to oblige you. My presence will be necessary in a certain ceremony in the Cathedral, that is fixed for a few weeks short of a year."

The Regent's eyes narrowed. "In the crypt, you mean?—your absence will, at least, postpone the ceremony—had you remained, I imagine it would have occurred much earlier."

Even Lotzen's calmness was disturbed by such a threat from a woman—and, momentarily, his color heightened and his eyes snapped in irritated surprise. Then he bowed.

"I am glad to have been shown the claws so early," he replied with sneering sarcasm; "I shall endeavor to keep beyond their reach. But I shall do my best to furnish the crypt another tenant, though I will not promise to put my Court in mourning for him."

The Princess shrugged her shapely shoulders.

"It is quite unnecessary to tell us what your barbaric nature told us long ago," she replied. "When do you wish to depart?"

"Within the week."

"And for where?"

"For France—Paris in particular."

"Very well—prefer your request through the regular channel, as any other officer, and I will grant it;" and with a perfunctory nod, she resumed her reading.

"I am permitted to withdraw?" he asked.

"You are always permitted to withdraw," she answered, without looking up.

"I like your spirit, Dehra," he laughed; "you and I would make an unconquerable pair; it is a pity you won't be my queen."

She pointed toward the door.

"Go, sir," she ordered, her voice repressed to unusual softness; "go! nor present yourself again until you have received permission."

And with a smile and a bow, he went; backing slowly from the room, in an aggravation of respect.

He had not come to the Palace for leave to go to France, or any where else; where he wanted to go, and when, he went. But his plans required that he be absolutely free and untrammeled, and so he had done this to insure himself against being ordered suddenly to some military duty that might hamper his movements even slightly. And his visit had been doubly successful—he had the permission, and in such a form that he was given the utmost liberty, and he had also learned the Regent's real attitude toward him, and that even with her it would be a fight without quarter. What the American would make it, the dead bodies in the De Saure house had indicated as plainly as spoken words—and, indeed, as such he knew they had been deliberately intended.

As he passed one of the windows in the corridor, he caught, far off amid the trees, the sheen of a white gown; he paused, and presently he recognized Mlle. d'Essoldé. With a smile of sudden purpose, he went quickly down a private stairway that opened on the Park below the marble terrace, and, eyes on the white gown, that showed at intervals through the bushes, he sauntered toward it.

There was, to be sure, a woman with raven hair and dead-white cheek at the Ferida, but there was also a woman yonder, and handier, with golden hair and shell-pink cheek; and variety was much to his taste, at times—and the picture on the stair still lingered with him, fresh and alluring. True, she had not received his advances with that flattered acquiescence he was rather used to, but he had no particular objection to temporary opposition; it gave zest to the victory—and, with him, victory had been rarely lost.

He encountered her in a narrow path, walled in by thick hedges of scarlet japonica, turning the corner suddenly and greeting her with a smile of well assumed surprise; stopping quite a little way off and bowing, his cap across his heart.

And she stopped, also; touched by fear and repugnance, as though a snake lay in her path.

"A happy meeting, mademoiselle," he said.

"For whom, sir?" she asked, turning half away.

"For me," he laughed, going toward her; "and for you, too, I hope."

She put her back to the hedge and made no answer.

"I owe you a very abject apology, for the other day," he said, standing close beside her, and leaning on his sword. "I fear I was brutally rude."

"There isn't the least doubt of it," she replied, and made to pass on.

He stepped before her.

"And are so still," she added.

"Come, Elise," he smiled, still blocking the way, "come; forgive me."

"Very well, I forgive you," she said, indifferently, and tried again to pass.

"Nonsense, my dear," catching her wrist, "put a bit of warmth into it—and then prove it by a little stroll with me toward the lake."

She recoiled at his touch, much as though the snake had stung her, and tried to wrench free, tearing her thin gown and scarring her flesh on the sharp thorns of the japonica, but making no outcry.

And this encouraged Lotzen; she was playing it very prettily indeed—to yield presently, the weary captive of superior strength. That a woman might be honest in her resistance, he was always slow to credit; but that one should actually be honest, and yet struggle silently rather than permit others to see her with him, was quite beyond his understanding.

He glanced up and down the path; no one was in sight, and the hedge was high—he would make the play a little faster. Hitherto, he had been content to hold her with a sure grip, and let her fling about in futile strivings; now he laughed, and drew her slowly toward him, his eyes fixed significantly upon her flushed face and its moist red lips, parted with the breath-throbs.

"Where shall I kiss you first, little one?" he asked—"on the mouth, or a check, or the gleaming hair?"—He held her back an instant in survey…. "Coy?—too coy to answer—come, then, let it be the lips now, and the others later, by the lake."

She had ceased to struggle, and her blue eyes were watching the Duke in fascinated steadiness. To him, it signified victory and a willing maid—he took a last glance at the path—then with a cry and a curse he dropped her wrist and sprang back, wringing his hand, the blood gushing from a ragged wound across its back, where Elise d'Essoldé's teeth had sunk into the flesh.

And she, with high-held skirts, was flying toward the Palace.

He sprang in pursuit—and stopped; she would pass the hedge before he could overtake her; and the open Park was no place for love making of the violent sort—nor with a wound that spurted red. The business would have to bide, for the present.... Over toward the terrace he saw the flutter of a white gown.

"Damn the little cat!" he muttered; "she shall pay me well for this."

Elise d'Essoldé, spent with running, her brain in a whirl, her hair dishevelled, weak-kneed and trembling now with the reaction, reached the marble steps near the pergola and sank on the lowest, just as Colonel Moore came springing down them, his eyes toward the japonica walk, searching for the girl in a white gown whom he was to have met there half an hour ago.

And he would have passed, unseeing, had she not spoken.

"Ralph!" she said, "Ralph!"

He swung around.

"Elise!" he exclaimed, "I'm sorry to be so late—I was—heaven, child, what has happened?"

The sight of him, and the sound of his voice, had calmed her instantly and put her pulse to normal beating; and now that she was with him, safe and unscathed, the coquette in her could not resist the temptation to torment him.

"Another kept the rendezvous," she answered, with affected naïveté.

He pointed to the torn gown.

"And that?" he asked.

"I did it."

"And the hair?"

"The penalty of an ill-arranged coiffure."

"And the red mark on your face—blood, it looks like."

"Blood!" she cried; "blood? where—where?"

"On your lips—around the mouth—"

The coquette vanished—the horror of it all flashed back upon her:—Lotzen's sybaritic leer—his easy confidence of assured success—the touch of his loathsome hand to her face—the sickening sensation as her teeth cut through his flesh and scraped the bones beneath—with a cry of disgust she sprang up, swayed unsteadily, and would have fallen had not Moore caught her.

"Water!" she implored, "water!" rubbing her lips frantically with her handkerchief—"water, oh, water!"

Amazed—mystified—alarmed, he stood an instant irresolute—then swinging her up, he bore her to where, near the sun-dial, a fountain played and splashed among the giant ferns. As they reached there, the nervous tumult subsided as quickly as it came, and she slipped swiftly out of his arms, and knelt beside the fountain, the spray powdering her hair with rainbow dust. And when she had bathed her face free of the blood-stain—though she could not wash away the red of her own embarrassment—she ventured to look at him.

He met her with a smile, that showed only sharp concern and tenderest sympathy.

"My child," he said, taking her hand, in the most gentle deference, and holding it in both of his, "tell me what has unstrung you so completely—you who are always merry and serene."

She gently freed her hand, and, gathering up the trailing ends of her skirt, turned toward the Palace.

"If I tell you," she said, "promise me that you won't make a scene nor try to punish him."

"Him!" he exclaimed, stopping short, "him! God in Heaven, was it that devil, Lotzen?"—he seized her arm—"where is he—where is he?"

She smiled at him very sweetly, loving the anger that blazed his face.

"I'll tell you nothing," she answered, "so long as you are in that humor—your promise first."

"No—no—I promised and forbore the other day; but now, with that"—sweeping his hand at gown and hair—"I'll forbear no longer."

She moved on.

"Come, Elise, who was it?"

She gave him another smile, but shook her head.

"Was it Lotzen—tell me, was it?"

Again the smile, and the motion of refusal.

"Very well, if you won't, I'll find out for myself."

"You cannot—the man won't tell—and no one saw it."

He laughed with quiet menace.

"I'll find him," he said; "I'll find him."

Quick fear seized her. He would succeed, she knew; and then, what would he do! Something, doubtless, to try to force the Duke to fight; and which would result only in his own disgrace and in being driven from the country. He must not suffer for her misfortune—and Dornlitz, without her dear Irishman, would be impossible; and she was not yet quite ready to go with him. She had told him something—as much as she might with proper reserve—of Lotzen's behavior that other morning; and it had been difficult enough to restrain him then. Now, with the dishevelled hair, and torn gown, and blood on her face, only his own word would hold him.

"Promise me, Ralph, promise me," she implored; "there is no reason for punishment—see," holding out her hand, "here is the only place he touched me—only on the wrist—I swear it, Ralph—"

He took the hand, and looked at the soft, blue-veined flesh, chafed and abraded with the pinch of iron fingers; and again the rage of hate swept him, and he put the hand down sharply and turned away his head, unwilling that she should see his face while passion marked it.

She touched his arm, almost timidly.

"Promise me, dear," she said—"please promise me."

She did not realize what she had called him; nor, indeed, did he, until days afterward, too late to turn it to account; though what he answered worked far more to his profit, than had he used the chance offered by an inadvertent endearment.

"I promise," he said; "I ought not to; but because you wish it, I promise—now will you tell me?"

She looked up at him gratefully—and such women as Elise d'Essoldé can say much with their eyes. They had mounted the steps and were on the terrace; she pointed into the Park.

"It was in the japonica walk," she said; "I was waiting for you, when Lotzen came upon me, seemingly by accident——"

"There are no accidents with Lotzen," Moore broke in.

"It may be, but he chose to treat it so;—I tried to pass—he stopped me and begged forgiveness for his brutal rudeness of the other day; I forgave him indifferently, hoping to escape quickly, and tried again to pass. He caught my wrist, and demanded a kiss, and that I walk with him to the lake. I was close against the hedge, and it was in my struggles to get free from him that the sharp thorns tore my gown. He let me thrash out my strength, holding me all the time by this wrist; presently, when he was about to kiss me by main force, I bit him in the hand, and escaped, running at top speed, and in fright and exhaustion collapsing where you found me.... That was all, Ralph," she ended.

Moore's intense repression found some relief in a long breath.

"All!" he said, rather huskily; "all! ... well, all I ask is, some day, to have him against me, sword in hand."

"Your promise!" she exclaimed.

He smiled down at her. "The promise holds, child, as you well know; but this affair of the Book may work an opportunity."

"If it does, take it," said she instantly.

"Trust me, my lady," he answered, as he left her at the small door used only by the Princess and her privileged intimates.

"Your lady?" she echoed across the sill—her natural witchery increased four-fold, in his eyes, by the tumbled hair—"your lady—perhaps."

In the hallway, just at her own room, she met the Princess, who, woman-like, marked at a glance every detail of her disordered attire.

"Good heaven, Elise," she exclaimed, "what has that Adjutant of mine been doing to you?"

"Practicing sword tricks on my skirt," said she, holding it up to show the rents, "and learning to be *un coiffeur*."

"He seems to be as uncommonly proficient in the one as he is deficient in the other,"—then looked at her questioningly; "but seriously, Elise, what happened?—if you care to tell me."

"The Duke of Lotzen found me alone in the japonica walk."

The Princess struck her hands together angrily.

"Lotzen! oh, Lotzen!" she exclaimed; "some day—did Moore come on him there? If he did, the some-day is already here."

"Fortunately, no, since I escaped unharmed."

"Unfortunately, you mean—it saved to the world another scoundrel."

"And Ralph would be a fugitive in disgrace," said Mlle. d'Essoldé.

"With the Lion and a Brigadier's commission as a punishment," the Regent answered.

"He wanted to go back, and it was I that kept him."

"It's a misfortune—more than a misfortune; it's almost a calamity—my dear Elise, if ever again your Colonel get so proper an excuse to kill that devil, pray don't intervene."

"I'm sorry—very sorry, I'm almost criminally stupid."

"Nonsense, dear," said the Princess; "there will be other chances—meanwhile, what happened?... Bit him! Oh, delightful, delightful!"

The other gave a shiver of repugnance.

"Disgusting, I should call it, now—I did it in the frenzy to be free. I shall never forget the horrible thing."

"Nor will he—you've marked him for life—the pity is it wasn't his face.—Go on; what happened then?"...

"The nasty brute," said Dehra, when she had heard the last detail—"and save for the punishment you yourself administered, he, for the time, must go scatheless; you cannot permit such a story to go through the Court and the Clubs; and you may be quite sure he won't tell it." She struck her hands together vehemently. "Lotzen! oh Lotzen!—Some day, Elise, your lover or mine is going to be granted the blessed privilege of putting a sword through his vile heart." She sprang up. "Come, dear, you need diversion—we will ride; and if I can get the Archduke, we'll take your Colonel, too." She went to the telephone.... "Is that you, Armand?"—when the recall bell rang.... "This is Dehra—Elise and I are off for a ride; if you can go with us, I'll have Moore go, too.... Bother your important appointment; break it.... You can't?... We can be back by four o'clock.... Have matters to see to; will they occupy all the afternoon?... They will?... And you need Moore, also?—all right, take him—what is your appointment?... Can't tell me over telephone?... Tell me tonight—well, I suppose I can wait—come for dinner.... Yes, stupid.... Good-bye, dear."

She hung up the receiver. "You heard, Elise; neither of them can go. I should hate to be a man and always busy. Come, we will go ourselves, and make an afternoon of it—and stop at the Twisted Pines for tea."

XIV
AN ENTICING RENDEZVOUS

The failure of Colonel Moore to keep promptly his appointment with Mlle. d'Essoldé to meet her that morning in the japonica walk was due to a letter that had come to him in the early post, and which had sent him, without a moment's delay, straight to Dornlitz and Headquarters; nor did he even stop to telephone the Archduke, but left it for one of the young officers in the outer office to do.

The Military Governor received him at once, and with a look of questioning concern.

"Anything wrong at the Palace?" he asked.

"Nothing, Your Highness," said Moore, with his graceful salute—so unlike Bernheim's stiff motion—"nothing; I brought this letter; it is for you, though sent to me."

The Archduke took it, without comment—he knew it must be of peculiar importance to bring Moore in person at that hour. When he had read it, he looked carefully at the envelope, and turning on his desk lamp, he spread the letter under it and examined it very slowly and critically; finally he re-read it aloud:—

> "'If His Royal Highness the Archduke Armand wish to know the whereabouts of a certain Book, let him be at the Inn of the Twisted Pines at four o'clock this afternoon. No harm is intended; and as a proof he is privileged to bring as large an escort as he desires. If he accept, let him stand in a window of his private office, overlooking the Avenue, for five minutes at exactly noon to-day. This is his only chance; there will be no second letter.
>
> "'One Who Knows.'"

"Well," said he, "the writer at least knows how to put up a very enticing bait—'privileged to bring as large an escort as he desires—at four o'clock this afternoon—at the Inn of the Twisted Pines'—surely, there is nothing in them to suggest danger, daggers or death.... I think we shall accept, Colonel; what's your notion about it?"

"If it is a plant," he said, "it's a very clever one—and hence spells Lotzen; but, for my part, I'll be charmed to go with you, whatever it is."

The Archduke smiled. "Of course you will, you peaceful citizen, and be sadly disappointed if there isn't a head for you to hit. It's just as well I gave you to the Regent, you would be leading me into all sorts of danger."

"And Your Highness has established such a splendid reputation for avoiding danger," Moore laughed.

"How so?"

"Did it never occur to you, sir, that the man who would deliberately force a sword fight with the Duke of Lotzen, has won a name for reckless courage that he can never live down?"

"But I disarmed him, thanks to your defense to his *coup*."

"Small good would my defense have been to one who hadn't the nerve and skill to use it; to fail means death, as you, of course, appreciated."

The Archduke nodded. "But the public knew nothing of all that."

"Just so, sir—all they know is that you, in sheer deviltry, took your chances against one of the two best swordsmen in Valeria; that you won, demonstrated your skill, but it didn't disprove the recklessness."

"I did not intend it that way, Moore; I assure you I had no idea of bringing on a fight that night at the Vierle Masque, when I went over to him and the Spencer woman."

A broad grin overspread the Irishman's handsome face.

"You couldn't make a single officer believe it," he said; "and seriously, sir. I wouldn't try. It is just such a thing as your great ancestor would have done, and it has caught the youngsters as nothing else ever could; they swear by you—only last night, I heard a dozen of them toast you uproariously as the next king."

"Which brings us back to the Book and this letter," Armand remarked; "shall we take an escort?"

"I'm a rather incompetent adviser, you think; but the very provision that you need not go alone, may be a trap to lull suspicion and bring you there with only an Aide or an orderly. If the letter is honest, it will be no harm to go well attended; if it isn't honest, you will lose nothing, and the escort may be very useful."

"You are becoming a very Fabius in discretion," the Archduke smiled; "and we will take the escort." He considered a moment. "Or, rather, we will have it on hand for need. I'll see to it that a troop of Lancers shall be passing the Inn a little before four o'clock, and halt there, while their captain discusses the weather with the landlord. And we will ride up with a great show of confidence or contempt, whichever way the One Who Knows may view it."

"Shall I tell Her Highness of the letter, and your purpose?" Moore asked.

"Not on your life, man! She would send a Brigade with us, even if she didn't forbid our going. I'll get you leave for the afternoon—and not a word to Bernheim, either; he would have nervous prostration, and load me down with a suit of plate-mail and a battle-axe. You and I will just have this little adventure on the side." He got up. "I tell you what it is, Moore, the pair of us could make a brisk fight of it if we had to—hey, man?"

The Irishman laughed joyously.

"And may we have to, sir!" he cried; "may we have to!"—and made as though he were sending home a finishing thrust.

The Archduke shook his head. "There can't be any doubt of it; you would have a most dangerous influence over me; it is well you're with the Regent. But for this afternoon, I suggest that you select your favorite sword, and see that it doesn't drag in the scabbard—and half-after-two at the Titian gate."

Moore paused at the door.

"Of course," said he, "Your Highness will wear the steel vest."

"I'll wear it," was the answer; and the Colonel went out, wondering at the ready acquiescence, where he had anticipated a curt refusal. Before he had crossed the ante-room, the Archduke called him.

"I saw you were surprised," said he. "I had a little adventure the other night that you don't know about. Sit down a minute, and I'll tell you of Bernheim's and my visit to the De Saure house at two in the morning."...

"I always said Bernheim was the man for a close pinch," Moore remarked, at the end, "but he is even better than I imagined. The chest is simply delicious." He paused, in sudden thought. "And, now, I reckon I understand why Count Bigler has his ear done up in surgeon's plaster. I noticed it at the Club yesterday, and heard him explain it as a 'sore.' To-morrow, I'll ask him if he caught the 'sore' in the De Saure house."

"And don't tell Bernheim," said Armand; "if he knows he had such a good chance at Bigler, and then missed him, it will make him miserable for days."

"Days! It will sour him for life. Next to the Duke of Lotzen, the Colonel hates Bigler most."

When Moore had gone, the Archduke took up the letter and envelope and again examined them; looked for a water mark—there was none; went over the writing—man's or woman's he could not decide; postmarked at the main office in Dornlitz at ten P.M. of yesterday; not a scintilla any place to indicate the origin. Well, it did not matter; he would accept the offer; and there was an end of it, now—the solution could come this afternoon at four. So he put up the letter, and pushed the button for his secretary, quite forgetting to telephone the Princess as to borrowing her Adjutant. Then, after a while, she, herself, called him; and as they finished their talk, the bell sounded the first stroke of noon.

He arose, and hooking the frogs of his dark green jacket, the gold braid of his marshal's insignia heavy on the sleeve, he went over to the large window, and raising the sash stood in full view of the avenue.

It was the hour when it was busiest; on the sidewalks a pushing, hurrying, good-natured crowd, at their mid-day recreation; in the road-way, a tangled mass of vehicles—not of the society folk, they came three hours later, but the wagons, and drays and vans of trade and traffic. He recognized an occasional face in the throng, usually some officer hurrying to Headquarters for the reception he always held for half an hour at noon. To-day it would have to start five minutes late.

Presently some one caught sight of him, and saluted with raised hat; others looked up, and did the same; and in a moment the crowd was passing in review, the men uncovering, the women greeting him with smiles. He answered with bows and handwaves; and if a bit of satisfied pride stirred his heart and warmed his face, small wonder. He was still new in his royalty; and even if he were not, at this critical period, such demonstration of esteem by the general populace would have been very gratifying and particularly welcome. And he stayed a trifle longer than the required time; then, with a last bow and a wave of especial graciousness, he turned away, and rang for the doors to be opened.

It was the Archduke's rule that entire informality should be observed at these affairs, and he emphasized it by sauntering around, speaking to everyone, and not obliging them to go up to him, for a stiff bow and a word. He laughed with this group, joked with another, argued with a third, until not a man but had come under his eye, at least for an instant, and he under theirs. He had begun the receptions soon after he became Governor of Dornlitz, more particularly for the purpose of getting acquainted with the officers on duty under him; but it was not limited to them—any one was welcome—and the result had been rather more satisfactory than even he had hoped for. There was not an official in his district to whom he had not given a hearty handshake and a pleasant word; and as he happened to have a truly royal knack of remembering faces, and the names that went with them, many a young lieutenant—and indeed, not a few higher in rank—had gone away with a flattered heart and an ardent enthusiasm, openly proclaimed, for the Marshal-Prince who would condescend to remember an unimportant subordinate, and seem glad to see him again, and to tell him so. And the contrast it offered to the Duke of Lotzen's ungracious and domineering ways was little to the latter's advantage; and the fruit of it had been ripening fast, within these last few weeks.

So, to-day, the room was crowded, and the welcome the Archduke received was such as might have made even Lotzen pause and think, had he seen it. And this thought occurred to Armand; and he ran his eyes over the many faces, wondering which of them belonged, to-day, to the Duke's spy; for that there usually was one present he had no doubt.

And presently he found him; and, catching his eye, motioned for him to approach.

"I am glad to see you, Monsieur le Comte," he said, relieving himself from offering his hand by readjusting his sword. "When was it I saw you last?"

Count Bigler's lips twitched with suppressed amusement.

"Here, Your Highness?" he answered, "I am ashamed to confess I haven't been here for many weeks."

"Yet, surely, Count, I've seen you somewhere since then, and very recently, too—where was it?"

Bigler feigned to think.—"One sees Your Highness so many times, it is difficult to remember the last … on the Field of Mars, last Monday, wasn't it?"

The Archduke shook his head. "No," he said, "no; it was in the evening—I recall that very distinctly." Then he looked with deliberate inference at the bandaged ear—"oh, I have it: it was at the De Saure's; you were there when I came, and you left first and—rather hurriedly. It all comes back to me now. Surely, Count, you can't have forgot such a pleasant evening!"

Bigler assumed a look of guileless innocence.

"It is not permitted to contradict Your Highness," he answered, "but I may, I think, at least venture the truism:—what one has not remembered, one cannot forget."

"Or restated, my dear Count, to be quite in point:—what is inconvenient to remember, is best denied."

"Just as Your Highness will have it," Bigler grinned, and impudently fingered his ear.

"And confidentially, Count," said Armand smilingly, "while we are dealing in truisms, I give you these two:—'every man's patience has its limit,' and, 'who plays with fire gets burnt'—fatally."

Bigler's grin broadened.

"Is Your Highness the man with the patience or the man with the fire?" he asked.

"Study it out, sir," said the Archduke, as he passed on; "and let your master help you; the answer may concern you both."

The last thing before leaving his office, that afternoon, he wrote a note to the American Ambassador, enclosing the anonymous letter, and telling him his intention in reference to it; and adding that if Courtney had not heard from him by morning he should do whatever he thought best. This he dispatched by an orderly; and then, choosing a long, light sword, he rang for his horse.

Just outside his door, he met General Durand and stopped for a word with him; as they separated he saw Ferdinand of Lotzen coming down the corridor.

Between them it had long been a salute given and acknowledged, but now the Duke halted, fingers at visor.

"May I have a word with Your Highness?" he said.

Armand's hand dropped slowly, and he only half paused in his walk.

"I'm in a particular hurry, cousin," he replied, "won't to-morrow do as well?"

Lotzen's eye-brows went up.

"Isn't to-morrow rather uncertain for—both of us?" he asked.

"Yes," said the Archduke instantly, "yes, it is; and hence what need of talk between us, at least so late in the day. Wait until we have a to-morrow."

"What I wish to say has nothing to do with futures, cousin, only with the past, with the De Saure house—oh! that surprises you, does it?"

"Not half as much as the amazing mess you made of it," said Armand.

"That, my dear cousin, is just what I came to explain," said Lotzen quickly. "I had nothing whatever to do with the silly affair; it was a clever idea, but sadly bungled; I heard of it only the next day, and I want to assure you it was not my work—

though, as I say, it was a clever idea—too clever, indeed, to be wasted so fruitlessly."

The Archduke regarded him in speculative silence;—just what manner of man was this; and what could be his ulterior purpose in such an astonishing avowal!

"Will you tell me, cousin," he asked, "why you should trouble to disclaim participation in an outrage, whose only offense, in your eyes, was its failure?"

Again Lotzen's eye-brows went up. "I thought you would understand that it is in justice to myself; I would not have you think me guilty of so stupid a piece of work."

"Doubtless, then, it will gratify you, monsieur, that I never doubted your complicity, however much I may have marvelled at the unskilled execution—you would have arranged it rather differently. Indeed, I was sorry that you, yourself, were not in command. I left a message, both upstairs and down, that I thought you might understand."

Lotzen smiled, rather warmly for him.

"I understood," he said; "your writing was exceedingly legible."

"And I sent you another message, a little while ago, by the man with the wounded ear," said the Archduke, his eyes upon the other's bandaged hand. "I suppose you got it?"

The Duke laughed and held up his hand, the back and palm covered with plaster.

"This wasn't made by a bullet, cousin;" he replied; "I got it this morning from a new pet I was trying to train.—No, I didn't get your last message."

"Better get it to-day, cousin," said the Archduke, as he turned away; "*to-morrow* is rather uncertain."

XV
FOUR O'CLOCK AT THE INN

Ten miles out, on the Titian Road, is the Inn of the Twisted Pines. Something more than two centuries of storms and sunshine have left its logs and plaster wrinkled and weather-beaten, yet the house stands as stanch and strong as the day the last pin was driven, and the painted sign and the bunch of furze hung above the entrance.

The old soldier who built it had lived long enough to marry a young wife, and leave it to her and a sturdy boy; and, thereafter, there was always a son to take the father's place; and with the heirship seemed to go the inherited obligation to maintain the house exactly as received. No modernity showed itself within or without; the cooking alone varied, as it reflected the skill or whim of the particular mistress; and it chanced that the present one was of unusual ability in that particular; and the knowledge of it coming to the Capital, had brought not a little trade of riding parties and the officers of the garrison.

And so Captain Hertz, of the Third Lancers, had not done quite the usual growl, when he got the order to march at once with his troop, selecting such a route as would bring him to the Inn a few minutes before four o'clock, taking care to approach it from the West; and to halt there and await further instructions.

He had confided to his subaltern that it was a crazy sort of proceeding to be manœuvring against old Scartman's Inn; but if it had to be done, it was at least considerate to choose as the objective point, a place where they could have a good meal to eat, and the keeper's pretty daughters to philander.

And between thinking of the victuals and the damsels, the Captain so hurried the march that they reached the Inn unnecessarily early; yet they had no reason to regret it, for the tap-room was cool and pleasant, the food to their taste, and the girls' cheeks prettier and softer than ever—though it would seem that, lately, the last were becoming much more difficult to taste.

"What's got into the hussies?" Hertz demanded, rubbing his face, as the Lieutenant and he went out into the courtyard; "They used to be mild enough."

"You've been falling off in looks the last year, my dear fellow," Purkitz laughed—"can't say I much blame the girl—I've no finger marks on my cheek, you see!"

"Huh!" grunted Hertz, "solid brass; wouldn't show the kick of a mule.—What in Heaven's name are we sent here for any way!—'await further orders'—that may mean a week."

"And why not," the Lieutenant laughed; "the victuals are delicious, and the girls——"

"Oh, go to the devil!"

"And even father, himself, will do for company in a pinch."

The Captain laughed, too. "Not if I can get away—did you ever see such a countenance? It positively makes me ill."

"Poor old Scartman," said Purkitz; "he's a good man, but there is no denying that 'the Lord made him as ugly as He could and then hit him in the face.'"

From the eastward, came the sound of a galloping horse.

"Our orders, I hope," Hertz exclaimed. He glanced at his watch. "A quarter of four—I wonder what silly business we're to be sent on, now."

The hoof-beats drew swiftly nearer, but from where the two officers were standing, the high wall of the courtyard obscured the road, and they sauntered slowly across toward the gateway. As they reached it, a big black horse swept around the corner and was upon them before the rider could draw rein.

Hertz gave a cry of warning and sprang aside, tripped on his spur, and sprawled in the deep dust; while Purkitz's wild jump landed him with both feet on his superior's back, whence he slid off and brought up on Hertz's head, thereby materially augmenting the fine flow of super-heated language that was bubbling from the Captain's dirt-filled mouth—nor did the loud guffaw and the shrieks of feminine laughter, that came from the house, serve to reduce either the temperature or the volume.

Meanwhile, the cause of it all—a slender, sinuous woman, black gowned and black veiled—sat the big horse motionless and silent, waiting for the human tangle to unloose itself.

Coated with dust—his uniform unrecognizable, his face smeared and dirty—Hertz scrambled up.

"What in hell do you——a woman!" he ended, and stood staring.

"Yes, my man, a woman," said she, "and one very sorry for your fall—you are the landlord, I presume."

Lieutenant Purkitz gave a shout, and leaned against the gate.

"Landlord!" he gasped, "landlord!—that face—oh, that face!" and went off into a fit of suppressed mirth.

The woman looked at him and then at Hertz, and though the thick veil hid her features completely, there was no doubt of her irritation.

The Captain bowed. "Madame will pardon the ill manners of my clownish servant," he said, indicating Purkitz; "I am Captain Hertz, of Her Highness' Third Lancers. Yonder is the landlord; permit me to call him."

She leaned down and offered him her hand.

"A thousand apologies, my dear Captain, for my reckless riding and my awkward tongue—there is small excuse for the former, I admit, but my veil may explain the latter.—You are not hurt?"

A voice so soft and sweet must have a face to match it, and Hertz went a step nearer.

"Madame can cure everything but my heart, if she but raise the veil," he said.

The voice laughed softly.

"Then, sir, I am afraid to raise it—your heart would not survive the shock. Good-bye, and thank you," and she spurred across to where old Scartman was standing near the stables.

"I am to meet some one here at four o'clock," she said; "has my party come?"

Boniface's shrewd little eyes had taken her in at a single glance.

"Gentleman, I suppose?" he asked.—"None of them?" jerking his thumb toward the two lancers.—"No? then he's not here yet."

She glided gracefully out of saddle, and hooked up her skirt.

"Put my horse in the stall nearest the door," she ordered; and herself saw it done. "Now, I want a room—the big one on the lower floor—for an hour or so."

The inn-keeper bowed.

"Certainly, madame—and the gentleman?"

She considered.... "He is one high in rank, very high—indeed, no one in Valeria is higher—tell him I'm here; and admit him instantly; but don't, do you hear me, don't tell him I'm a woman."

Old Scartman coughed and hesitated.

"But please you, madame," he ventured, "if I'm to tell him you're here, but not to tell him you're a woman, how's he to be sure you are you?"

"True, O patron of rendezvous!" she laughed. "If he ask for proof, you may tell him I'm *the one who knows*."

"Now, that's more to rule," he said, with a nod and a chuckle.

They went into the house, and he opened the door into the big room.

"This is what madame wishes?"

"Yes," said she—"and remember, no interruptions, now nor later—understand?"

He bowed with rather unusual grace, for one of his appearance and calling.

"Perfectly, madame—does madame think I look so like a fool?"

She surveyed him an instant.

"No, my good man, I don't," and closed the door; "but I wouldn't care to tell you what you do look like," she ended.

Going over to the window, she fixed the curtain so as to permit her to see in front of the house, and then, removing her veil, she drew out a tiny mirror and deftly touched to place the hair that was disarranged. As she finished, she heard horses approaching, and she saw, through the open gateway, a sudden commotion among the Lancers who were lounging at ease by the roadside, their mounts picketed under the trees. She knew that her man was coming.

A sergeant ran in and said a word to Hertz who, free now of his dust and anger, was sitting on the steps with Purkitz, hoping to get a glimpse of the face behind the veil, and staring at the windows with calm persistency.

"My God!" she heard Hertz exclaim, as both sprang up, and, frantically buttoning tunics and drawing on gloves, ran out into the road and swung to horse. There was a snap of commands, a stamping of hoofs, and the lances rose high above the wall in a line of fluttering pennons; they dipped, and the next moment the Archduke and the Regent's Adjutant drew up before the gate.

The former raised his hand, and Hertz rode forward and saluted.

"How long have you been here, Captain Hertz?" he asked.

"Since a few minutes after three, sir."

"Has any one come to the Inn in that time?"

Hertz's spine went cold, and his voice trembled—*she* was the Archduke's, and he had dared to ogle her.

"No one, Your Highness," he answered—"no one but a woman—only a few minutes ago—on horseback—alone."

"Did you happen to look at her, Captain? If you did, you might describe her."

"I cannot, Your Highness; her face was covered with a thick, black veil."

The Archduke smiled. "You're a good soldier, I see; a pretty face comes first."

"But her figure, sir—it's wonderful, black habit and black horse—and she can ride—and her voice—"

"At least, Captain, your inability to describe her isn't due to lack of observation," the Archduke remarked dryly. "You have aroused my curiosity; I must see this remarkable woman—and do you remain here. I may have need of you presently; if you hear a whistle, come to me instantly."

"Very clever, my lord," Hertz muttered; "but you can't cozen this bird; you're here to meet her, and we are not expected. If the Regent knew it—whew!" and dismounting, he nodded to the sergeant.

"This looks about as harmless as a game of ping-pong," said Armand, as they went into the courtyard; then, suddenly, an amazing idea flashed upon him; and he swung around, and motioned Hertz to him.

"What color was the woman's hair?" he asked.

"Black. Your Highness, black as her gown."

He dismissed Hertz with a look.

"Moore," he said, and without moving on, "this plot is tangling fast. Can you guess who this woman is?"

"'The one who knows,'" said the Colonel promptly.

"Yes, and more—it is Madeline Spencer."

"Impossible!"

"I hope so, God knows," the Archduke answered; "I've had enough of that devil—Scartman, is any one awaiting me?"

The old fellow had come up at a run.

"Your Highness' pardon," he cried, bowing almost into the dirt; "had I known you were coming I would have been at the gate to receive you——"

"Never mind the reception, my man, answer my question—is any one awaiting me?"

"I think so, Your Highness—"

"Don't you know—what name did she give for me?"

"'The one who knows,' sir—but I wasn't to tell you, sir, she is a woman—she was most particular as to that."

The Archduke laughed. "Well, you didn't; I knew it—where is she?"

"I will conduct your——"

"You'll do nothing of the sort," said Armand, dismounting and flinging his rein to his orderly; "where is the lady?"

Old Scartman knew enough to palaver no longer.

"The large room on the right, Your Highness," he answered promptly.

"Come along, Moore," said the Archduke, "let us have a look at her—and pray heaven it isn't Spencer."

But the landlord shook his head dubiously.

"It's queer doings, sure enough!" he muttered;—"leastwise, it's no love meeting they're up to;" and he followed them as far as the hall, to be within call if needed.

Shielded by the curtain, Madeline Spencer had watched the scene in the courtyard, laughing quietly, the while, at Hertz's confusion and at what she knew was in his mind, as to the Archduke and herself; now she flung the veil lightly around her head, and put her chair where the sun would be behind her. Moore's presence had surprised and disappointed her; but, on the whole, she preferred him to Bernheim—and particularly if one of them were to be at the interview. Though she had rather counted upon Armand coming alone, if only to show his contempt for the permission to bring an escort—that he had sent the troop of Lancers she did not credit for a moment, though it might do to twit him with it.

Cool player that she was, and skillful beyond most women, yet even her heart beat a little faster, and her hand showed the trace of a tremble, as she heard the rattle of swords and spurs in the hall-way, followed by the sharp knock upon her door. And she let the knock come a second time before she answered it. She had not seen Armand since that night in her reception room in the Hotel Metzen, when the King and he had surprised her and Lotzen together, and, after tumbling the Duke's schemes about his ears, had sent him to Lotzenia in disgrace and her across the border; and, now, the sight of him, and the sound of his voice, had stirred again the old fondness that would not down. And though, to his face, she might laugh at his anger and mock at his contempt, and feel it so then, yet afterward, in the depression that in such natures always follows periods of excitement, the recollection of it hurt her sadly, scorn it as she might, despise it as she did—destroy him as she meant to do, and would.

"*Entrez!*" she called, "*entrez!*" and with the words, the tremble passed, and she was serene and undisturbed again.

"Your Royal Highness!" she said, very low, and swept him a quick curtsy.

Instead of offering his hand to raise her, he answered with a slight bow.

"Madame desired to see me?" he asked; and crossing over obliged her to turn so that the light from the window fell upon her sideways. And, despite the heavy veil, that gave him only a black mask of crape instead of her face, he was satisfied he had surmised correctly.

Suddenly she caught the veil and flung it away.

"You know me, I see," she laughed, "so we will dispense with this covering—it is very warm."

For a little while, he looked at her in forbidding silence.

"What ill wind blew you back to Dornlitz?" he asked presently; and she almost cried out in surprise at the deliberate menace in his voice. And Moore marvelled and was glad—the old Henry was being aroused, at last.

"Ill wind?" she said—leaning carelessly against the window ledge where the sun played through her wonderful hair, and tinged the flawless face from dead-white to a faint, soft pink—"ill wind for whom, Armand?—surely not for you; why am I here?"

The Archduke gave a sarcastic laugh. "That is precisely what I should like to know."

"You doubt the letter?"

A shrug was his answer.

She leaned a bit toward him.

"If I show you the Book of Dalberg Laws, will you believe?" she asked.

"That they are the Laws, yes."

She smiled rather sadly.

"The facts will have to prove my honest motive, I see; and I came from Paris, hoping that I could render you this service, as a small requital for the injury I did you a little while ago."

The Archduke laughed in her face.

"And for how much in gold coin of the realm, from some one of my enemies?" he asked.

She put the words aside with another smile.

"I've been in Dornlitz for more than two weeks," she went on; "can you guess where?—yes, I see you can; the only place I could have been, and you not know of it."

"And you mean to say the Book is in Ferida Palace?" said Armand.

"I do."

"And you are ready to restore it to the Regent?"

"No," said she, "I'm not ready to restore it to the Regent; I'm ready to give it to you if I were able, but I'm not—it will be for you to recover it."

"How do you know it is the Book of Laws—did the Duke tell you?"

She laughed her soft, sweet laugh. "Oh, no, he didn't tell me—he has no idea that I know he has it; I saw it by accident——"

"How could you recognize the Book?" he interrupted; "only three people in the Kingdom have ever seen it."

"By intuition, mainly; and by the secrecy with which the Duke handles it—let me describe it:—a very old book; leather-covered, brass-bound and brass-hinged; the pages, of parchment—those in front illumined in colors with queer letters, and, further on, more modern writing—it *is* the Book, isn't it, Armand?"

"Or Lotzen has described it to you," he answered.

She made a gesture of discouragement.

"You are hard to convince," she said—"you will have to be shown—will you take the trouble?"

The Archduke smiled. "Now we come to the kernel," he remarked; "the rest was only the shell. Quite candidly, madame, I'm not inclined to play the spy in Ferida Palace; there are easier deaths to die, though doubtless none that would be more sure."

"You didn't used to be so timid or careful, Armand," she mocked; "there are no dangers other than those of my boudoir—and if you fear them you may send a substitute—even one of your friend Courtney's secret agents.—For the last few nights the Duke has been going over this Book page by page; his apartments are across a small court from mine, and his private cabinet is directly in view from my boudoir. Send some one there this evening at eleven, and with my field glass he can see everything the Duke does, and every article on his desk. Surely, that should be enough to satisfy the most suspicious."

"Rather too much," said he; "it brings us back to the question of motive:—why should you, who have had so much of my dear cousin's money, and have enjoyed his kind and courteous hospitality for so long, suddenly turn against him, and betray him?—for believe me, madame, I take no stock in your pretty story of requiting injury, and coming all the way from Paris to help me find the Book."

"But, my dear Archduke, what matters my motive, if you recover the Book—besides, now you can send the police this instant and search the Palace and seize the Book, if it's there, and they can find it—doesn't that in itself attest my honesty?"

"Not in the least. You know very well that I would not venture to take such drastic action against the Duke unless I were sure, not only that he had the Book, but that it would be found—hence it's safe to tell this story. And as your motive—it all comes back to that—can't be to assist me, it must be to assist the Duke; and so—" he shrugged his shoulders.

It had never occurred to her that he would be so difficult to convince; she had thought that her bait, and particularly the privilege to send any one to verify it, and her description of the Book, would capture him instantly. But she had failed to appreciate how thoroughly Armand despised her, and how deeply he mistrusted her, and, more than all, how intensely repugnant it would be to accept a service from her, or to have any dealings with her except *à outrance*.

She bent forward and looked him in the eyes.

"Why might it not be to assist myself?" she asked—"to revenge myself, if you please, Armand."

"Yes?" he said questioningly.

"Ferdinand of Lotzen and I have come to the parting place," she said with quick bitterness—"the brute struck me yesterday; no man ever did so twice—and none ever once, that I didn't punish promptly. I did come from Paris thinking I might aid you, for some how I was sure he had that book; he was glad enough to have me; and then he was so kind and liberal I—you won't believe it I know, Armand, but it's true—I couldn't bring myself to betray him; nor should I, but for yesterday. Now I want revenge; and I can get it quickest and best through you. There, you have my true motive; and even you should not doubt it, for, God knows, a woman hates to confess that a man has struck her."

She turned away and looked through the window, her fingers playing nervously on the sill; while the Archduke, doubtful, yet half convinced, glanced at Moore uncertainly.

Instantly the Colonel motioned to accept, and that he would go to the Ferida; and Armand smiled, and indicated that both would go—if any went; then he crossed to the great fireplace and stood before it, staring thoughtfully into the cinders. Suddenly he straightened his shoulders, and faced around—and Moore knew that the decision was made, and finally.

"Mrs. Spencer," he said, "we will lay aside the questions of motive and personality: You, an individual, come to me, the Governor of Dornlitz, and offer information which, if true, will lead to the recovery of an article of great value, that belongs to the Government and has mysteriously disappeared. It is my duty, as Governor, to investigate the story, and I will do it, either in person or by subordinate. If the story be true, and the article in question be recovered by your aid, then you will be entitled to the proper thanks of the Government and a suitable recompense.—So much for that. But I also wish to assure you that Armand Dalberg, himself, declines your offer and your aid; and should your information result to his personal profit and advancement, it will be a life-long regret."

She heard him without turning—and Moore thought he detected the faintest shiver at the end; and, in truth, the words and tone were enough to chill even a colder heart than hers.

But when she faced him, it was with one of the soft and caressing smiles she could use with such fatal fascination, and which made Moore catch his breath and stare, though it touched the Archduke not at all.

"I thank His Royal Highness, the Governor of Dornlitz," she said, dropping him another curtsy, "for his consideration and trust, and the promised reward; the latter I decline.... As for Armand Dalberg, I can assure him he will owe me no obligation: it will give me a life-long pleasure to be the means of causing him a life-long regret."

The Archduke smiled indifferently.

"To that extent, then, I shall feel less obligated," he replied. "Meanwhile, let us be seated, and receive madame's instruction for to-night. I shall want the Book seen by more than one person—how many can you arrange to admit?"

"How many do you wish?"

"Three, possibly four."

"You may bring half a dozen if you like," she said, "though the fewer, the less chance of failure."

"Very good—how is it to be managed?"

She drew off her gauntlets, and from one of them took a sheet of note paper—stamped with the Duke's arms—on which she had sketched roughly so much of the Ferida and its grounds as entered into her plan. Spreading it out, she explained how they were to gain entrance to her apartments; and that there might be no mistake, she went over it again, cautioning them that it must be followed with the most careful precision. At the end, she gave the map to Moore.

"Of course, I shall not expect Your Highness to-night," she said; "but I hope you will send Colonel Moore; it will be well to have some one who can, if necessary, use both head and sword—though I don't anticipate the remotest difficulty in your——"

A volley of cheers from without drowned her voice. It could only be the soldiers, and yet it was such an extraordinary thing, and with the Field-Marshal, himself, within sound, that the two men looked at each other in puzzled surprise; and when the noise not only continued but actually grew louder, the Archduke frowned and went to the window.

And what he saw made him frown still more, and he swore softly to himself, as a man does, sometimes, when unpleasantly surprised and obliged to think quickly, and to act on the thinking, with a heavy penalty awaiting a mistake.

Crossing the courtyard, with Hertz and Purkitz walking on either side, were the Regent of Valeria and Mlle. d'Essoldé. And even as Armand stood there, they were out of saddle and Dehra was running lightly up the steps.

"Send Scartman to us in the big room, if you please, Captain," she called—then stopped, her eyes fixed on two horses standing a little way off—a Field-Marshal's insignia on the saddle cloth of one and a Colonel's of her Household on the other. So! so! and they were too busy with appointments at four to ride with them. She caught Mlle. d'Essoldé by the arm.

"Look, Elise!" she said, "look at those saddle cloths yonder."

The Archduke followed her motion, and understood. It was a most infernally unfortunate contretemps, but it would have to be met, and at once.

"The Regent is on the porch," he said. "I do not care for her to know of this meeting nor its purport, until after to-night. Madame, will you please be good enough to conceal yourself; the door is the only exit, and it is impossible now—I will try to prevent Her Highness entering here, but I may fail; I likely shall. Come, Moore," and he hurried out.

But Madeline Spencer only laughed, and, winding the veil into place, went and stood by the chimney—here was a very god-given opportunity, and assuredly she had no notion to let it pass unused.

And the landlord, slumbering in the hall, had been tardily aroused by the cheering, and coming forth, still half asleep, he met the Princess just at the entrance.

"Scartman," she said sharply, "where are His Highness and Colonel Moore?"

The landlord awoke with a suddenness that was painful, and which left him staring at her in silly-eyed speechlessness.

"What ails you, man?" she demanded—"tell the Archduke I'm here—we shall be in the large room."

This brought back a bit of his senses, and he bowed to the ground, hoping to get back more of them before he need come up.

"I will find His Royal Highness at once," he said; "I did not know he was here—I've been asleep—but if Your Majesty—Your Regency—Your Highness, I mean, will permit—the large room is occupied, I will——"

At that moment, Armand and Moore came out.

"So it would seem," the Princess remarked dryly.

"Don't blame the poor fellow, Dehra," the Archduke laughed; "he did the best he could, doubtless, and at my order. We are here on the business I spoke of this morning—it's finished now, and we will ride back with you, if we may."

Dehra held out her hand, and gave him the smile she knew he loved.

"Of course you may," she said, "and gladly; but first I want a cup of tea—Scartman, the kettle instantly!"—and before Armand could detain her, she was past him and into the room.

As she crossed the threshold, she caught the faint perfume that a woman always carries, and which often-times is so individualized, as to betray her identity instantly. It was a peculiar odor—the blended fragrance of many flowers—and she recognized that she had known it before;—but what was it doing in this room, now!—it was too fresh to be many minutes old.

"Armand," she said, "what woman has been here?" glancing laughingly around.—"And is here still!" and pointed with her crop to the veiled figure in the shadow near the chimney.

The Archduke ground back an oath, and stepping forward bowed to Madeline Spencer.

"Madame," said he, "will you do the Governor of Dornlitz the favor to excuse him, and to accept his thanks for your service? Colonel Moore, madame's horse."

"*Je vous remercie, Monsieur le Prince,*" she murmured, taking Moore's arm, and moving with sinuous grace toward the door. But as she passed the Princess Regent, who had stepped aside to give her way, the veil slipped from her face, and the two women looked into each other's eyes—the one with a smile of mocking impertinence, the other with a calmly ignoring stare, and showing, by not so much as the quiver of a muscle, her anger and surprise.

And when they had gone, the Princess turned her gaze upon the Archduke, the blue eyes ominous in their steadiness; and as he would have spoken, she repelled him with an imperious gesture, and gave him her back.

"Come, Elise!" she said, and left the room.

In the courtyard, Colonel Moore had just swung Mrs. Spencer to saddle, and was fixing her skirt. Dehra paused in the entry until the black horse had passed the gate; then she went leisurely down the steps, waved Moore to Mlle. d'Essoldé, and let the groom put her up.

Acknowledging Moore's farewell salute, with her crop, but no smile, and with never a glance toward the window, behind whose curtain she must have known the Archduke would surely be, she rode away—the Lancers again cheering her devotedly as she passed.

XVI
A TOO CONVINCING ARGUMENT

Colonel Moore went slowly up the steps and into the room, through the half open door of which he saw the Archduke standing, with chin on breast and back to the fireplace. He looked up, as the Adjutant paused at the threshold, and nodded for him to come in.

"Ordinarily it would be proper now for us to have a good, stiff drink, may be several of them," he remarked, "but the only kind that fits this situation, so far as I'm concerned, is straight whisky, and I don't believe this cursed place can supply it."

"Quite right; it can't," said Moore; "I tried the other day—won't anything else do?"

"No—nothing else; and it's just as well I can't get the whisky; I may need a clear head to night."

"You are not going, sir!"

Armand nodded. "Going? of course I'm going—why not? and I only hope I'll get a chance at my sweet cousin. We promised only to look—to raise no disturbance—and on Spencer's account it is right enough that we should do nothing to betray her; but if Lotzen get in the way, Colonel, we are not obligated to avoid him."

"Why should Your Highness walk deliberately into the tiger's lair—when another can go quite as well, and without danger?" Moore protested.

The Archduke took a cigarette and tossed the case across to the Adjutant.

"Because I'm really hunting the tiger," he laughed; "and I like excitement in good company—though I fear it will be a very tame affair."

The other shook his head dubiously. "It's not right, sir, for you to expose yourself so unnecessarily—let me go in command."

"Nonsense, Ralph, you're getting in Bernheim's class; quit it. What I wish you would tell me is whether Spencer dropped her veil intentionally or by accident."

"It seemed so accidental it must have been intentional," said Moore.

"If I were sure of it, that would cancel a trifle more of my obligation."

"Her Highness will know—" the Colonel began, and stopped abashed at his blunder.

"And so will Mademoiselle d'Essoldé," said Armand. "I may have to depend on you for information."

"Then Your Highness will likely have to get it, yourself," Moore laughed. "We're not speaking either, it seems; she let me put her up, because the Regent sent me to her, but—I'm chilly yet. Did you ever notice, sir, how disconcerting it is to think you're talking to a woman, and then find it's a mistake and that really you're talking only to yourself?"

The Archduke smiled. "Yes," said he, "I've noticed it; and we may have a rather frigid atmosphere for a few moments this evening until I can explain—we are to dine with Her Highness and Mademoiselle."

"If you don't mind, sir, I'll violate propriety and let you arrive first; your explanation will do for both—and besides, I fancy such things are best done *à deux*."

"You fancy!—you innocent-Irishman-afraid-of-a-woman!" He drew on his gloves. "Come along—put on a brave front and I'll take you home. Five minutes talk will set matters right."

"If you're not talking to yourself," Moore observed.

The landlord was awaiting them in distress and trepidation almost pitiful. Such ill luck had not befallen the Inn in all its years of busy life. The Regent and the Governor! It was the end of his favor—the end of the Twisted Pines. To-morrow—may be to-day—would come the police, and the nails would go into the doors, and boards across the windows, and the big gates, that had always swung open at daybreak, would swing no more, and in disgrace and shame he and his would be turned out, with the curt admonition to seek a harbor in another land.

He almost dropped as the Archduke's hand fell on his shoulder.

"Scartman," said he kindly, yet incisively, "doubtless your mind is much too occupied to remember everything that happens here—but let me suggest that it would be well even to make a special effort to forget what has occurred this afternoon. I have known such forgetfulness to merit special reward."

The landlord looked up in bewildered joy.

"But Her Highness, sir—she will not——"

"Tush, man," Armand interrupted, "I'll answer for the Regent."

The old man began to cry, and through his tears he groped for the Archduke's hand and kissed the gauntlet fervently.

"God bless Your Highness!" he said—and was still repeating it when the latter passed the gate.

The Archduke rode slowly along the line of Lancers, scrutinizing every man as he went; then motioned the officers to him.

"Messieurs," he said, "my compliments on your troop.—Captain Hertz, you may return to barracks."

Hertz saluted, faced his men and raised his sword. And Armand, galloping down the road, turned in saddle and with his cap answered the wild cheer they sent after him.

"Purkitz," said the Captain, before giving the order to break into column, "now is your opportunity to prove you can actually know something and not tell it."

"And yours also, O wiser than serpents," the Lieutenant laughed, "to prove you actually do know something that you tell."

But the Archduke had not deemed it necessary to caution either of them; here, even the dullest witted soldier in the Army would have the sense to hold his tongue.

Where the road for the Summer Palace took off at the old forge, the Colonel left him, and Armand went on to the Capital. He rode these last few miles at a slow jog, and thoughtfully. It was well enough to treat the matter lightly to Moore, but, none the less, it troubled him. Dehra's conduct had been so extraordinary for her—who had refused to credit, for an instant, Madeline Spencer's claim to be his wife, though actually supported by a marriage certificate—that he was puzzled and all sorts of doubts and fears harassed him. It suggested some untoward influence; what he could not imagine, nor how, nor whence it had come; but, even then, everything would be very easy to explain, if she would give him the opportunity, and not, in the natural perversity of a woman, refuse to see him, and so make herself miserable, altogether needlessly. He had yet to learn that sometimes it is well to let a woman inadvertently discipline herself; it is more effective than if the man does it; and usually saves him a vast amount of recrimination. Then, too, he did not want Dehra to know of this intended night visit to the Ferida, where the natural prospect was duplicity and murder, and only Madeline Spencer's worthless word to guarantee its safety. As it was now, if he explained at all, it would have to be down to the minutest detail, and he could foresee what the Regent would have to say about any such adventure on his part. Yet if the Ferida party went he must lead it—and the Ferida party was going.

So when he reached the Epsau, he was almost hoping to find a message from the Princess that he was not expected for dinner. But it was not there, nor had it come when he started for the Palace, though he waited until the very last moment.

He found Moore pacing the corridor, on watch for him, but with nothing to clear up the situation.

"And I've spent most of the time since I got back," he ended, "in prancing up and down here, trying to get a glimpse of Mademoiselle, or some one, who might give me an inkling of the temperature inside—all on your account, sir, of course; I'm getting used to this freezing and thawing process."

"Very good, Colonel, then we will go right in, and you can be thawing while I am explaining—come along, man, come along," and taking him by the arm they went on down the corridor, and entered the Princess' small reception room next her boudoir.

"Announce us," said the Archduke to the footman, "but say to Her Highness that I would like a few minutes private speech with her—and to Mademoiselle d'Essoldé say that Colonel Moore has a message from me and awaits her here.... I leave that message to your Irish wit," he remarked, when the servant had gone.

But the man was very slow in returning, and presently Moore laughed.

"It's getting chilly," he observed—"notice it?"

The boudoir room swung open and Mlle. d'Essoldé came in.

"Can't say I do," said the Archduke aside, as he acknowledged her curtsy; "looks very charming to me."

She gave the Archduke a smile, Moore a look of indifferent greeting, and then Armand another smile.

"My mistress receives Your Highness," she said, holding back the door; and quite ignoring Moore's effort, as he sprang forward to relieve her.

Under the chandelier, where sixty candles fluttered their mellow light about her, the Regent of Valeria was standing; but her eyes were on the red rose she was slowly pulling apart, nor did she lift them when Armand entered. Having come in a little way, slowly and with purposeful deliberation, he stopped, and leaning on his sword tarried for her to speak; and willing that she should not, for a while, that so, he might have this picture long enough to see it ever after—this white-robed, fair-headed daughter of the Dalbergs, waiting to pass judgment on her betrothed.

The last petal fell; she plucked another rose—a white one—from her corsage, and looked up.

"You may speak, sir," she said, in voice an impersonal monotone.

The Archduke bowed.

"I have nothing to say," he replied.

She raised her eye-brows in polite surprise.

"I thought you had requested ten minutes private speech with me."

"I did," said Armand, "but I withdraw the request; explanations are vain, when one has been already judged, and judged unheard."

"One who is taken red-handed can have no explanation that explains," said she.

Then, of a sudden, out flashed the adorable smile, and she laughed, and flung him the white rose.

"There, dear," she said, "there, is your pardon—now, come," and she held out both hands; "come and forgive me for this afternoon."

And when he had forgiven her, she put him in a chair and perched herself on the arm beside him.

"Tell me, Armand," she said, "are we never to be free of that awful woman?—where did she come from?—how did she happen to be at the Inn?"

"And how did I happen to be with her there, you want to know," he laughed.

She nodded. "That more than all—yet I didn't ask it."

He took out the anonymous letter, which he had remembered to get from Courtney; and when she had read it, he tore it into bits.

"Will you have the explanation that explains now or during dinner?" he asked.

She sprang up.

"I forgot I was hungry! Come we will get Elise and Moore—that girl is a rare coquette; she makes my poor Adjutant's life very miserable."

"It looks like it!" said Armand opening the door just as Moore caught Mlle. d'Essoldé and kissed her, despite her struggles.

"I warned you, my lady," he was saying, "you would tempt me too far some day … will you forgive me now, or shall I do it all over again?"

The Princess laughed. Moore's arms dropped and he sprang back, while Mlle. d'Essoldé, flaming with embarrassment and anger, buried her face in her hands.

"Forgive him until after dinner, Elise," said Dehra; "you can retract then, and resume the situation, if you wish."

"O wise and beneficent ruler!" said Moore, bowing to the ground, "I agree to the compromise."

Mlle. d'Essoldé looked at him in contemptuous scorn—though, in truth, she was more inclined to laugh; she never could be angry with her Irishman, for long.

"You savage," she said, "you brutal savage; don't ever speak to me again."

He stepped forward and offered his arm, with all the suavity he knew so well.

"Never again after dinner, mademoiselle," he said sadly; "meanwhile, the pleasure is mine."

And to his surprise she took his arm; and when the others' backs were turned, she looked up and smiled, the impudently provoking smile he had suffered under so long, and had at last punished.

"My compliments, Monsieur Ralph, on your adroit proficiency,"—and the tone and manner were as provoking as the smile—"it is quite unnecessary to refer to what it proves."

"As much so, as to refer to what enables one to recognize proficiency," he agreed.

"And if all the men I know are like you, sir—"

He bent down.

"Now *that* is an inference I'm curious to hear."

"Do you want them to be like you?" she asked, eyes half closed and glances sidelong—"because, if you do, it would be rather easy to oblige you—and may be not unpleasant—and I can begin with His Highness of Lotzen—truly it's a pity, now, I ruined my frock so needlessly this morning, in the japonica walk;" and giving him no time for reply, she dropped his arm and glided quickly into the chair the bewigged and powdered footman was holding for her.

No mention of the Twisted Pines was made until the coffee was being served; then the Princess motioned for the liqueur also to be put on the table, and dismissed the servants.

Drawing out her case, and lighting a Nestor, she smiled at the Archduke, and at his nod passed the cigarette across;—and when Colonel Moore looked inquiringly at Mlle. d'Essoldé, she shrugged her pretty shoulders and gave him hers.

"You know what it implies, Elise," Dehra remarked.—"No?—then ask Colonel Moore to tell you sometime—now, we're to hear the explanation that explains—the Tale of the Veiled Lady of the Inn," and she looked at Armand....

When he had finished, the Princess offered no comment, but frowned and played with her cigarette; and the Archduke, ever glad for any excuse to look at her, and very ready to be silent the better to look, watched her in undisguised devotion.

"What's the plot behind it?" she demanded, suddenly; "I can't make it out—it's absurd to fancy that woman honest, though I'm perfectly sure Lotzen has the Book. But why—why should he want to show it to us? Not out of love nor friendship, surely; nor bravado, either; our dear cousin isn't given to any such weakness. So it must be simply a rather clumsy attempt to lure you to the Ferida for slaughter—and that, again, seems unlikely; for Ferdinand isn't clumsy, nor would he want you murdered in his Palace; and as to the provision that you need not go—or that you may take a dozen with you if you wish—and if you don't go, that she preferred Colonel Moore, or some one with brains and a sword—all that, I say, is too amazingly inconsistent with anything except entire honesty for my poor brain to solve."

"Don't try, my dear," the Archduke laughed. "We will give you the solution to-morrow."

She laid aside her cigarette, and, folding her arms on the table, surveyed him in displeased surprise.

"Surely, Armand, you don't mean that *you* are going?" she asked.

He nodded, smilingly.

"Why not?" he asked—"the Colonel and I, with a few good blades, and the Veiled Lady's promise to protect us."

"But it's absurd, perfectly absurd, for you to take such risk. At the best, you are obligated only to look, to make no attempt to-night to recover the Book; and at the worst you can only fight your way out of the trap. In the one case, Colonel Moore can do the looking as well as you—in the other, their plot to kill you will have failed and your substitutes will be given some excuse by Spencer and let go in peace—oh, it's worse than absurd for you to go, Armand,"—she saw from his expression that her argument was futile—"and you know it, too; and you're going only because you like the excitement, and to show Lotzen, like a big boy, you're not to be dared."

The Archduke laughed at her indulgently.

"May be I am, little girl," he said; "but I've made up my mind to fight this business out myself, and that sends me to the Ferida to-night. I'll take every precaution——"

"Except the proper one of staying away," she interrupted. "You're struggling for a Crown, man, and mad rashness has no place in the game. Play it like Lotzen, in the modern way, not like the Middle Ages—he uses its methods, true enough, but lets others execute his plans and face the perils."—She put out her hand to him.—"Come, dear, be reasonable," she begged; "be kind; even the wildest idea of leadership does not obligate you to go."

He took her hand and held it, with the firm, soft pressure of abiding affection, looking the while into her fair face, flushed now with the impetuous earnestness of her fear for him.

"I think it does, Dehra," he said gravely. "It is our duty to the country to find the Laws and settle the Succession at the quickest possible moment——"

"Yes, it is, but——"

"And there are but three in the Kingdom who have ever seen the Book, you and Lotzen and myself; and there must be no question as to its absolute identification, before you as Regent resort to force to recover it—force that may necessitate the taking of the Ferida by assault. Therefore, dear, I must go, for *I* must see the Book. Assume, just for illustration, that Colonel Moore brings a description that seems to correspond to the Laws; you, as Regent, formally accuse the Duke of Lotzen of having the Book and demand its instant surrender; and upon his indignant denial that he has it, and his offered readiness to have his Palace searched, you order me, as Governor of Dornlitz, to have my rival's residence invaded and subjected to the ignominy of *a mandat de perquisition*; or, again, he may deny the Book without demanding a search, and submit to it only under protest; or he may refuse to permit the search and oppose it by force. And whichever the case may be, the Book will not be found—he will take very careful precaution, as to that, you may be sure. And what will my position be then, with the House of Nobles?—when our only explanation, for such fruitless insult, is that some one saw a book, which he described to us, and which we thought was the Laws. Indeed, though it hadn't occurred to me before, it may be just such a condition that he is playing for——"

"But, my dear Armand," the Princess interrupted, "would it be any advantage even if we could say that *you* saw it?"

"An incalculable advantage, Dehra; I know the Book—there could not be any chance for mistake; and it would then be my word against Lotzen's, an even break, as it were; whereas, otherwise, it will be his word against our guess. Yet, indeed, in this aspect, it's very doubtful if we ought to resort to open measures against him, even if I saw the Book. It would be a question for careful consideration and counsel with all our friends—and it is but right that I should be able to assure them that I, myself, saw it, and recognized it beyond a doubt. It's worth all the danger it may involve; though I don't anticipate any—the more I think, the more I believe we have solved the riddle. Lotzen wants some one to see the Book—he much prefers it shouldn't be I; he fancies I will gladly send a substitute; and he takes me for a hot-headed fool, who then will promptly play out for him the rest of his game, landing him on the Throne and myself beyond the border."

The Princess had listened with growing conviction that he was right; now she turned to Moore.

"And what is your best judgment?" she asked.

"That His Highness has the argument," was the prompt reply; "and I confess I was hitherto of your mind, and urged him, all I might, to let me go in his stead. Now, I am convinced not only that we should verify Mrs. Spencer's story, but that the Archduke must do it."

"And because he has seen the Book, and can identify it beyond doubt?"

"Exactly that, Your Highness; such identification is vital."

Dehra nodded and sipped her cordial meditatively; while Armand watched her in sudden disquiet; he had seen that look on her face a few times only, and it always presaged some amazing decision that was immutable—and not always to his approval. When she raised her eyes, it was with the conquering smile that he had never yet stood out against for long.

"Armand," said she, "you and Colonel Moore have persuaded me; it is right for you to go, and I'll go with you——"

"What! *You!*" the Archduke cried—"are you crazy, child?"

"Not in the least, dear; only very sensible to your cogent logic—who can identify the Book so well as I, who have known it all my life; you have seen it but once, you know."

"But the danger!"

"There isn't any danger, you said—and if there were, the Regent of Valeria will be the best sort of protector for you."

"But you will have to—go into Madeline Spencer's apartments—may be remain there half the night," he protested.

"And much more seemly for me than for you, my dear, and much less—tempting."

He joined in her laugh, but shook his head and turned to Moore.

"Colonel, will you oblige me by telephoning Mrs. Spencer we shall not be there to-night; word it any way you wish."

"Colonel Moore," said the Princess sharply, "you will do nothing of the sort. The Regent of Valeria requires the attendance of the Governor of Dornlitz and yourself to the Ferida Palace this night—and in the interval, you both will hold yourselves here in readiness."

Armand would have protested again, but she cut him short with a peremptory gesture.

"It is settled," she said; then added, almost vehemently: "surely, you can't think I want to see that awful woman!—but it's the only sure way to block Lotzen's game. The Nobles will take my word as to the Book—and so will the Army, and the people, too. No, I must go."

XVII
INTO THE TIGER'S CAGE

They had gone into the library for a rubber of bridge, until it was time to start for the Ferida. Now there came a chime from the mantel, and Dehra glanced at the old French clock that her Bourbon ancestress had brought with her—among wagon loads of clothes and furniture—when she came to be wife to Henry the Third.

"Well, Armand," she said, "if we are to be at our dear cousin's rear gate at eleven, I suppose it's the last moment for me to change my gown, this one isn't especially appropriate—have you anything in particular to suggest?"

"Nothing," he smiled, "nothing; except that you don't make yourself any more attractive than is absolutely unavoidable."

"And that I conceal my identity as much as possible, I suppose?"

"Undoubtedly—and the more effective the concealment, the better."

She laid aside the cards she was shuffling and arose.

"Will you come with me, Elise?" she asked. "You can help me with the disguise."

Moore closed the door behind them, and going over to a side-table poured out a very stiff drink.

"I don't like it!" he said, turning around, the glass half emptied, and tossing off the remainder; "I don't like it, a little bit!"

"Then it's appalling to think what you would take if you did like it," the Archduke commented.

The Colonel laughed and poured out a trifle more.

"The liquor is all right," he laughed; "it's this notion of Her Highness I don't like."

Armand had begun to deal solitaire, but he stopped and tossed the cards together.

"I wonder if Mademoiselle d'Essoldé could persuade her to give it up?" he said.

"She wouldn't try—she, too, wanted to go. I blocked that, however; I told her that one foolish virgin was as much as we could look after in this mess, and that she would best stay home and trim the lamps. It wasn't a happy remark, I fear, but it did the business—you will have to give me another message for her to-morrow. Meanwhile, I must go over and do a bit of dress changing myself—shall I need a mask?"

"I don't know; better take one."

The Archduke was in the uniform of a general officer, dark green evening coat and trousers, with buff waistcoat; and unadorned save for the narrow gold cord on the shoulder, the insignia on the sleeves, and the braid on the leg seam. Because Dehra liked him best in the Red Huzzar dress, he always wore it when he dined with her; for to-night, however, it was entirely too showy and hampering, and he had chosen the one quietest in tone and best suited for quick action.

Left alone, he tried the solitaire again; but it got on his nerves, and after a minute of listless playing, he sprang up, with an exclamation of disgust, and began to pace the floor. Presently Moore returned, in the fatigue uniform of the General Staff, with its easy-fitting jacket, and was immediately sent back to telephone the Secret Police to spread a loose cordon around the Ferida, with a dozen men loitering in close vicinity to every gate. There was no anticipating what they were about to encounter, so it was well to provide for the worst. It was his duty to protect the Regent whether she wished it or not; and though he might not take them inside with her, yet if the occasion arose, a pistol shot would bring them very quickly.

"It's growing late," he remarked, as the Adjutant came back; "if we are to be there on time we must start."

He was going toward the bell when voices in the next room told him the Princess was coming; and she entered—a slender officer in a long military coat, and a soft felt service hat.

The two men mechanically raised their hands in salute, and she acknowledged it with formal motion and a merry laugh.

"Will I pass?" she asked.—"See, the hat covers my hair, and its wide brim shadows my face; the coat reaches almost to my feet, and its big collar quite hides the back of my head; and, as for what's under the coat, see again"—and loosing the frogs, she swung it back, disclosing the tunic of her Blue Guards, and, below it, the close-fitting knee skirts, and high spiral puttees of a shooting suit.

"And is that as unattractive as you could make yourself?" the Archduke asked, with affected seriousness, as he fastened her coat and adjusted her sword.

"It's as unobtrusive as I could make myself—some day, if you wish, sir, I'll show you just how unattractive I can be."

But he only laughed, and, taking her hand, hurried her to the carriage.

On the drive, he told her briefly how they were to reach Mrs. Spencer's apartments, and cautioned her, as tactfully as he could, against doing anything which might serve to disclose her identity.

"Don't worry, dear," she said, "I'm going simply to see the Book; I shall not even speak without permission—you are in command, not I;" and she found his hand, and held it; rather sorry now that she had ordered her Adjutant inside with them, when he was about to mount his horse to follow.

"Will there be others with us?" she asked, presently.

"Yes, Captain De Coursey and Lieutenant Marsov, of the Cuirassiers; both guaranteed by Colonel Moore to be skillful swordsmen, and friendly to me as against Lotzen."

"And besides," the Adjutant added, "devoted to an adventure, and in discretion unsurpassed."

"Will you tell them who I am?" she asked.

The Archduke hesitated.... "No, not unless it becomes necessary; it would only make them unduly nervous; but if trouble come, they must know."

"I can protect myself, a little while," said she, slapping her sword in laughing bravado; though indeed she was very clever with the foils.

To her quick eye and natural talent had been added years of careful training under expert *maîtres*; for, to Frederick, she was both son and daughter, and he had encouraged her in everything that went to strengthen body or mind. Yet she was so very modest about it, that only very lately had even Armand known of her proficiency; and now, he regularly put on the mask and plastron with her, and had her present when Moore and he were practicing.

"And for more than a little while," the Archduke replied; "and if you do have to draw, try to forget you're fencing with pointed weapons, and bear in mind only that you must not be touched."

She leaned closer to him.

"Goodness Armand, you make me afraid," she said, with a little shiver; "I don't want to fight any one."

"Please God you won't have to, dear, but if you do, remember that the surest way to save your life is to take the other fellow's."

She shivered again. "I shouldn't want to be a man."

He slipped his arm around her and bent down.

"Let me send you back to the Palace, sweetheart," he whispered—"for my sake go back."

"It is for your sake I'm going on," she answered, "and—I'll kill the other fellow if I have to—but I don't want to."

The carriage drew in to the curb and stopped. It was on a side street near the rear gate of the Ferida, and as the Archduke got out, two officers in quiet uniforms and capes, who were walking slowly along, halted, and, after a glance, came up and saluted. They were De Coursey and Marsov.

"I thank you for your attendance," said the Archduke; and leaving it for Moore to acquaint them with as much of the business in hand as was necessary, he linked arms with the Regent and they went leisurely on; there was ample time, and they reached the entrance as the Cathedral bell rang the hour.

The great gate was closed and locked, but in it was a small one, so cleverly hidden among the frets and ornaments that the

Archduke had trouble in locating it, and still more in finding the catch, which Mrs. Spencer had engaged would not be fastened.

Across the street a number of men were loitering, and two came hastily over; but recognizing Colonel Moore, who had stepped out to meet them, they made a quick salute and were returning, when he called them back.

"It will be for you to see that we are not locked in," he said, and following the others, who had already entered, he closed the gate behind him.

The drive ran between great oaks straight toward the house, but, a little way in, a narrow walk branched from it on either side and wound through trees and between hedges to the side gates, and thence on to the front. Mrs. Spencer's apartments were in the wing on the right, and her instructions were to proceed by the path on that side until opposite the rear of her suite; then by another path that bisected the first, and which, crossing the driveway between the rear and side gates, led to the house and close under her windows; there, at the first small door, they were to knock.

Eleven o'clock was a very early hour at Ferida Palace, and the Archduke looked dubiously at the lighted windows and the flitting figures inside, with the music of the orchestra, in the main hall, throbbing out irregularly in bursts of rhythmic melody. It seemed rather absurd for five people to attempt a surreptitious entrance into such a place; and again he urged the Princess to return at least to the carriage, and await him there; but without success; and in deep misgiving he went on.

They gained the small door unseen, and, with a quiet word of warning, he knocked.

From within came an answering knock, to which he responded with two quick taps, twice repeated; the door opened a little way and Mrs. Spencer's maid peered out; then, assured, she swung it back and curtsied them inside.

"*Suivez de près, messieurs*," she whispered, finger on lips, and hurried down a narrow but rather brightly lighted passage, and up a stairway, and into a room on the second floor, where she prayed that they wait until she could announce them to Madame.

"And say to your mistress," the Archduke ordered, "that it is our pleasure not to intrude upon her until everything is arranged as intended."

"If Spencer will respect the request, it will be much easier for you, dear," he said to Dehra; "when we are watching Lotzen, the boudoir will have to be in darkness, and I'll take care that we leave the moment you have seen the Book."

"Do you think she will recognize me?" the Princess asked.

"I don't know; it's hard even to think what she can do or will do."

"At least, it has been easy thus far," she laughed; "almost so easy as to indicate a trap."

The same thought had naturally been in his mind, and he had hoped it would not occur to her.

"Everything has worked so smoothly it rather suggests the reverse," he said confidently; "but whatever happen, you must keep with me or Moore.—Gentlemen, I neglected to say that you will retain your caps until I remove mine.—Lieutenant Marsov, will you oblige me by turning off all the side lights?"

Presently, from somewhere down the corridor, came the ripple of Madeline Spencer's laugh, and the ring of her clear voice.

"Good-night, Monsieur le Comte! I thank you for the dance, and all the rest;"—then in quieter tones: "no, you may not come in; you have annoyed the Duke quite too much to-night, as it is—to-morrow? well, may be—*tout à l'heure!*" and the laugh again, and the closing of a door.

The Princess looked at Armand and gave a faint shudder, but made no comment.

In a moment the maid returned. "It is as you wish, Monsieur le—Monsieur," as the Archduke's gesture stopped the title. "Madame awaits you at once."

In the room adjoining the boudoir, the Archduke left the others and went in alone.

Mrs. Spencer curtsied.

"Your Highness honors me," she said.

"Pray, madame," said he, returning her greeting with the curtest of military salutes, "let us eliminate unnecessary ceremony—this is an official visit, made at your particular request; if we are ready to begin, I will call my witnesses."

She watched him smilingly, pressing down the roses that lay across her breast—red roses, on a black gown that ended far below the dead-white neck and shoulders.

"What a cold-blooded brute you are, Armand," she mocked. "Can it be, that the pretty, innocent, little doll, out yonder in the Palace, has found a drop that is warm even when fresh from the heart?"

He looked at her in steady threat.

"Madame, I have told you I am here for but one purpose; beyond that, even in conversation, I decline to go. I tried to make it clear to you at the Inn, how I would come, and why. I do not remember your record, nor even know your name; if I did, it would be my duty to send you immediately out of Valeria, and under escort. If, however, you presume to use this occasion to become offensive, I shall be obliged to remember, and to know."

She laughed scoffingly, and taking a cigarette lighted it.

"As a token of peace," she said softly, and proffered it to him.... "No?—I thought Ferdinand said he had learned it from you and—but, of course, it does make a difference whose are the lips that kissed it."

The Archduke turned abruptly and went toward the door; another such word and he might forget she was a woman. She might be able to show him the Book, but, even could she give it to him, he would not have it, if its price were the Princess on her tongue.

She saw she had gone too far.

"Armand!" she cried, "Armand! stay—I'll be good—I'll be good."—She sprang forward and caught his arm—"Don't go—think of what I can show you."

"Then show it, madame," he answered, facing her and so displacing her hand; "show it; and leave off personalities."

Without replying, she went to a window, and drew the shade aside a little way.

"Yes, he is there," she said, "but Bigler is with him ... ah! he is going—now, we shan't have long to wait."—She motioned the Archduke to her. "See—there shouldn't be any doubt of the identification, if he give you a chance to see it."

He went over and looked. She was right; nor would they need the field glass to recognize it. Fifty yards away, in the opposite wing, were Lotzen's apartments—his library windows raised, the shades high up, the curtains drawn back; and he, himself, at the big table under the chandelier, a twin drop-light focused on the writing pad.

And even while the Archduke looked, Lotzen arose and from the safe behind him took out a package wrapped in black.

"That's it!" Madeline Spencer exclaimed, "that's it!—Here is the glass——"

He lingered for another glance, before summoning the others—and Mrs. Spencer forestalled him.

She ran to the door and flung it wide.

"Come," she said, "come——His Highness needs you."

The Princess had been talking to Colonel Moore, her back to the door; as it opened, she threw up her head, and turned with an eager smile, thinking it was Armand—and so gave Mrs. Spencer a full view of her face. Then Moore stepped quickly between them and suavely bowed Mrs. Spencer into her boudoir; the next moment the Archduke was there.

"With your permission, madame, we will extinguish the lights," he said, "and raise the shades."

She smiled maliciously, deliberately moving near enough to see the Princess over Moore's shoulder.

"Extinguish the lights?" she laughed, "certainly; darkness will be better for the business, and will conceal—*everyone*," and herself went over to the main switch at the corridor door and pushed it open.

The Princess caught Armand's hand.

"She recognized me," she whispered.

"Oh, no, dear; you're only nervous," he answered—though he was satisfied she was right. "Keep your hat well down, and don't look at her; the moment you have identified the Book, we will leave; you go with Moore; I'll engage the vixen until you're out of range."

He had led her to a window and raised the shade. The lights from the Duke's library leaped across the garden court at them, but he, himself, was not visible, though on the table lay the package, still wrapped in black as when taken from the safe. Some one came behind them, and Armand glanced over his shoulder—it was Mrs. Spencer, and she was looking at the Princess; nor did she cease, though she knew his eyes were on her; instead, she smiled and shot him a quick glance, and resumed the looking. He felt Dehra begin to tremble—whether with anger or nerves, he could not tell—and Mrs. Spencer spoke.

"Your Highness' companion is evidently unused to adventures, despite his uniform; he is actually twitching with excitement."

"Or with the temptation of your proximity," Armand replied giving her his back. And Dehra laughed softly.

Colonel Moore had been at another window; now he came over, and, in the most casual way, found Mrs. Spencer's hand and gave it a familiar squeeze.

"You're pretty enough to-night to give even an old-stager like me a flutter," he whispered in his most caressing tones, and, in the darkness, slipped his arm around her waist.

She pushed it away, though not very vigorously it seemed to him.

"You are impertinent, sir," she said.

"I meant to be; it's the only way to get on with you," and he deliberately put his arm around her again, and rather more tightly. "Come along to my window," he urged.

She knew very well that his purpose was to divert her from the Princess, but she went—nor appeared to bother that his arm remained. Here, was a new sort of man, with a new sort of method, and she was, if the truth be told, very willing for them both. Besides, her time would come presently.

"Moore is a wonder," Armand commented—and broke off, as the Duke came into view and sat down at his table.

But Lotzen was in no haste to unwrap the package; he drew it over and slowly loosed the cords, then suddenly laid it aside, and coming over to the window, seemed on the point of drawing the shade; but he changed his mind, and after staring into the garden and toward Mrs. Spencer's apartments, he returned to the table.

Without more ado he removed the black cloth, but pushed it in a heap, so that it hid the book—that it was a book, they could distinguish, but nothing else—and went to examining some papers he took from it.

The Princess stirred restlessly; her nerves were not attuned to such tension; and the Archduke reassured her by a touch and a word. Over at their window, Mrs. Spencer and Colonel Moore were whispering, and laughing softly, the latter, however, with a wary eye across the courtyard. The swinging cadence of a Strauss waltz came, brokenly, from the orchestra still playing in the great hall, with, now and then, a burst of men's voices in noisy hilarity from the card rooms or the main guard.

Presently the Duke put down the papers, and, pushing aside the black cloth, disclosed the back of the book—black, with heavy brass hinge-bands across it.

"Look," the Princess exclaimed, "look! it's very like it—why doesn't he lift the cover ... there!—see, the pages, too!—it must be!—it is!—it——"

"Run away, girl!" came Count Bigler's voice from the corridor, "run away, I say—you're pretty enough, but I want your mistress now." There was a moment's scuffle, and the door swung back——"Dark! well, 'let there be light!'" and he snapped the switch.

It all was done so quickly and unexpectedly that Mrs. Spencer was caught half way to the door, as she sprang to lock it; Armand had time only to push the Princess away from the window and step in front of her; while Colonel Moore, with De Coursey and Marsov, tried to get across to cover the Archduke.

But they failed. Bigler saw him instantly.

"The American!" he shouted, "the American!" and wrenching back the door, he disappeared down the corridor.

"The fool!" Madeline Spencer exclaimed; "he has spoiled everything—quick, you must get away; I don't want another De Saure house here," with a look at Armand—"the way you came will still be open."—She hurried ahead of them through the rooms to the stairway.... "I've been honest and I want to prove it, but," she laughed sneeringly after them, "the next time Her Highness plays the man, let her wear a mask and a larger shoe." The noise of men running came from below. "Hurry!" she cried, "they are trying to cut you off."

With the Regent between them, and De Coursey and Marsov behind, the Archduke and Moore dashed down the lower passage to the small door and out into the garden.

"Come along!" said Armand; "we don't want a fight; make straight for the gate."

Holding Dehra's arm, he ran across the drive and, avoiding the winding path, cut over the grass—to bring up, in a moment, at a fountain in a labyrinth of thick hedges and walks, none of which seemed to lead gateward.

With a muttered imprecation, the Archduke chose the one that pointed toward the winding path by which they had entered, only to discover that it curved back toward the house.

"Take the hedge!" he ordered; and he and Moore tossed the Princess over the seven foot obstruction, and were swung up, themselves, by De Coursey and Marsov, whom they then pulled across.

But this took time; and now Bigler's voice rang from the garden.

"Make for the side gates—I'll look to the rear one!" he cried; and almost immediately they heard him and his men between them and their exit.

The Archduke stopped.

"There is no need to tire ourselves by running," he said; "we shall have to fight for it, so we may as well save our wind.—Gentlemen,"—turning to De Coursey and Marsov—"to-night you are honored above most men—you will draw swords for the Regent under her very eye—behold!"

He lifted the hat from the Princess' head, and the light of a near-by street lamp, that shone above the walls, fell full on the coils of high piled hair, and the fair face below it.

Both men cried out in astonishment, and, kneeling, kissed her hand.

Then they pressed on, finding almost immediately the path by which they had entered.

Meanwhile, the commotion in the garden near the palace had increased, and now the Duke of Lotzen's stern voice cut sharply into the night, from one of his windows.

"What the devil is all this noise?" he demanded.

"Thieves, Your Highness," some one answered from below—"five of them in madame's apartments—they escaped into the garden."

The Duke made no reply, at least which they could hear; and the Princess laughed.

"He's off for madame," she said; "and we are thieves—rather clever of Bigler to have us killed first and recognized later."

"He didn't see you," said Armand; "he recognized me, and thinks this is the chance he missed at the De Saure house."

A moment later they came into the wide drive-way, and face to face with the Count and a bunch of a dozen men.

He gave a shout that rang through the garden.

"Seize them!" he cried; "kill any that resist!" knowing very well that it would require the killing of them all. He, himself, drew his revolver and stepped to one side—a safer place than in the fighting line, and one where he could get a surer shot at the Archduke, if it were necessary.

But even twelve men hesitate to close with five, whose swords are ready; and in the instant's pause, Dehra, flinging off her hat, sprang between Bigler and the Archduke, and covered the former with her pistol.

"God in Heaven! the Princess!" he cried, and stared at her.

"Will you play with treason, my lord Count?" she asked. "Drop that revolver!—drop it, I say!—and you men, stand aside!—into line, so!—return swords!—now, by the left flank, march!—fall in behind, Count, if you please—march!"

With a laugh and a shrug he obeyed.

"The Regent commands," he said.—"Attention! salute!" and with hands to visors the column went by; while Dehra, fingers at forehead in acknowledgment, watched it pass and go down the drive toward the Palace.

Then she turned, and put out her hand to the Archduke.

"I'm tired, dear," she said, "very tired——Captain De Coursey, will you bring the carriage to the gate?"

XVIII
ON TO LOTZENIA

"It is a most amazing situation," said the Ambassador—as he and the Archduke sat in the latter's headquarters, the following morning—"and one guess is about as likely to be right as another. It's difficult to believe Spencer honest, and yet she seemed to play straight last night. She is of the sort who fiercely resent a blow and go to any length to repay it. And you think Bigler's interruption was not prearranged?"

"It impressed me that way," said Armand. "In fact, I'd say I am sure of it, if I had any but Lotzen or Spencer to deal with."

"And you saw enough of the book to be satisfied it is the Laws?"

"To satisfy myself, yes—if that fool, Bigler, had waited a little longer, I would have known beyond a doubt."

"And, as it is, you can't be absolutely certain?"

"No; at least, not certain enough to make an open issue of it with Lotzen."

Courtney shook his head decisively.

"It is a great misfortune you were not able to make sure," he said; "for I'm persuaded it was not the Book. As I told Her Highness that day at luncheon, if the Duke ever did have it, he has destroyed it to get rid of Frederick's decree; and if there were no decree, then he would have produced it instantly as establishing his right to the Crown."

"If that be true—and I grant the logic is not easy to avoid—what was it I saw? I would have sworn it was the Book; it resembled it in every particular."

Courtney's fingers went up to his gray imperial, and for a long while he smoked his cigarette and stared thoughtfully at the ceiling.

"It is a fine mess," he said, at length; "Spencer mixes it so abominably. What really brought her to Dornlitz?—how long has she been here?—did the Duke strike her—if there is a plot back of it, why should she have been selected to do the open work with you, of all people?—why, if Lotzen have the Book, doesn't he destroy it?—why does he want you to see it in his very hands?—why, if he haven't the Book, does he want to convince you that he has?—... If it's a plot, then its object was either the one you suggest: to tempt you to violent measures against him to recover the Book, and so to discredit you with the Nobles when it's not found; or—and this may be the more likely—to inveigle you into a death trap by using the Book as a lure."

"Either of which," observed the Archduke, "would explain his preservation of the Book."

"Or sentiment," Courtney laughed. "Her Highness thinks the Duke would never destroy the Laws of his House."

"I fancy she wouldn't be quite so strong on that now," Armand observed. "I wish you had seen her last night; she was magnificent, simply magnificent.—Richard, she is the Dalberg of us all!—it's she, not I, nor Lotzen, who ought to wear the Sapphire Crown."

Courtney nodded in hearty acquiescence.

"And as she may not, it is for you," he said, gravely, "to make her a Queen by wearing it yourself—and, as I believe I've admonished once or twice heretofore, to do that you must keep alive—dead Archdukes are good only to bury."

"I'm very much alive," the other laughed, "more alive than I've been since I shed cadet gray."

"The Lord knows it is not from lack of effort on your part to get killed; you've tempted death in every dare-deviltry you could find—and this De Saure house affair is the limit—though last night was about as idiotic. The Princess has more discretion in an eye-lash than you have in your whole head—but for her, you would be surrounded now by tapers and incense—what fresh atrocity against common prudence will you perpetrate next, I wonder!"

The Archduke pushed the decanter across.

"Take another drink, old man," he grinned, "you must be dry, with such a warm bunch of ideas jostling one another for exit—I'll promise to be as discreet hereafter as a debutante. I admit the De Saure business appears foolish now, but then, at that hour of night, in darkness, rain and storm, would you, or any other man, have denied a woman's call for help? I couldn't."

"Nor anything else that promises adventure," said Courtney. "If Lotzen doesn't make an end of you——" he shrugged his shoulders and lit another cigarette.... "I've sworn a dozen resolves to quit advising you; and then, every time I see you, you've gone and done some other foolish thing, and I blow off—if you will forgive me this time, and may be a few more times, I'll not do it again."

"My dear Dick," said the Archduke, "the one thing I'll not forgive is for you *not* to do it again. You're the only man in all this land who would speak out his mind to me; and do you think it isn't welcome—to have something of the old life occasionally?"

For a while both men smoked in silence, the Marshall thoughtfully, the Ambassador waitingly; and in the midst of it Colonel Bernheim entered with a letter for the Archduke, which, he explained, he had just received, enclosed in another envelope addressed to himself and marked "Immediate."

Armand glanced at Courtney for permission, got it, and read the letter:

"A——

"We are leaving Dornlitz before daybreak by special train, ostensibly for Paris, really for Lotzen Castle. The Duke guessed instantly why you were in my apartments, and what you saw. We had a fearful scene, and he struck me again—the cur! It is the B.; he admitted it, in his rage—and he has it with him. I am a prisoner now, and compelled to accompany him because I know too much, he says. I'm not asking you for rescue, I can manage him in a few days; but if you want the B. you will know now where to get it. I owe you this, for the fiasco last night, due to that fool, B——, though I don't advise you to follow; Lotzen Castle isn't Ferida Palace, and I can't aid you there; and besides, now, he is bent on your death, and intends to kill you at the first opportunity. I will find some way to have this mailed, sending it to Col. Bernheim so it will reach you promptly and not be delayed by official routine.

"M. S."

"3 A. M."

Without a word, the Archduke passed the letter over to Courtney; and without a word Courtney took it, read it twice, and passed it back; and fell to blowing smoke rings through each other.

"Well," said Armand presently, "when you're satisfied with the rings, and it seems to me they couldn't be bettered, I shall be glad to have your opinion of the letter."

The other shook his head, and went on with the rings.

"What is the use?" he answered. "You are going to Lotzenia."

"I'm sorely tempted, I admit—but I don't know——"

Courtney flung his cigarette at the fireplace, and got up.

"Then, if you don't know, I'll tell you what I think,—throw that damn letter into the fire and stay right here in Dornlitz; if you let it lure you to Lotzenia, you are an unmitigated fool."

"But the Book!—and Spencer only confirms what my own eyes told me."

"Lies, lies, rotten lies!" said Courtney. "He hasn't the Book—it's all a plant—you escaped last night because Bigler blundered in, and because the Regent was with you—but in that wild land of the North, you will last about a day, or less. Why don't you forget the miserable Book, for a while, and get to work on your vote in the House of Nobles?—there is where you will likely have to fight it out any way, even if Frederick did make your decree. Play politics a bit, and you will have Lotzen back in Dornlitz on the jump—and the Book with him, too, if he has it."

The Archduke went over and put his hand on Courtney's shoulder.

"Dick," he said, "it's something worth living for to have known a man like you, and to have had him for a friend and companion; and if I don't follow your advice you will understand it is because I can't. You have called me headstrong; I grant it, it's bred in the bone I think; and I'm not of those who can sit, and wait, and play politics. I shall find the Laws of the Dalbergs, somewhere, somehow, long before the year is over; and if necessary I'm going to kill Lotzen in the finding—or be killed—" he broke off with a laugh and a shrug. "Positively, old man, I'm ashamed of myself; I seem to have become a braggart and a swash-buckler."

"Who is the braggart and swash-buckler, my dear Marshal?" asked the Princess, entering suddenly, with Lady Helen Radnor, Mlle. d'Essoldé and Colonel Moore, "not Mr. Courtney I hope."

"Unfortunately, no; Your Highness," said Armand. "Candor compels me to admit that I was characterizing myself."

She pointed her crop at the decanter, and nodded questioningly to the Ambassador.

"No," said he, "no; it's only a sudden rush of remorse for deeds past and to come."

"To come?" said she, and looked at the Archduke inquiringly.

For answer he handed her Madeline Spencer's letter.

She glanced at the signature, smiled, and with a word of excuse, she carried it over to a window; and Armand, chatting with Lady Helen, watched her curiously as she read and re-read it; and then she looked up quickly, and gave him the glance of summons.

"Have you shown it to Mr. Courtney?" she asked. "Did he say what he thought of it?"

"He did—and at some length, and also what he thought of me.—Briefly, it was to the effect that the letter is a snare, and that I'm several kinds of a fool if I let it lure me to Lotzenia."

The Princess tapped her crop softly against her boot, and considered.

"Of course," said she, in momentary interruption of her thought, "I know what *you* think—you think you're going,—but I don't know——" and the tapping of the crop began afresh....

Presently a soft light came into her eyes, and she flashed him the adorable smile. "Are you willing to wait the year for our wedding, dear?" she asked.

He bent down over her, as though looking at something in the letter.

"You know I'm not, sweetheart," he said, "that's why I want to find the Laws—to make you Queen the sooner."

"Your Queen?"

"Mine—yes, either here in Valeria, or over the seas in old Hugo's land—as the Book decides for Lotzen or for me."

"And do you honestly think, Armand, that he has the Book?"

"What do you think?" he asked.

"Women don't think—they have only intuition, and mine says that he has."

"Then I shall go this night——"

"And I with you."

"Then I won't go."

"Nonsense, dear—why not? Dalberg Castle is always ready, and I shall take the Household, or part of it. I most assuredly would not let you go alone, to be butchered by our dear and loving cousin."

He knew it was useless to protest.

"Well, come along, little woman," he said; "and may be, together, we can devise a way for me to get the Book out of Lotzen Castle."

She turned upon him, full faced and emphatic.

"But I'll not go, nor shall you," she declared, "unless you promise you won't do anything without consulting me. I'm going because you need some one to curb your recklessness; and I have no mind to see you throw your life away just because you won't take a dare."

The Archduke gave her cheek a surreptitious pinch.

"I promise," he laughed; "you're something of a Dalberg daredevil yourself when the fever is on—and you're the finest little comrade and commander God ever made."

Again she gave him the smile—and they went back to the others.

"Mr. Courtney," said she, at once, "we are about to spend a short while at Dalberg Castle, going to-night by special train, with a few members of the Household; it will be a great pleasure to Armand and me to have you with us."

"I am honored," said the Ambassador, with a grave bow; "I shall be glad to go."

"Even if you do disapprove," said she lightly—"but, what would you, monsieur! I don't want to imprison Armand, so the best thing I can do is to go along and try to take care of him; and that's where you can help me."

"And that, Your Highness, is precisely the reason I'm going," he answered;—"Warwick will stick to his work to the end."

"The end!" she exclaimed, with sharp seriousness.

"In the great Cathedral yonder," he answered.—And the Princess, thinking only of the coronation, smiled and glanced with proud faith at the Archduke.

But to the latter the real inference went home, and sharply.

"The crypt, you mean?" he muttered aside.

And Courtney nodded curtly.

"The crypt I mean," he said. "Even Warwick and Margaret of Anjou together could not save the silly Henry."

But the old, lean-faced Prime Minister did not deal in inferences when—having come at the Regent's summons, from his office in the Administration wing of the same building—he was advised of the matter, and that he was to assume charge of the government during her absence.

"Has Your Royal Highness forgot the Chambers meet this day week, and that the Regent must open them in person?" he asked.

"I had forgot," said she, "but I shall return for it."

The Count shrugged his shoulders.

"It is not for me to question the Regent's movements," he said; "but if you will accept the advice of one who was your father's friend and trusted servant, and who ventures to think he can, at least in this instance, speak with his dear, dead master's voice, you will abandon this astonishing intention, that can profit nothing to His Highness' cause, and will lead him only into dire and awful danger."

"Will there be no profit in recovering the Book?" she demanded.

"You will not recover it in Lotzenia."

"The Duke has it; I saw it last night."

The Count shook his head. "I feel sure that Lotzen hasn't the Book; but if you are positive, beyond a doubt, then formally demand it as Regent; if he refuse, take half the Army, if need be, and batter down his Castle and get it."

The Princess laughed. "Now, Count, you know very well that would be the one sure way not to get it—he would destroy it."

"And himself with it," said Epping; "for then your testimony would be enough to convict him, and lose him his last chance for election by the Nobles. It would be as effective as to find the Book itself."

"Your plan does not please me for two reasons," she answered, promptly and decisively. "It contemplates the destruction of the Laws of the Dalbergs, which I would rather die than be the cause of; and it would permit the House of Nobles to determine the succession to the Throne, a thing hitherto unknown, and to my poor mind subversive of the rights of my House. What we want is the Book, and the way to get it is to take it quietly and by stealth. Hence, I was willing that His Highness should go to Lotzenia, and I with him, to see what might be done."

"In other words," said the Count incisively, "you deliberately stake the Archduke Armand's life for the preservation of the Book."

The Princess gasped, and her face went white.

"Don't say it, my child!" the old man exclaimed, "don't say it!—think a moment first—and then forgive me for having let my affection for you drive my tongue too far."

And instantly her anger passed; and she went to him and laid her hand on his, where it rested on his sword hilt—while the Archduke spoke quickly.

"Your Excellency does not quite appreciate that the Regent is dealing with a very unruly subject, and one who will not countenance the assault on Lotzen Castle. Neither Her Highness nor myself could stand before the Nobles and affirm on honor and unreservedly that the Duke has the Book, though we think we identified it. But more vital still is the fact that I will not consent to any measures which would drive the Duke to destroy the Book. I am determined to establish my right to the Throne by the Laws of the Dalbergs, and not to owe it to the vote of any man nor set of men. Frankly, my lord, I care so lightly for it, that, but for this little woman here, and to make her the Queen which by birth she ought to be, I would not lift a finger nor move tongue to gain the Crown. And if we are to have it—she and I—it must be with all its ancient rights and authority, unsmirched and unimpaired by the politics and obligations of an election."

The old Count raised his thin, white hand—his lean face flushed, the fine fire of a hotspur youth glowing in his eyes.

"Go, Sire!" he said, "go; and win your crown as a Dalberg should—and would I were young enough to go with you—as it is, I will hold things stanch for you here."

XIX
LA DUCHESSE

Madeline Spencer, lying in a languorous coil among the cushions in the deep embrasure of an east window, was gazing in dreamy abstraction across the valley to the mountain spur, five miles away as the bird flies, ten as the road runs, where, silhouetted against the blue of the cloudless sky, rose the huge, gray Castle of Dalberg.

For the last hour, she had been training a field glass on it at short intervals, and presently she levelled it again, and this time she saw what she was waiting for—from the highest tower of the keep the royal standard of Valeria was floating.

For a little while she watched the Golden Lion couchant on its crimson field—lashing its tail in anger with every undulation of the fresh west wind, as though impatient to spring into the valley and ravage and harass it, much as the fierce first Dalberg himself had doubtless done—then she slowly uncoiled herself, and gliding from the ledge swished lightly across to the far door, that led into the Duke of Lotzen's library.

"Ferdinand," she said, "they have——" he was not there, though she had heard him a moment ago singing softly, as was his wont when in particularly good spirits.

She went to his desk and sat down to wait, her eyes straying indifferently over the familiar papers that covered it, until they chanced upon a slender portfolio, she had never before seen, and which, to her surprise, contained only a sheet of blotting paper, about a foot square, folded down the center. Curious, she opened it, to find, on the inside, the stamp of the royal arms, and the marks of a dozen lines of heavy writing, most of it clear and distinct, and made, seemingly, by two impressions, one at each end of the sheet.

What was it doing here?—and why so carefully preserved?—She looked at the writing more attentively—and suddenly one word stood out plain, even if inverted, and under it a date.

Instantly blotter and portfolio were replaced, and she hurried to her boudoir for a mirror. Laying it face upward on the desk, she held the writing over it. A single glance proved her surmise true. Here and there words and letters were missing or were very indistinct, but there could be no doubt that this was the blotter used by King Frederick when he wrote the decree the night before his death. Her hasty reading had found nothing to show the purport of the Law—indeed, it seemed to be only a few lines of the beginning and of the end, including the signature and date—but possibly a closer inspection would reveal more; and so she was about to copy it exactly, when she heard the Duke's voice in the adjoining room and had time only to hide the mirror and to get the blotter to its place until he came in.

His cold face warmed, as it always did for her, and as it never had done for another woman, and he bowed to her in pleasant mockery.

"Good morning, Duchess," he said; "what are your orders for the day?—you occupy the seat of authority."

She got up. "Having no right to the title," she said, giving him her most winning smile, "I vacate the seat—do you think I look like a duchess?"

"Like a duchess!" he exclaimed, handing her into the chair and leaning over the back, his head close to hers, "like a duchess! you are a duchess in everything but birth."

"And title," she added, with a bit of a shrug.

He stroked her soft black hair, with easy fingers.

"The title will be yours when Ferdinand of Lotzen reigns in Dornlitz," he said.

She bent back her head and smiled into his eyes. It was the first time he had held out any promise as to her place in event of his becoming king, though she had tried repeatedly to draw him to it.

"Would you do that, dear?" she asked, "do you really care enough for me to do that—to acknowledge me so before the world?"

"Yes, Madeline, I think I do," he said, after a pause, that seemed to her perilously long. "It appears rather retributive that you, who came here, at my instance, to play the wife for the American, should thus have been put, by my own act, into a position where our friendship must be maintained sub rosa. You are quite too clear headed not to appreciate that now, at least, I may not openly parade our relations; to do so would be to end whatever chance I have with the Nobles. But once on the Throne and the power firm in my hand, and they all may go to the devil, and a duchess shall you be—if,"—pinching her cheek—"you will promise to stay away from Paris and the Rue Royale, except when I am with you."

She wound her lithe arms around his neck, and drew his face close to hers.

"I promise," she said presently, "I promise…. But what if you should miss the Crown?—you could not make me duchess then."

"Why not, *ma belle?*" he asked, holding her arms close around his neck. "I shall still be a Duke, and you—*la Duchesse de la main gauche.*"

She could not suppress the start—though she had played for just such an answer, yet never thinking it would come—and Lotzen felt it, and understood.

"Did that surprise you, little one?" he laughed. "Well, don't forget, if I miss the Throne, and live, I shan't be urged to stay in Valeria—in fact, whatever urging there is, will likely be the other way."

"Banished?" she asked.

He nodded. "Practically that."

"Paris?"—with a sly smile upward.

He filched a kiss. "Anywhere you like, my dear; but no one place too long."

She was thinking rapidly—"duchess of the left hand";—never his duchess in name—never anything but a morganatic wife to whom no title passed; but what mattered the title, if she got the settlements, and all the rest. And Ferdinand was easy enough to manage now, and would be, so long as the infatuation held him; afterward—at least the settlements and the jewels would remain.

Truly she had won far more than she had sought or even dreamed of—and won it, whether Lotzen got the Crown or exile. The only risk she ran was his dying, and it must be for her to keep him out of danger—away from the Archduke and his friends, where, she knew, death was in leash, straining to be free and at him. Hitherto she had thought her only sure reward lay in Ferdinand as king; in his generosity for a little while; and so she had been very willing to stake him for success. Now she must reverse her method—no more spurring him to seek out the Archduke and dare all on a single fight; instead, prudence, discretion, let others do the open work and face the hazards.

She gave a satisfied little sigh and drew him close.

"May be you doubt it, dear," she said, "but I can be very docile and contented—and I shall prove it, whether as duchess of the right hand or the left."

He laughed, and shook his head.

"You, docile and contented! never in this world; nor do I want you so—I prefer you as you are; you may lose me, if you change."

"Then I'll not change, dear," she whispered, and kissed him lightly and arose.

He reached out quickly to draw her back, but she eluded him.

"Nay, nay, my lord," she smiled; "I must not change, you said."

"Don't go away," he insisted; "stay with me a little longer."

She sat down across the desk from him.

"I almost forgot what I came for," she said. "Do you know *they* have come?—the flag went up a little while ago."

He nodded. "Yes, I know—a whole train load and half the Household:—the Regent, the American, Moore, Bernheim, De Coursey, Marsov, the scheming Courtney, damn him, and a lot of women, including, of course, the Radnor girl. For a pursuit with deadly intent, it's the most amazing in the annals of war. Under all the rules, the American and a few tried swords should have stolen into Dalberg Castle, with every precaution against our knowing they had come; instead, they arrive with the ostentation of a royal progress, and fling out the Golden Lion from the highest tower."

"What are you going to do first?" she asked.

"Nothing—it's their move. They have come for the Book, and they must seek it here."

She was idly snapping the scissors through a sheet of paper and simply smiled her answer.

"Give me a cigarette, dear," she said, after a pause, "I've left mine in my room."

He searched his pockets for his case; then tumbled the papers on the desk, she aiding and very careful to leave exposed the portfolio that contained the blotter.

"Oh, there it is," she exclaimed, "on the table, yonder;" and when he went for it she drew out the blotter and feigned to be examining it.

"Here, little one," he said, tossing her the case—then he saw what she had, and for the shadow of an instant, which she detected, he hesitated—"fix one for me," he ended, and sat down, seemingly in entire unconcern.

"Bring me a match," she ordered, eyes still on the blotter, as she opened the case and took out a cigarette.... "There, I spoil you." She laid down the sheet and lit another Nestor for herself. "Ferdinand," said she, turning half around in her chair and looking up at him, "just where is this wonderful Book of Laws?"

"Here, in this drawer," opening one beside her, showing the same package wrapped in black cloth that Armand and Dehra had seen in Ferida Palace.

"I don't mean that one," said she. "I mean the *real* Book."

He sent a cloud of smoke between them.

"I wish I knew," he said; "but the American won't tell me."

She scattered the smoke with a wave of her handkerchief.

"Are you quite sure he could tell you?" she asked.—"In fact, my dear boy, do you need to be told?"

He looked at her with a puzzled frown; and for answer she tapped the open blotter, and smiled.

"Even though inverted, a few words are very plain:—a King's name and a date.... And the King died the next day."

"And what is your inference?" he asked.

"It's rather more than an inference, isn't it?" she laughed; "I should call it a sequitur:—that he who has the Book's blotter, has the Book."

She had expected either cool ridicule or angry denial; instead, he laughed, too, and coming around to her, gave her an admiring little caress.

"You're quite too clever, Madeline," he said; "it is a sequitur, but unfortunately it's not the fact—now. I haven't the Book; I did have it, and I know where it is, but I can't get it."

"You had it—and let it get away?" she marveled.

"Yes."

"And know where it is, and yet can't get it?"

"Yes, again."

"Surely! surely! it can't be that I am listening to the Duke of Lotzen!... But, of course, you know what the decree is."

And now he lied, and so easily and promptly that even she did not suspect.

"No," said he, "I don't; I lost the Book before I had a chance to open it. All I know is what that blotter tells. Damn it, why couldn't it have had the middle of the decree instead of both ends!" and in marvellously assumed indignation he seized the soft sheet, and tore it into tiny bits. He had no mind that even she should have the chance to copy it, and delve into all that the words and blurred lines might imply.

"May I know where the Book is, dear?" she said, after a pause; "may be I could help you."

An hour ago he would have balked at this question; but now her interests had become so bound up with his that he could trust her.

"Know, little one? of course you may know," he said instantly; "I shall be glad for a confidant. The Book is exactly where it belongs:—in the box, and it is in the vault of the King's library at the Summer Palace."

She laughed merrily.

"Ferdinand, dear Ferdinand!" she cried, "I'm ashamed of you—to tell me such a clumsy lie."

"It isn't a lie—that's the pity."

"Then why all this bother as to the Succession, and search for the Book?" she asked incredulously.

"Because, my dear, I'm the only one who knows it's there—listen, and I'll tell you how it happened."

At last! at last! she was to know—and she nestled close to him and waited. Truly, this was her day. And he told all, not even omitting the killing of the valet.

Her first question was typical of her mind, it went straight to the crux of the whole matter.

"But why can't you get the Book?" she asked.

"Because I can't get at it. The infernal American has put a cordon of troops around the Palace, so that it's impossible to pass at night without declaring myself; Moore occupies the library; and finally the combination on the vault has been changed."

"Isn't it absurd?" said she; "the Book actually in its place and yet lost."—She sat up sharply. "Do you really want it, Ferdinand?—because, if you do, may be I can help you."

"Assuredly I want it. If the decree is against me, we will destroy the Book and go on with our game."

"Then, dear, let us go after it—and *now, now!* The Regent is absent, hence less vigilance in the Palace; Moore is with her, hence the library is deserted; it should be easy for you to get us in it by day and unsuspected."

"And having blown open the vault, be caught in the act," he smiled.

"That is where I come in, dear; I will engage to open it, noiselessly, and in less than fifteen minutes, too."

"Is it possible that you are one of those wonder workers who can feel a combination?"

"Yes," said she, "though I've not tried it for years."

"Come, come, try it now!" indicating a small iron safe in the far corner.

She went to it, and sinking to the floor with sinuous grace, she put her ear close to the dial plate and fell to manipulating the knob with light fingers; turning it back and forth very slowly and with extreme care.

And the Duke, leaning against the safe, watched her with eager eyes—could she do it?—if she could——

SHE FELL TO MANIPULATING THE KNOB WITH
LIGHT FINGERS.

Mrs. Spencer sprang up.

"That was easy," she said.

Lotzen reached over and seized the handle; the bolts snapped back and the door swung open.

With the first burst of impulse she had ever seen him display, he whirled and caught her in his arms.

"We will win now, my duchess!" he exclaimed, "we will win sure. No burglarious entry—no explosion—no flight; instead, the Duke of Lotzen and his Aide will go openly to the library, and then in a trice will we have the Book and be gone.... And I shall owe it all to you, dear—*ma chérie duchesse.*"

She closed her eyes; truly, this was her day!

"Let us go to Dornlitz this very night," she said.

He shook his head. "We must wait a day, little one; until our friends across the valley have assured themselves that I am here. But to-morrow night we will steal away to the Capital, and get the Book; and then, if necessary, we will come back, and send our dear cousin to the devil where he belongs."

XX
THE PRINCESS TURNS STRATEGIST

The Archduke put up his field glasses and, turning to the Princess, waved his hand toward the open country, and around to the Castle behind them.

"So, dear," he said, "this is home—the Dalberg aerie and its feeding grounds. I like them well. And particularly do I like the way the nest itself has been kept up to the time in comforts and appointments."

"Do be serious, Armand," she protested; "haven't you any sentiment! Look at the wonderful blue of the Voragian mountains; and the shifting shadows on the foot-hills; and this spur, and Lotzen's yonder, trailing out from them like tendrils of a vine; and the emerald valley, streaked through the center by the sparkling Dreer; and the fair lands to the south, as far as eye can carry, and yet farther, league upon league to the sea—yours, my lord, all yours—the heritage of your House—the Kingdom of your Fathers."

"You have forgot the loveliest thing in all the landscape," said he, "the one thing that makes the rest worth while."

She sprang from him. "No, sir, not here on the wall in view of the bailey and every window; confine your sentiment at present to the inanimate portion of the landscape."

He went over and leaned on the parapet beside her.

"I fear I have quite too much sentiment," he said; "I have already expended far more than you would believe—on the Castle, and the mountains, and the valley, and all the rest. Now I'm done with it, except for animate objects; the business we have in hand promises to be sufficiently occupying. Yonder is the Book; and how to get it, and quickly." He leveled his glasses at Lotzen Castle and studied it a long time.... "A pretty hard proposition," he remarked. "Have you ever been in it?"

"Unfortunately, no; but Major Meux has been Constable here for two years, and surely must have been there often—yonder he is now, by the gate tower."

The Archduke caught Meux's glance and motioned for him.

"Major," said he, "can you give us an idea of the plan of Lotzen Castle?"

"I can do better than that, Your Highness, I can show you a plan, drawn to scale and most complete. I came upon it in the library only last week. It's more than a hundred years old, but I think it is still in effect accurate."

"I wonder how it happens to be here?" said the Princess, with the peculiar curiosity of a woman as to non-essentials.

"At the time it was made Lotzen was also a Royal Castle," the Constable explained; "it was very natural to deposit the draft here with the King's own records."

As they crossed the main hall, they chanced upon Colonel Moore, and, taking him with them, they went into the library—a great, high-ceilinged room, on the second floor of the keep, the walls hidden by massive, black oak cases, filled with books and folios, in bindings of leather stamped with the Dalberg Lion—and from a shelf in a dark corner the Constable brought a small portfolio, made to resemble a book, in which the draft was folded.

"This is admirable," the Archduke remarked, examining it with the trained eye and instant comprehension of the engineer officer; "it could not be done better now.... See, Dehra, it is the whole fortification, as plain as though we were on the high tower, here—" indicating on the draft.

"I suppose so," she smiled; "but to me it looks only like a lot of black lines, flung down at random and with varying degrees of force; sort of an embroidery pattern, you know."

Armand, bending over the sheet, did not hear her.

"What did you make out of this, Major?" he asked; "there seems to be nothing on the key to explain it—might it be intended to indicate a secret passage from the second floor of the keep to the postern?"

"That puzzled me also," said Meux, "but your explanation, sir, seems very likely.—Possibly old Jessac might know something;

he has been here for more than seventy years, as a boy, and upper servant, and steward, and now as sort of steward emeritus and general reminiscer; and he has the legends and history of this castle at his tongue's end."

"Yes," said the Princess, "if anyone know, it's Jessac, and I think he served for a time in Lotzen Castle—have him here, Major, if you please."

The old man came, tall, slender, shrivelled of face, white and thin of hair, yet erect and vigorous, despite his almost four and a half score years. They raised men, and kept them long, in the tingling, snapping, life-giving air of the Voragian mountains.

"Don't kneel, Jessac," the Regent exclaimed, giving him her hand.

He bent and kissed it with the most intense devotion.

"My little Princess! my little Princess!" he repeated; "God is good to have let old Jessac see you once more before he dies." Then he straightened, and, turning sharply toward the Archduke, scanned him with an intentness almost savage. Suddenly his hand rose in salute. "Yes, you're a man, and a Dalberg, too—the finest Dalberg these old eyes ever saw."

And Armand understood, and went to him, and took his hand, and held it.

"Every one loves her, Jessac," he said, "but none quite as you and I." Then he drew him over to the table. "Do you know the interior of Lotzen Castle?" he asked.

"As I know this one, my lord—I lived in it for twenty years in my young days; even now I could go blindfolded from gate to highest turret."

"Is this plan accurate now? See, here is the gateway, and this is the keep."

"I understand, sir."—He studied it for a little while, following the lines with his finger, and muttering brokenly to himself, under his breath. "Yes, Your Highness, it's about the same, except that here is an outer building for servants, and here a storehouse; and the arrangement of the rooms in the main part is some different, particularly on the second floor, where several have been made out of one; but the stairway and hall are still as they always were. Indeed, sir, there has been small change or improvement since long before the present lord's father died. Duke Ferdinand had never visited it for more than a score of years, until a few weeks ago, just a little while before our gracious master was called———"

The old man was garrulous; so far, age had not missed him; and here the Archduke interrupted.

"Jessac," he said kindly, "you have made all that very clear; now can you tell us if there is any secret passage in the castle?"

"One, sir," was the prompt answer; "leastwise, I know one, there may be others."

"And it?"

"From the library to the postern gate, near the west tower—this is it, sir," indicating the line on the plan; "many is the time I've used it, his lordship being absent, when I wanted to get out at night; indeed, sir, there is a key to the postern still here, as well as duplicates to almost every door. They were not surrendered when King Henry gave the place to the late Duke—all the locks had been changed shortly before that. Would Your Highness care to see the keys?—they are in the armory."

"Bring them here," said the Constable quickly.... "I know by experience, sir, that if Jessac get you into the armory, you won't escape for hours; he has a story for every piece in it, and wants to tell them all."

The old man came back, a dozen large keys jangling; and laid them on the table.

"This is to the postern," he said; "it's smaller than the others, so it could be carried more easily, you know, sir—these brass tags, sir, show where they belong."

The Archduke looked them over.

"I don't see the key from the library to the secret passage," he said.

"There is none, sir; the big stone in the middle of the side wall of the library, and the one on the right just inside the postern arch, revolve when pushed at the upper edge—this way, Your Highness," and he demonstrated, using a book as the stone.

"Thank you, Jessac," said Armand, with a smile and a nod of dismissal; "we may want you again to-morrow. I'll keep the keys," and he swept them into a drawer of the desk.

Then the Constable withdrew, and for a while Armand and Moore studied the plan, and went over the problem confronting them; and which, though greatly simplified now, was still difficult and delicate beyond anything either had ever been obliged to solve. Perilous it was, too—but that neither regarded for himself; and Moore would gladly have assumed it alone could he have insured thereby the Archduke's safety.

Through it all the Princess watched them, harkening carefully to what was said, and saying a few things herself, mainly in the shape of questions which showed that, even if to her the draft did resemble an embroidery pattern, she was astonishingly apt at following the discussion. But when Armand remarked that he would make the attempt that very night, she interposed promptly.

"Wait until to-morrow," she urged; "take at least one night's rest; you need it; and the extra day may disclose something as to the situation in Lotzen Castle."

"To-night is the proper time," said the Archduke; "we may not be expected then; we shall be most assuredly to-morrow; it's our one chance for a surprise."

"And with our dear cousin that chance is no chance, as you are very well aware," said she; "he knows you are here, and why you are here, and he is ready for you this instant. No, no, dear, it's simply your natural impetuosity, which I came along to moderate; and here is my first veto: not to-night." She put her hand on his arm. "Please, Armand, please; don't you understand—I want to be sure of you a little longer; the day you enter Lotzen Castle may be our last."

Moore turned quickly away—and the Archduke looked once into the soft eyes, and at the adorable smile; and the eyes and the smile conquered, as eyes and smile always will when the one woman uses them, as the one woman always can, if she try.

"I ought not to let you persuade me," he said, with a half serious shake of his hand, "but—you're pretty hard to resist. At least, you won't prohibit my riding over toward the Castle, and having a look at it now, in broad day, if I promise not to venture inside nor very near."

"On the contrary, I should like to go with you; come, we will all go—you tell the Ambassador, and I'll get Helen and Elise," with a nod and a smile at Moore.

"A reconnaissance in force!" the Archduke laughed, when the Regent had gone; then he ordered the horses, and he and Moore went off to get into riding uniform.

A wide, macadamized avenue wound sharply down from the castle to the valley, where the roads were of the soil, soft and sandy. Once there, the six loosed bridle and sped away across the level country; nor drew rein but thrice until they came to the forks, where the road to Lotzen took off for its mile of tortuous ascent.

Here they halted, and Armand and Moore scanned through their glasses the Castle and its approach; and by riding a very little way up toward it, they were able to see the postern gate, which was on the edge of the hill about a third of the distance around from the bridge, and was approached by a narrow, rain-washed, boulder-strewn path, leading almost straight up the side of the acclivity. The moat ran only across the front, the almost sheer descent on the other sides of the wall having been deemed, even in the old days, quite sufficient protection against assault.

"Well," said the Archduke, as he shoved the glasses back into their case, "thank God, we have old Jessac to tell us how to find that postern path—and, Colonel, before we start, it might be wise for each of us to make his will, and to say good-bye to his lady, for, of a truth, it is going to be a rather serious business."

They rode back by way of Porgia, the garrison town, five miles down the valley. It was also the railway station for both Castles, though some years before, King Frederick had run a track over as close as possible to Dalberg, so his own train could always be at hand to hurry him away. And there it had brought the Regent that morning, and was now waiting, ready for instant use.

A regiment of Uhlans were at drill on the edge of the town, and the Princess waved her cocked hat to them as she cantered by. The Colonel in command answered with his saber, while from two thousand lusty throats went up a wild cheer of passionate devotion.

Armand reached over and patted her on the arm.

"Surely, dear, the soldiers love you," he said.

"They seem to,"—then out flashed the smile again; "but there is only one I'm sure of," leaning over close.

"You little temptress!" he said, "I've a great mind to prove it now."

She laughed merrily. "You may—but catch me first;" and as her horse had the heels of his, she never let him get quite on even terms, no matter what the pace.

"Come, dear," he said, "I'll promise to wait until we are at the Castle."

"As you wish—but the bend in the road yonder would have hid the others, and there I was—but until the Castle, then."

And when Armand promised double punishment later, she tossed her head, and told him she was always ready to pay for her crimes—and sometimes rather willing.

As they turned from the valley road into the avenue, they came face to face with the Duke of Lotzen and Count Bigler, both in full uniform.

The Princess was passing on, with a curt return of their salutes, when the Duke drew around in front of her.

"Your Royal Highness and myself seem to be unfortunate in our visits to each other," he said; "I missed yours the other evening, and now you have missed mine."

"You have been to Dalberg Castle?" she asked. He bowed. "For my call of ceremony upon the Regent."

She reined aside. "You are not on the Regent's list, sir," she said; "if you wish to save your dignity, you would best not present yourself until summoned."

"I assumed it was restored by your own informal visit," he smiled.—"Will you not honor Lotzen Castle, also?—and you, too, cousin Armand!"

But neither answered him by so much as a look, and with a mocking laugh he went on, saluting the American Ambassador with easy formality, and bestowing upon Mlle. d'Essoldé a leeringly suggestive smile, that made Moore frantic to strike him in the face.

The Princess' toilet was finished very early that evening, and then she sent for her Adjutant.

"Colonel Moore," said she, motioning him to be seated, "I am resolved that the Archduke shall not venture into Lotzen Castle to-morrow night, and therefore, I am going myself to-night; will you go with me?"

Moore's amazement deprived him of an immediate answer.

"But, Your Highness!—" he stammered.

"It is quite useless to protest; I'm going; if you do not care to escort me, I shall get Bernheim."

"Let me go alone," he urged.

"No."

"And the Archduke, what of him?" he asked.

"The Archduke stays here, serenely ignorant of it all."

"He will never forgive me——"

She cut him short. "Very well, monsieur, you are excused—be so good as to send Colonel Bernheim to me at once—and I trust to your honor not to mention the affair to any one."

He had done all he dared; more, indeed, than he had fancied she would tolerate. A subordinate may not argue for long with the Regent of a Kingdom, however sweet-tempered she may be.

"Your Highness misunderstands," he said; "if you are determined to go, there is an end of the matter; naturally, your Adjutant goes also."

She smiled. "Now, that is better—and I'm glad—and we will take De Coursey and Marsov, and slip away at midnight, with old Jessac for guide. The secret passage opens into the Duke's library, we get the Book and retire."

"Vault and all?" Moore asked.

"You don't remember the draft, Colonel, there isn't a vault."

"Doubtless, however, there is a safe."

She waved her hand impatiently. "It will be time enough for that when we get there."

"And if we can't find the Book in the library?" he persisted.

"Then we will seek it elsewhere—it's just that contingency which sends me. If I were sure it is in the library, I might let the Archduke go."

"Yet will you not take some precaution for your own safety, in event of Lotzen overcoming us?" Moore asked.

"I can't bring myself to believe that he would venture to harm the Regent, but, if he should, these," pushing two papers across to him, "ought to be sufficient."

"Your Highness is a strategist," said the Colonel, when he had read them. "I have nothing to suggest; and I'm ready now to go with a more willing spirit and a lighter heart."

She held out her hand, and flashed him the smile, usually reserved for Armand, alone.

"And we will save the king, Ralph—you and I; and give him the Book, and speed him to his crowning. I leave the details to you, to see the others, and instruct and caution them; remember, for the Archduke to get the slightest suspicion would ruin everything. It will be for me to see that he retires early to-night. Now, do you, yourself, seek out Bernheim and send him to me quickly."

"My good friend," said she, acknowledging Bernheim's stiff military salute with one equally formal, "I need your aid in a matter of peculiar importance and delicacy—and which must not, under any circumstance, be known to any one in the Castle, and above all not to His Highness the Archduke—not a whisper of it, Colonel Bernheim."

Bernheim's answer was another salute, but he could say as much with it, in an instant, as some men in an hour of talk.

"Here are two sealed orders," she continued; "immediately after dinner you will ride down to Porgia; there, not before, you will open the one addressed to yourself, and deliver the other to the Commanding Officer of the garrison. For the rest, the orders will speak for themselves."

Once more, the martinet's hand went up.

"Yes, Your Highness," he said; "but how am I to go without getting leave from the Archduke?"

"I will get it for you—you need not say anything to him—just go——Ah! there he is now—Armand," said she, when he had greeted her, "I want to borrow Colonel Bernheim for a little while after dinner, may I have him?"

"Take him," said the Archduke, with a smile at his Aide; and when Bernheim had gone: "but why don't you borrow me instead?"

"Because, sweetheart, one doesn't need to borrow what one has," she answered, and gave him both her hands.

XXI
IN THE DUKE'S LIBRARY

The Princess managed so well that by a little after eleven o'clock the card games were over, and she, laughingly, had escorted Armand to his own door and received his promise to retire at once.

Then she went to her apartment and dismissed all the attendants except her maid. To-night she must ride as a man, so she donned a close-fitting divided skirt, high boots, and her Blue Guard's jacket, and topped it with a long military overcoat that came almost to her spurs.

Colonel Moore met her at a side entrance, and they hurried across the courtyard and over the bridge to where, a little way down the avenue, were waiting De Coursey and Marsov, with Jessac and the horses. They had thought to send the old man in a carriage, but he would have none of it; so they let him have his way, when he assured them he could ride twice the distance without fatigue—and he proved it that night.

In calm persistence of purpose Dehra was a typical Dalberg; she had determined that the Archduke should not expose his life in Lotzen's castle, and so she was assuming the risk, without the least hesitation; just as the same Dalberg spirit sent the Archduke to recover the Book, heedless of the peril entailed. And so now, after a word of inquiry as to the general arrangements and the time required to reach the postern gate, she made no further reference to the business in hand. Instead, she chatted with Moore as unconcernedly as though she rode for her pleasure, and not upon a desperate mission where death was likely waiting for them all.

There was no moon, but the stars burned with double brilliancy in the wonderful mountain heavens; the road lay fair before them; and far off to the front the lights of Lotzen Castle beckoned. And as they crossed the valley, the lights gradually grew fewer, until presently there was but one remaining, which Jessac said was the big lamp on the bridge in front of the gate-arch, and which always burnt until sunrise.

A little way from the Lotzen road they met Colonel Bernheim, alone. He bent forward in sharp scrutiny.

"Thank God, Moore, you persuaded her not to come!" he exclaimed, as they drew up.

The Princess' light laugh answered him, and he actually cried out in distressed disappointment, and forgot the eternal salute.

"I wasn't to be persuaded, Colonel," said she. "Is everything arranged?"

This time the salute came.

"The dispositions are made as Your Highness ordered," he answered.

She thanked him, and he rode beside her to the cross-roads.

"I must leave you here.—Heaven keep you safe this night," he ended, with broken voice.

She reined over close to him and held out her hand.

"My good Bernheim, nothing is going to happen to me," she said; "but if there should, it will be for you and Epping to seat the Archduke where he belongs, and to confound Lotzen and his satellites—promise me."

The Colonel's face twitched, and his eyes glistened, and for a moment he bowed his head on his breast; then he leaned over and kissed her gauntlet.

"As God reigns, it shall be done, my mistress," he said; "and though I have to kill Lotzen with my own hand."

Instead of taking the road to the Castle they continued up the valley a little way, to where a narrow brook tumbled noisily across the track, eager to reach the foaming Dreer. Here Jessac dismounted, and, leading his horse, turned upstream. There was no path, and the starlight availed nothing in the heavy timber, yet the old man never hesitated, winding his way among the trees and around the rocks as readily as though it were day. After half a mile, the ground began to ascend sharply; almost immediately he halted, and at his direction they turned the horses over to the orderlies, and followed him on foot.

"The postern path, such as it is, is yonder," he said, and a few steps brought them to it, just where it ended its plunge down the bald side of the hill from the Castle that now towered almost straight above them, a mass of black forbiddingness respoussé against the sky-line by the reflection of the gate-way lamp.

Colonel Moore made a last appeal to the Princess to abandon her purpose to accompany them, and was good-naturedly overruled, and peremptorily ordered to lead on.

"Would you have a Dalberg retire with the enemy in sight?" she ended.

The postern path was now no path—only a narrow, water-washed gully; yet, even so, it was the only means of access to the summit from that side,—or indeed, from any side save in front—elsewhere the tangle of brambles and the rocks, with the almost perpendicular elevation, made ascent practically impossible by daylight, and absolutely impossible by night. In fact, this way had long been abandoned, and the present course lay close under the wall, and over the moat by a narrow foot bridge, and then along it to the road just below the main gate. Jessac had not ventured to use it, however, because it was exposed to the light of the lamp, and so was in full view of the porter on duty in the tower.

It was rough climbing, and half way up Moore called a halt, to give the Princess a short rest; then they went on, stumbling, slipping, scrambling, trying to go quietly, and yet, it seemed, making noise sufficient to wake every one in Lotzen Castle.

But at last they reached the top, and the Princess leaned against the wall, breathless and trembling from the unaccustomed exertion.

Moore raised his hand for silence. In the intense calm of the night, the lightest noise would have echoed trebly loud, yet the only sound they heard was the splashing of the Dreer among its rocks, in the fog strewn valley far below. He drew out his watch, and after much looking made out the time.

"It's after one o'clock," he whispered; "when Your Highness is ready——"

"I'm ready now," said she, and turned at once to the gate.

"Quiet, man, quiet!" Moore cautioned, as Jessac's key scraped into the lock, and suddenly turned it with a loud snap. The old man pushed the door back slowly; the arch was twenty feet through, and the darkness impenetrable; but he entered unhesitatingly, and the others with him, Moore's hand on the Regent's arm.

"Can you find the stone without a light?" he asked.

"Easily, sir! ... here it is—stand back, my lord, or it may hit you ... there!"

There was a slight creak, and Moore was sensible of something swinging up by his face.

"It's open, sir," said Jessac; "but best not show a light until we are inside, it might be seen in the courtyard—I'll go in first—bend low or you'll strike your head."

The Adjutant took Dehra's hand and having located the stone and the opening, he guided her through. Jessac closed the stone into place and then, by the light of Moore's electric torch, he showed them how it was so balanced that by pressure at the top (from without) or at the bottom (from within) it would swing around parallel with the floor.

The passage was large enough for two of them to walk abreast and without stooping, and extended through the heart of the wall, about a hundred feet, until opposite the keep, as Jessac informed them; here it narrowed to half, and by a dozen stone steps descended below the level of the bailey, and thence under it to another set of steps leading up inside the wall of the keep.

Thus far they had come rapidly and without incident. Suddenly a drove of rats, blinded by the light and squeaking in terror, ran among their feet, and the Princess instinctively caught up the skirts of her long coat, and, with a little shriek of fright, tried to climb up the side of the passage.

The cry, slight as it was, let loose all the echoes of the vault with appalling resonance; instantly Moore extinguished the torch and laid his hand on her arm.

"What a fool I am!" she exclaimed in a whisper; "now, I've spoiled everything."

"Not likely," he assured her; "the castle is asleep and the walls are thick, but we best wait a bit."

Presently the rats commenced to squeak again, and to scurry about, and the Princess beginning to tremble, he switched on the torch and motioned Jessac to proceed.

Treading as lightly as one of his own mountain cats, the old fellow went swiftly up the stairs, and when the others reached the top he was not to be seen. Moore shot the light down the passage; thirty feet away, if the draft were correct, were the stairs that ended at the library; when they reached them, Jessac was on the landing signaling to come on.

He drew the Colonel over to the big stone.

"There used to be a crack along the edge here," he said, very low, "where I could listen, and also see a very little, but it seems to have been closed. Shall I swing the stone, sir?"

Moore hesitated. What lay behind the stone? His last look at the library windows, from far down the hillside, had shown no light within; yet was it really so, or was it only that the curtains were drawn? If the Princess would but consent to remain here, at least until he had gone in and inspected. He glanced at her uncertainly, and she read his mind, and shook her head.

"I follow *you*," she said.

With a sigh, he adjusted his mask; she and De Coursey and Marsov did the same.

"Does the stone move easily?" he asked.

"It did when I used it, sir," said Jessac.

"Can you open it only a trifle at first?"

"No, my lord, once started it must make its swing."

"And if there be something in the way?"

"There never used to be, sir; it was always kept clear."

"Then pray Heaven it is so still." He loosed his sword and shut off the torch. "Open!" he ordered.

"It seems to hold, sir," said Jessac presently; "I can't move it—may I have the light a moment?... Now, I'll try again."

They heard him pushing; gently, then harder, finally with all his strength.

"I can't do it, my lord," he said; "it's either out of balance or has been closed on the inside."

The Princess gave an exclamation of alarm.

"What!" said she impatiently, "it can't be opened?—we have failed? impossible, it must be opened—try again, Jessac."

"May be it's only jammed," said Moore; "come, I'll help you."

But still the stone refused to stir—suddenly it moved a very little—caught—moved a little more—caught again—then wrenched itself free, with a grinding scrape, and swung slowly around.

They heard it collide with something; the next moment came a terrific crash of shattering glass, and the resounding clatter of a metal tray.

Moore ground back an oath.

"Close the stone!" said he instantly, "quick, man, quick!"

But though it seemed to take an eternity to shut down, there was not the slightest sound, or other indication that any one had been aroused.

"What shall we do?" he asked the Princess; "that din must have been heard; shall we wait and risk another try, or escape now by the postern before we could be cut off?"

"We will risk another try," said she, at once. "Give the word whenever you wish."

For himself he was well content; his fighting blood was up, and here might be his opportunity to have it out with Lotzen, so he settled back to wait, harkening for the sound of any one coming by the passage; the location of the broken glass would tell the Duke instantly the cause, and his first act, naturally, would be to send a party around to intercept them; though, being a stranger in his own castle, he might not know of the secret way, in which case the accident would have no materially adverse result save, possibly, to startle those within hearing from a sound sleep.

And while they delayed, Moore gossiped in whispers with the Regent, hoping to divert her, if only a very little, from the heavy strain she must be under—the blackness was enough, in itself, for a woman to endure, without the danger. And he marvelled at her calmness and ease, and the light laugh which came at times.

"It's good of you, Colonel," said she finally, "but I think I'm past fearing now. I was horribly afraid at first, and the rats almost made me faint with terror, but now I'm sort of dazed, dreaming, automatic, whatever it is—when the reaction comes, there likely will be hysterics—but that shan't be until all this is ended—it's this inaction that is the most trying."

Moore touched Jessac.

"How long have we been waiting?" he asked.

"Well on to half an hour, sir."

"Then swing the stone."

This time it moved instantly and noiselessly. Moore put his head through the opening and listened;... save for the ticking of a clock, somewhere across the room, there was perfect quiet.... Suddenly it chimed twice; when the last reverberation had died, he stepped carefully inside; the Princess and the others followed.

The library was as dark as the passage; with a touch of warning to the Regent, Moore pressed the torch and flashed the stream of white light around the walls—fortune favored them; the room was unoccupied, and every door was closed. Then the light struck the iron safe, and the Princess, with the faintest exclamation of apprehension, grasped her Adjutant's arm and pointed at it. If the Book were in it, their visit would be barren; there was neither opportunity nor means to break inside. For the first time, the idea of failure touched her—she had been so full of assurance, so confident that once in the Duke's library and success was certain. Even when Moore suggested a safe she had waved it aside heedlessly. Her mind had been centered on the desk—that the Book must surely be in it. The light reached the big, flat-topped one in the middle of the room; with a quick spring she was at it, and Moore beside her.

Swiftly they went through the drawers—nothing ... nothing ... nothing ... ah! a bundle in black cloth—she tossed it out and fairly tore loose the strings—a glance was enough—leather—metal hinges—the Book! the Book! at last!

In an agony of delight she flung the cloth around it.

"Come!—come!——"

A shrill whistle—the doors were thrown open wide; in bounded three men, a lighted candelabra in each hand, and behind them a dozen more with rifles leveled. At the same moment, the Duke himself stepped from behind a curtain, and closed the stone into place.

At the whistle, De Coursey, Marsov and old Jessac had sprung to Dehra's side and, with Moore, ranged themselves around her—and now they stood there, five masked figures, swords drawn, the center of a circle of impending death, every man ready to fling himself upon the guns and chance it, but restrained because of her they were sworn to guard.

AT THE WHISTLE, DE COURSEY, MARSOV AND OLD JESSAC HAD SPRUNG TO DEHRA'S SIDE.

The Duke gave a chuckling laugh.

"Altogether a very striking picture," he remarked, with a wave of his hand around the room; "the candles—the masks—the swords—the guns—the attitudes;—it is a pity, Cousin Armand, you cannot see it as I do."

"He thinks I am the Archduke," Moore whispered to the Regent; "let him think it."

"Your coming to-night was a surprise," the Duke was saying, "I admit it—I had not expected you before to-morrow at the earliest—my compliments on your expeditiousness." He drew out a cigarette and lighted it at one of the candles—then flung the box over on the desk; "help yourselves, messieurs, *la dernière cigarette*," he laughed with sneering malevolence.

"Keep perfectly still," Moore cautioned, very low. "If it come to the worst, I'll try to kill him first."

"Did you address me, cousin?" Lotzen asked; "a little louder, please—and keep your hand outside your coat; the first of you who tries for his revolver will precipitate a massacre—even poor marksmen can't well miss at such a distance, and on the whole, these fellows are rather skilful." He smoked a bit in silence, tapping the splintered glass on the floor with the point of his sword. "Behold, cousin, my preservers—a decanter and some slender Venetian goblets; queer things, surely, to decide the fate of a Kingdom. But for their fall, you would have won. Now——" he glanced significantly toward the ready rifles. "Yet, on the whole, I wish you had waited until another night—it could have been done elsewhere so much more neatly—before you got here—or saw that, the package in the black cloth. You came upon me so suddenly, I had time only to take you—and now that I have you, frankly, cousin, I'm at a loss how to dispose of you—and your good friends.... Come, I'll be generous; choose your own way, make it as easy as you like—only, *make it*."

A slight stir caused him to turn. Madeline Spencer, in a shimmering white negligée, was standing in the doorway.

"Ah, my dear, come here," he said; "this is altogether the best point of view for the picture: 'The End of the Game' is its title—is it not, cousin?"

In this woman's life there had been many scenes, strange, bizarre, fantastic, yet never one so fiercely fateful as was this. And for once she was frightened—the flickering candelabra held aloft—the leveled guns—the masked group around the desk—the lone man leaning nonchalantly on a chair, smiling, idly indifferent, as much the master of it all as a painter, brush poised before his canvas, able to smear it out at a single stroke.

He held out his hand to her. She shook her head, meaning to go away; yet lingering, fascinated and intense. Armand Dalberg was yonder—on the brink of the grave, she knew. Once she had loved him—still loved him, may be—but assuredly not as she loved herself, and the power of wealth and place. Nor could she save him even if she try; so much she knew beyond a question, so, why try.

The Duke faced his prisoners.

"Come, cousin mine, what shall it be: swords, bullets, poison? Time passes. You have disturbed me at an unseemly hour, and I must to sleep again.... No answer, cousin? Truly, you have changed; once your tongue was free enough; and it's not from fright, I'm sure; that, I will grant—you're no more afraid than am I myself. However, if you won't choose, I'll have to do it for you.... You came by the secret passage, and by it shall you return—part way—bound, but not gagged, it won't be necessary; please appreciate my leniency. Then, while you are lying quietly there, the revolving stones shall be sealed so tight that mortal man can never find them. Is it not a fine plan, cousin, to have been devised so quickly; and are you not proud of the mausoleum that you, a poor, unknown American, will have: the titular castle of Valeria's new King?"

At first, the Princess had been cold with terror—the muzzles of loaded rifles at ten paces, are not for women's nerves; but as the Duke talked she grew calmer, and the fear subsided, and anger came instead. And even as he seemed to take a devilish pleasure in grilling his victims with rage-provoking words, so she let him run along, to dig his own grave the deeper.

Now she stepped out from the group, and dropped her mask.

"Which cousin do you think you have been addressing, my lord of Lotzen?" she asked, taking off her hat.

The commotion in the room was instant; but the Duke stayed it with an angry gesture. His men were foreigners, and free of any sentiment beyond the sheen of gold.

"So, you little fool," he laughed, "you have dared to come here, too! Do you fancy that even you can save your upstart lover?"

"If you mean His Royal Highness the Archduke Armand," said she, very quietly, "he needs no saving—he is not here."

There was but one person in all the world whose word Ferdinand of Lotzen would accept as truth: he knew the Princess Dehra never lied. And now he sprang up.

"Not here!" he cried, "not here!"

She turned to her companions.

"Messieurs, will you do me the courtesy to unmask?"

The Duke ran his eyes over the four, and shrugged his shoulders.

"I thank you, messieurs," said he, "I shall not forget you, believe me I shall not.—But where, cousin, is His Royal Highness the Archduke Armand?" (sneering out every word of the title). "Did you lose him on the way?—or is he skulking in the passage."

Dehra laughed scornfully. "You change front quickly; a moment since you doubted his courage no more than your own. This is my own adventure; neither the Archduke, nor any one else in Dalberg Castle, is aware of it."

Lotzen bowed. "My thanks, cousin, for that last bit of news—I know the better, now, how to dispose of you and your friends."

The Princess walked over and sat on the corner of the desk.

"Am I to understand, my lord, that you would attempt to restrain me and my escort from leaving this castle?"

"Those who enter a residence with criminal intent, and are apprehended in the act, can hardly expect to escape unscathed. You have overlooked the fact, doubtless, that the privilege of high justice still attaches to this domain, though long since unexerted. Just what that justice will be I have not decided— enough, at present, that you are prisoners awaiting sentence, and since none will ever seek you here, I can let events determine when and where it will be pronounced."

And Dehra understood just what was in his mind.

"Which is another way of saying, cousin, that when you have killed the Archduke or made him prisoner, it will be time enough to pass judgment on us."

The Duke gave his chuckling laugh.

"Your Highness has the wisdom of a sage," he said; "and I advise you to employ it during your sojourn here, in ascertaining just what attitude is likely to be the best for yourself, after the American has been—eliminated."

And now the anger, which had been burning hotter and hotter, burst into flame.

"Do you fancy, Ferdinand of Lotzen," she exclaimed, striking a chair with the flat of her sword, "that I would venture into this den without first having made ample provision for our safe return? Around this place, at this moment, stretches a cordon of three thousand soldiers with orders to let no one pass the lines, and if by sunrise I have not returned, to take this Castle by assault and show no quarter. Colonel Bernheim is in command. I fancy you will admit that he will execute the orders."

"I will," said Lotzen.

"And if you doubt as to the troops, you can send and———"

"I will admit the troops also, cousin."

The Princess put the cloth-wrapped book under her arm and stood up.

"Then, if you will clear the doorway, we will depart."

"Not so fast, my dear," he smiled; "you seem to have missed the fact that a written command is quite as effective as an oral one; therefore, you will oblige me by taking of the paper and ink on the desk beside you, and inditing to Colonel Bernheim an order to withdraw instantly all the troops to Porgia, and himself to join you here—but first, you will favor me by returning that bundle to the drawer where you got it."

The Princess glanced uncertainly at Moore, hesitated, then handed the bundle to him, and turning to the desk wrote rapidly for a few minutes—read over the sheet, and held it out to the Duke.

He took it with a bow, and went back to his place.... The order was clear and unequivocal, almost in his own words, indeed. Her ready acquiescence had amazed him—now doubt came, and then suspicion—was he being outwitted? Had she provided for just such a contingency? He read the order again—then put it in its envelope and went toward the corridor door. He would have to chance it.

"One moment, cousin," said the Princess; "you may as well know that the only effect of that order, or any other, save from my own lips, will be to bring the assault forthwith, instead of at sunrise. It's for you to choose which it shall be."

He turned and regarded her contemplatively; and she spoke again.

"What is the profit now in restraining us? You have been playing for a Crown—you have lost;" (pointing to the book) "but why lose your life, too—though, frankly, as to that, save for the nasty scandal, I have no concern."

His face hardened. "There could be a few lives lost here before sunrise," he answered.

She smiled indifferently, though her heart beat faster at the threat; she had risked everything on her firm conviction that his cool, calculating brain would never be run away with by anger nor revenge—and the test was now.

"Assuredly, my dear Ferdinand," said she, "you can have us killed—and then the sunrise."

But he stared at her unrelentingly, and fear began to crowd upon her fast.

"Have we lost?" she said very low to Moore. "Have I brought you all to death?"

"It depends on the next minute," he replied; "if we live through it we're safe. He will have quit seeing red then."

And Madeline Spencer saw that he was hesitating; swiftly she went to him, and taking his hand, spoke to him softly and with insistent earnestness.

Gradually the frown faded; the fell look passed; at last, he smiled at her and nodded.

"We win," said Moore.

The Duke turned toward the corridor door and gave an order; the men drew aside into line, rifles at the present. Then he bowed low to the Princess.

"Since I know I may not do the honor myself," he said, "I pray you will accept my Constable as my substitute.—Captain Durant, escort Her Royal Highness the Regent to the main gate."

Durant stepped forward and his blade flashed in salute. Dehra acknowledged it with her own, then snapped it back into its sheath.

"Lead on, sir!" she said very graciously, and gave him her hand.

Without so much as a glance at the Duke, she passed from the room; and on the other side of her went Colonel Moore, sword in one hand, the cloth-wrapped book in the other.

When they had gone, Lotzen dismissed every one with a nod, and sitting down drew Madeline Spencer on his knee.

"You're my good angel," he said; "you came at the psychological moment; another instant and I would have sent them all to the devil."

She slipped her arm around his neck, and kissed him lightly on the cheek.

"And then the sunrise," she whispered, with a shudder.

He caught her to him.

"And even Paris is better than that, my duchess!" he cried; "Paris or anywhere, with you."... Presently he laughed. "I should like to see Dehra's face when she opens that book," he said.

Madeline Spencer sprang up, pointing to the clock.

"We are wasting time," she exclaimed. "Don't you see that we must go to Dornlitz this very night—that, now, to-morrow will be too late."

"You're right!" he said; and, with wrinkled brow and half-closed eyes, sat, thinking—then: "We may not use a special train, for we must go disguised; but the express for the South passes Porgia at four o'clock; we will take it; if it's on time we shall be in Dornlitz at seven in the evening, which will allow us an hour to get to the Summer Palace—after eight o'clock not even I would be admitted, in the absence of the Regent. Should we be delayed, as is very likely, we can go out early the following morning. The American won't know we left here, and will not be in any state to return—and even if he is, it's not probable he will leave before late to-morrow night, which will bring him to the Capital about noon—long after we have been in the library and got the Book." He strode to the door and shouted into the corridor for Durant.... "Captain," said he, "have the fastest pair and strongest carriage before the door at once. Madame and I are off instantly for the Capital; but see that no one in the Castle knows it; close the gates, and let none depart. In half an hour, send four of your trustiest men to cut the telephone line, in various places, between Porgia and Dalberg Castle; keep it cut all day, and prevent, in every way possible, any messages reaching the Castle. If the Regent, or the American Archduke, leave by train before to-morrow night, wire me immediately. Do you understand?—then away.... Come along, Duchess, only ten minutes to dress!"

With a laugh he swung her up in his arms and bore her to the doorway, snatched a kiss, and left her.

XXII
THE BOOK IN THE CLOTH

As is usually the case when a man retires before his accustomed hour, the Archduke's slumber was capricious and broken, finally ending in complete wakefulness and an intense mental activity that defied sleep. At length he switched on the reading lamp beside his bed and looked at his watch. It was only three o'clock. With an exclamation of disgust he got up and dressed, and went down to the library. The draft of Lotzen Castle was not as distinct in his mind as it should be; he would have another careful look at it and then, alone on the ramparts, with plenty of room to walk and think, he would work out the plan of campaign for the morrow.

He had put the plan and Jessac's keys together in the desk, the top drawer on the right.—They were not there—nor in the next one—nor the next—nor the next—they were not in any of them. He searched again, and carefully ... they were gone. He went to the far corner where Major Meux had got the portfolio; its place was empty. He frowned in puzzled irritation; who would have presumed to meddle with them? Moore, possibly, to study the draft, but he would not have taken the keys; they would be wanted only when——

"God! might it be!" he cried aloud, "might it be!"

His mind flashed back through the day: Dehra's solicitude that he should not go to-night—borrow Bernheim—early to bed—a dozen other trifles now most indicative. With a curse at his stupidity, he ran to Moore's quarters—empty—the bed untouched; then to Bernheim's—the same there; to De Coursey's—to Marsov's—both the same. He burst unannounced into the ante-chamber of the Princess' apartments, bringing a shriek from each of the sleepy maids.

"Your mistress—is she here?" he demanded.

"Her Highness retired hours ago, sir," one of them replied tremblingly, fright still upon her.

"But is she there now?—Send Marie here instantly."

The French girl came, wrapped in a long chamber robe.

"Is your mistress asleep?" he asked.

"Yes, Monsieur le Prince, hours ago."

He reached over and flung back her robe.

"Then why are you still dressed and waiting up for her? Don't lie to me, girl; where is Her Highness?"

"Monsieur doubts me?"

The Archduke made an angry gesture.

"Go to her—say I must speak with her at once."

"Wake the Regent! I dare not, sir."

He pushed her aside and went on into the next room. She sprang after, and caught his hand.

"Your Highness!" she cried, "you would not!—you would not!"

He seized her by the arm. "You little fool! the truth—the truth—if your mistress isn't here, she is in awful peril—may be dead." He shook her almost fiercely. "The truth, I say, the truth!"

With a cry the girl sank to the floor.

"Peril!—death!" she echoed. "She but went for a ride, sir; I do not understand——"

The Archduke was gone; he required no further information.

A quarter of an hour later, with thirty of the garrison at his back—all that could be provided with horses—he set out for Lotzen Castle; leaving it for Courtney, whose official position denied him the privilege of going along, to telephone the Commandant at Porgia for troops.

"She went to save me, Dick," he said; "now I will save her or——good-bye," and the two men had gripped hands hard, then the Archduke rode away.

At first, his anger had been hot against Moore and Bernheim, but now that sober second thought was come, he knew that they were not to blame, that the Regent herself had ordered them to the service and to silence. And presently his hope rose at the thought of the one's skilful sword and sure revolver, and the other's steady head and calm discretion; together, with De Coursey and Marsov, there might be a chance that the Princess would come out alive. But the hope grew suddenly very slender, as he reached the valley road and saw the great light of Lotzen Castle shining far away, and remembered his own sensations as he had stood under it that afternoon, and who its master was and what.

They had been obliged to go slowly down the steep and winding avenue, now he swung into a gallop and the six score hoofs went thundering through the valley, leaving the startled inhabitants staring, and wondering at the strange doings of all who came from the South. But them the Archduke never saw—nor anything, indeed, save the track before him and the light ahead, riding with hands low on the saddle, face set and stern; implacable and relentless as the first Dalberg himself, the day he rescued his lady from that same Castle of Lotzen and hung its Baron in quarters from the gate tower.

Only once did the Archduke pause; at the Dreer, a moment to breathe the horses and let them wet their throats. In the darkness he did not see a bunch of horsemen round the turn in front and trot slowly toward him, nor could he hear them for the thrashing of his own horses in the water. The first he knew of them was Colonel Moore's peremptory hail:

"What force is that yonder?"

With a shout that rang far into the night, Armand sent his mare bounding through the stream.

"The Princess? the Princess?" he cried, "is she safe?"

And her own voice answered, joyful and triumphant.

"I'm here, Armand, I'm here."

What need to tell what he said, as reining in close he drew her over to him! The words were a bit incoherent, may be, but Dehra understood; and presently she put her arms around his neck and kissed him.

"Come, Sire," she said, "let us go on—and when we get to the Castle, Your Majesty shall have again the Book of Laws."

"The Book! you cannot mean you've been in Lotzen Castle?"

She laughed her merry little laugh. "And out again—and the Book with us, from under our dear cousin's very eyes."

"You brave girl!—you foolish child!—you wonder among women!" he marvelled.

She put out her hand, and took his; and so they rode, back through the valley and up the avenue to the Castle, and as they went she told him the story of the night.

"But better than the Book, sweetheart," she ended, as they drew up before the entrance, "it saves you for Valeria and for me; had you been there, helpless under his guns, not all the troops in the Kingdom would have held Lotzen's hand."

"And better than all else," he said, as he swung her down, "is your own dear self."

"Nonsense," she replied, "I'm but a woman—you are the Dalberg and a King.... Colonel Moore, bring your package to the library, and summon all our friends."

When they had come, the Princess took the bundle, still wrapped in its black cloth, and handed it to Armand.

"Sire," said she, "the Laws of the Dalbergs—found this night in Lotzen Castle."

Without a word he bent and kissed her hand,—then, laying the package on the desk, he cut the strings and removed the cloth, exposing the big, leather-covered, brass-bound volume.

"Read the decree, Sire!" she exclaimed.

He opened the book—stopped—turned a page—then slowly closed it.

"Suppose we wait, Your Highness, until the Royal Council is present," he said.

But something in his voice alarmed her—she sprang forward, pushed aside his restraining arm, and seized the book. One glance inside—an exclamation of bewildered incredulity; another glance—and the book dropped to the floor.

"False!" she cried, "false!" and flung herself across the desk in an hysteria of tears.

Instantly Courtney turned and quitted the room, and the rest after him, leaving her and the Archduke alone together.

It was evening when the Princess appeared again. She came just as the clock was striking nine, and taking the American Ambassador's arm, led the way in to dinner, which here was *en famille*, and without any ceremony of the Court.

"Tell me, Mr. Courtney, that I don't look quite so foolish as I feel," she laughed.

He let his eyes linger on her—this lovely woman who was a nation's toast—the imperially poised head, with the glorious, gleaming hair, and the haughty, high-bred face that, when she willed, could be so sweet and tender; the slender, rounded figure in its soft white gown of clinging silk—he shook his gray head.

"If you feel as you look," he answered, "you are not of this world, but of Paradise."

"O——h, monsieur! and Lady Helen just across the table."

He fingered his imperial a moment, then leaned close.

"Helen is an angel, too," he said.

"You mean—?" she exclaimed.

He smiled. "Yes, I mean—on our ride this afternoon—but don't tell it, now."

She took his hand low under the board.

"I'm so glad," she said; "Helen's a dear—and so are you." Then she gave a little laugh. "This seems to have been a rather busy afternoon for Cupid."

"Another?—Mlle. d'Essoldé and Moore?"

She nodded. "Yes, but not a word of it, either—not even to Helen," quizzically.

"No, not even to Helen," he said with well affected gravity, his lips twitching the while.

A footman entered and passed a note to Colonel Bernheim, but the Princess' eyes had caught the pink of the envelope and she knew it was a wire, and of exceeding importance to be brought there now—and it was for the Archduke; if it were for her, Moore would have got it. Chatting gayly with Courtney, she yet watched Bernheim, as he read the message, holding it down, out of sight.

It seemed to be very brief, for almost instantly he glanced at the Archduke—hesitated—then sent it to him.

"What is it, Armand?" she said, as he took it. "What has Lotzen done now?"

"Why Lotzen?" he laughed, spreading the sheet on the cloth before them.

It was dated Dornlitz:—

> "The Duke arrived here at eight-thirty this evening on the express from the North. He was in disguise.
>
> "Epping."

"I don't understand," said she.

"Neither do I," he answered; "that's the trouble with our cousin, he is always doing queer things."

"But he was at Lotzen Castle this morning."

"And is in Dornlitz now;—" he shoved the wire across to Courtney.—"Dick, what do you make of this—what's doing now?"

Courtney read it, then stared thoughtfully into his wine glass, twirling it slowly the while, the amber bubbles streaming upward.

"I make enough of it," he said, "to urge that you hurry back to the Capital. The false Book was intended primarily to lure you here, where you could be killed more easily, but its purpose also was to get you away from Dornlitz. The first failed, because Her Highness forced Lotzen's hand so quickly he was unprepared; the second, however, has won,—he has eluded you. I have always insisted that he hasn't the Book, but now I am persuaded that he knows where it is, and has gone for it."

"Let us go, Armand!" the Princess exclaimed—"let us go instantly."

He put his hand on her arm.

"We will go, dear," he said—"see—" and turning over the sheet, he wrote:—

"Epping,

"Dornlitz.

"Keep him under surveillance. We leave to-night; reach Dornlitz by ten A. M.

"Armand."

"Yes," said the Princess, "and add that he is to call the Royal Council for half after ten at the Summer Palace.—I'm going to give Lotzen a chance to explain a few things."

XXIII
THE CANOPY OF SWORDS

When the train had crossed the Lorg and the towers of Dornlitz shone far off to the front, the following morning, the Princess sent for the Archduke.

"Armand," said she, "I have been thinking—much of the night, indeed—and I am persuaded that this day will see the end of our quest; don't smile; wait, wait until the day has passed. Lotzen knows where the Book is—he hasn't it—he never has had it—he would not have needed a counterfeit if he had; besides, do you fancy he would have left it behind when he went to Lotzenia—or that he would have come back here if he had it with him? If he knows now where the Book is, he has known all along—then why hasn't he got it? Because it's been impracticable, no adequate opportunity. Where is the opportunity now that he hasn't had before?—the Summer Palace—with the Household gone, he can spend a day in it without explanation or interruption—and the King's suite is vacant. There Adolph hid the Laws—and Lotzen knows where—and they are what he has gone for; that is why he left his Castle night before last, within an hour after me; he realized the false book would send us back to Dornlitz and that he must go instantly if he would be there first. Oh, it's all plain now—to me at least."

The Archduke went over and stood beside her, stroking her fair hair softly with his finger tips.

"Sweetheart," said he, "there is much force in what you say, and you will also remember that Elise d'Essoldé saw Lotzen come from the library the day you charged him with killing Adolph and stealing the Book. Yet the answer to it all is, that the entire Palace has been searched and vainly—and the King's suite torn almost into bits. Hence, under the facts, your theory seems unavailing."

She looked up at him with a half disappointed smile, but with an insistent shake of the head.

"You go too far with your facts, dear," she said; "I, too, thought that every inch of the King's suite had been searched, but I've changed my mind; it hasn't been—if it had, we would have found the Laws."—She gave a cry and sprang up. "The box, Armand! the box! the Book's in it."

He looked at her in amazement.

"The box was empty," he said.

"Yes—*was! was!* but is not now! When did you look in it last?"

"At the Council."

"Exactly—so did I—and Adolph brought it to us, lid down and 'locked,' she said. Oh, I see it all now:—it wasn't locked, and he put the Book back in it, and told Lotzen, and Lotzen killed him—and then, when he came for the Book, he found the combination changed—you did it, you know—and as long as Moore was in the suite he could not break the vault; so he lures us all away: if he can kill you, he will be King and can get the Book at his leisure; if he fail, as he has done, then it's the Laws before we return." She flung her arms around his neck. "Don't tell me I'm mistaken, Armand! don't tell me I'm mistaken!"

He held her off, and looked at her in wondering admiration.

"Oh woman!" he said, "oh faith, and intuition, and loyalty beyond the stars! No, Dehra, I will not say you are mistaken; I do not know; we will test it. We will go straight to the Palace—you and I, without a word as to our purpose—and we will open the vault, and the box—and if the Laws are in it, yours be the glory."

"And yours the Crown!" she cried, and kissed his hand.

Then the train ran into the station and stopped, and the Archduke stepped out and gave his hand to the Princess. The platform was empty save for Count Epping.

"Your Royal Highness will pardon the informality of your reception," the Prime Minister said, when the greetings were over; "I assumed you did not want Lotzen to know of your coming; I even waited until nine o'clock to call the Council;—and I did not notify him, and so warn him that we had penetrated his disguise."

"Where is he now?" the Princess asked.

"At Ferida Palace—he went there last night and has not left it since."

"I think I want him at the Council," she said; "Colonel Moore, will you and Colonel Bernheim please go and summon him; then follow us at once; and do you, my dear Count, come to me as soon as the Ministers have assembled."

The brougham flashed away, and the Archduke drew down the blinds.

Dehra gave a satisfied little sigh and sank back in the corner.

"We seem to have beaten him," she said; "we shall have the first look into the box."

Armand put his arm around her, and drew the fair head to his shoulder.

"I have already beaten him," he said—"we fought first, for you, little girl. A fig for the box, and the Book and the Crown!"

At the gate of the Park the Princess signaled to halt, and raised the blind.

"Who of the Royal Council have arrived?" she asked the officer on duty.

"His Royal Highness the Duke of Lotzen, General Du———" he got no further.

"To my private entrance! quick, quick!" she called, and the carriage shot away....

"What does it mean?" she demanded; "Epping said Lotzen had not left the Ferida."

"It means that you have solved the riddle. Lotzen has not come to the Council, he does not even know of it; he has come for the Book."

They drew up at the door, the Archduke opened it with Dehra's key, and they dashed up stairs. She snatched a master-key from a drawer of her writing table, and they crossed the corridor and entered the King's suite through the small reception room, between which and the library lay a cabinet and a bedroom.

As they entered the latter, treading cautiously, they heard the Duke of Lotzen's voice in the library, the door of which stood ajar.

"It's a pity to break it," he was saying, "but——" and there was a snap and crack.

Under the Archduke's hand the door opened noiselessly, and through the narrow rift, between the hangings, they could see within.

The Duke, no longer disguised but wearing the undress uniform of his rank, was standing at the large desk; beside him an officer in a long cape and a Cuirassier helmet; and before him the big, black box of the Laws. He had just forced the lock; now he laid back the lid, and took out the Book.

"We win, Duchess!" he said, "we win! thanks to your marvellous fingers and quick brain," and lifting the helmet from Madeline Spencer's high piled hair, he kissed her ardently.

"Not so, cousin!" said the Princess, flinging aside the curtain, "you lose—it is we who win."

For a moment the Duke stood staring, too amazed to speak, and Mrs. Spencer, with a sharp cry, fled to his side; then, as he saw the end of his dream, the passing of his hopes, the fierce and fiery spirit, that was always burning deep in his soul, burst through the gyves of studied equanimity his stern will had imposed.

"Not yet!" he cried, "not yet!" and turning quickly he tossed the Book into the big chimney behind him where a wood fire burned.

"Come on!" he taunted, flashing out his sword, "come on, cousin Armand!—there's your crown, come get it!"

"Look to the Book, Dehra!" the Archduke called, and sprang at Lotzen, with a joyful smile. "At last!" he said, and the fight began.

"Push the Book farther into the fire, Madeline!" the Duke ordered, the words timed to the beat of the steel.

Dropping her cape Mrs. Spencer, with the easy hand of a practiced fencer, whipped out the sword she was wearing, in her disguise as an officer, and was speeding to obey, when Dehra caught up one of Colonel Moore's swords from the corner and rushed upon her.

"Guard yourself, Duchess!" Lotzen cried; and she swung around just in time to throw herself between the Princess and the fireplace. Instantly their blades rang together.

The Archduke heard, and out of the side of his eye he saw, and his brow wrinkled in anxiety. Spencer was no novice; she, too, he knew, had learned the gentle art of the foils in her youth, and under French *maîtres*, and she was not to be despised even by one so skilful as the Regent. He had little doubt that he could kill the Duke, but what profit in it if Dehra died. He hesitated to speak, it might disconcert her, and yet he must warn her.

"Watch her play in tierce," he said, in the most casual tone; and almost shouted for joy, when he heard Dehra's little laugh, and her voice calm and easy.

"Thank you, Armand!"

But it very nearly cost him his own life, for in trying to catch a glimpse of her he had loosed his eye-grip, and Lotzen's point shot out viciously, and only a lucky swing aside sent it scraping along the skin instead of through the neck.

"Rather close, cousin!" he remarked.

"The next will be closer," said the Duke softly. "Meanwhile, the Book burns."

But the Archduke did not fall into the trap, and loose the eye-grip a second time.

"Let it burn!" he answered, "I'd rather kill you than save it—but I will do both."

"If you can, cousin! if you can—" and the swords rang on.

And the Duke was right—the Book was burning, slowly, but burning none the less. His throw had been a trifle short, and instead of being in the heart of the fire it was on the outer edge, where the coals were not so glowing. There the leather and metal cover had protected it for a short while, but now the tiny flames were crawling along the edges, shooting up quick pencils of light that flared ever higher and more frequent.

And Dehra caught the gleam when it flashed the brightest, and in a fury of desire she drove at Madeline Spencer. Hitherto she had aimed only to disarm her, now it was the Book at any price.

But the American woman's defense was still impenetrable; defence was her forte—trick, feint, attack, she knew every one, and always her sword blocked them or turned them aside. But there she had stopped; never once had she herself assumed the offensive. She would take no chance of killing the Regent; and she had soon discovered the Regent was not aiming to kill her. But now she felt the change, and she knew that it was a matter of only a little while until she would have to yield or be sped. She could hear Lotzen and the Archduke, at the other end of the room, still fighting as fiercely as at the beginning;—the taunting laugh; the quip given, and returned; the crash of a chair as one of them kicked it away; but all she saw was the flitting steel before her, and the Princess' glowing eyes.

Of a sudden there came a burst of voices, the door toward the Council Chamber was dashed open, and Count Epping rushed in, and all the Ministers behind him.

Madeline Spencer drew back and lowered her sword; the Princess sprang to the fire-place and rescued the Book, smothering the flames with the hearth rug; but Lotzen ground out an oath and flung himself with fresh fierceness at the Archduke.

At first even the imperturbable Prime Minister had been too astonished to act; now he came slowly forward, his old, lean face aglow with the joy of the combat and the music of the steel. Then he stopped and stood, watching, head slightly forward, lips half parted, eyes shining, fingers playing lovingly over his own hilt. Ah! it was a good fight to look upon; a noble fight, indeed; such masterly sword play he had never seen, nor was ever like to see again; the swift attacks, the fierce rallies, the marvellous agility, the steady eye, the steel wrist. And then, the nerve of him who was losing, and must know it; for Lotzen was losing—surely losing. Twice the Archduke had driven him around the table; now he forced him slowly back ... back ... back ... to the wall ... against it ... tight against it.

"Yield, cousin!" he said; "it's your last chance."

But the Duke only smiled mockingly and fought on.

With an appealing cry Madeline Spencer darted toward them.

"Spare him, Armand!" she pleaded, "spare him!"

The Archduke stepped out of distance, but with point still advanced.

"Take him!" he said, "take him, and joy with him!"

Ferdinand of Lotzen slowly raised his sword in salute.

"My thanks, cousin!" he said, "I can accept from her what I could not from you. You have bested me—the game is over. I shall not be needed at the reading of the decree.—Your Royal Highness—Messieurs of the Council—I bid you fare-well." He held out his hand to Madeline Spencer. "Come, my Duchess, we will to your Paris and the Rue Royale.—Monsieur le Comte, the door!"—and with all the stately grace and courteous deference of a minuet he led her down the room, and bowed her out, and himself after.

There was a moment of silence; then the Archduke spoke.

"My lords, the Book of Laws is found, or so much of it as the fire has spared. How we chanced to come upon it here will best be told another time; enough now that but for the daring and quick wit of Her Royal Highness, it would have been forever lost." He glanced at the clock. "The hour for the Council has already passed. Your Excellency, the Laws are before you, will you do us the favor to read the decree?"

The Count stepped forward and lifted the Book from the rug; of the heavy cover little remained but the brass hinges; the first few pages were scorched and half consumed, and all the edges charred and split and eaten into by the flames; but otherwise it seemed to be without hurt.

Yet Dehra's hand went to her heart, and her breath came sharply, as slowly and carefully Epping turned the leaves, holding them together the while, lest they break apart. Was the decree there! Might Lotzen have destroyed it—torn it from the Book, before they came upon him!

Then the Count stopped, and bending down read for a moment. When he looked up there was a strange expression on his face; he did not speak at once; and when he did his voice was repressed and almost trembling.

"It is here," he said; "executed the day before King Frederick died. I read it:

> "'Section one hundred thirty-first.—It is hereby decreed that His Royal Highness the Archduke Armand shall be eligible to the Crown of Valeria, and he is herewith restored to his proper place in the Line of Succession, as the right heir male of Hugo, second son of Henry the Third.'"

For an instant Armand's brain whirled—then he awoke to Dehra's hands in his, and her voice in his ear, and the shouts and waving blades of the Ministers.

"The ritual, Epping! the ritual!" the Princess cried, and caught up the sword she had tossed aside to rescue the Book—then gasped in wondering fear, as the old Count raised his hand and shook his head.

"Wait!" he said; "there is another decree that comes before the ritual. Attend!—

> "'Section one hundred thirty-second.—Whereas, for the first time in a thousand years the Dalberg has no son: It is hereby decreed that the succession as Head of the House of Dalberg, and, ipso facto, to the Crown of Valeria, together with all their hereditary titles, powers, possessions and privileges, shall be vested in our only child and daughter, Dehra, Princess Royal of Valeria. And all and every decree conflicting therewith is hereby specifically revoked and annulled.'"

And now the swords were up again, and the Archduke's with them, and the wild huzza roared through the Palace and far into the Park; and Bernheim and Moore, coming down the corridor, dashed into the library and stopped, amazed; then joined in, knowing that it must mean victory.

But Dehra, herself, pale-faced, tear-eyed and trembling, turned and flung her arms around Armand's neck.

"It's wrong, dear! it's wrong!" she cried; "you are the King!—you are the Dalberg!"

"No, sweetheart, it is right!" he said, releasing her arms, and bowing over her hand until his lips touched it. "Praise God! it is right."

Then he stepped back and flashed his sword above her head; and all the others sprang to meet it, and locked there, a canopy of steel.

"Valeria hails the Head of the House of Dalberg as the Queen!" he cried.

And from every throat came back the answer:

"We hail the Dalberg Queen!"

And now the trembling had passed; she looked up at the swords proudly, and stretching out her hand she touched them one by one; but touching Armand's last—and her eyes sought his, and over her face broke the adorable smile, and she drew down his blade, and kissed it.

"Hail, also, to the King!" she said; "your King and mine, my lords!—the King that is to be."

THE END

Milton Keynes UK
Ingram Content Group UK Ltd.
UKHW030623061024
449204UK00004B/381